SOCIAL WORK
AS HUMAN RELATIONS

SOCIAL WORK AS HUMAN RELATIONS

Anniversary Papers
of the New York School of Social Work
and the Community Service Society
of New York

COLUMBIA UNIVERSITY PRESS · *New York*

1949

PUBLISHED IN GREAT BRITAIN, CANADA, AND INDIA BY GEOFFREY CUMBERLEGE
OXFORD UNIVERSITY PRESS, LONDON, TORONTO, AND BOMBAY

MANUFACTURED IN THE UNITED STATES OF AMERICA

Foreword

TWO COINCIDENT MILESTONES of significance to the broad field of social welfare were marked by the papers comprising this book and its companion volume, *The Family in a Democratic Society*.

In observing the one hundredth anniversary of the Community Service Society of New York and the fiftieth anniversary of the New York School of Social Work in the spring of 1948, the purpose was not so much to review the past as to look ahead. Accordingly, a program of three scientific symposia was offered. These were designed to increase understanding of the present problems of social welfare and contribute to a more effective approach to these problems, by drawing upon knowledge and experience now available in the medical and social sciences and in the practice of social and health work.

Most of the papers in this volume were presented at the third symposium, on "Professional Social Work: Its Substance and World Significance." This marked particularly the half-century anniversary of the School as the first professional training institution of its kind, which is not only a division of the Society but also a graduate school of Columbia University. Some other relevant papers, presented at the Society's anniversary dinner and at the first symposium, are placed with them. The other symposium papers make up the companion volume.

The Society and the School welcome this opportunity to make these papers more widely available, and in lasting form. One purpose of our program itself was to bring to a broad public a clearer concept of the place of social welfare in tomorrow's world and thus to strengthen the forces which give impetus to forward-looking social and health programs. Many laymen and professional workers have desired copies for study. The sessions were designed for the free interplay of thought and knowledge, and therefore the papers present the views of their individual authors rather than representing necessarily those of the Society or the School.

For their participation in making this twofold anniversary observance meaningful to the field of social welfare generally, gratitude is due to the authors and to the members of the boards of trustees of the Society and of the School, of their committees and their staff. Our whole community is indebted, I feel, to Walter S. Gifford, chairman of the board of the Society, Bayard F. Pope, its president, and Morris Hadley, chairman of the board of the School, for their devoted and wise leadership.

GUY EMERSON, *Chairman*
Committee on the 100th Anniversary,
Community Service Society of New York

New York, New York
March 1, 1949

Contents

PART III: VISTAS IN HUMAN RELATIONS

Part I: Theory and Techniques

Helping People—the Growth of a Profession

GORDON HAMILTON

HOW TO BE A GOOD NEIGHBOR WISELY AND EFFECTIVELY remains the most challenging of the fundamental problems of civilization. It is probable that the principles of living in peace and fellowship in family, civic, national, or international relations are the same, if they can but be discovered and applied. Everyone is aware that unless a great human principle is found which can be made to work for intergroup and interclass tensions in community, international, and interracial problems, civilization itself is doomed.

In the Westward-facing nations, indications of such a principle are thought by many to be found in an evolving concept of democracy, one of the central ideas of which is a deep conviction as to the worth of the individual and belief in his capacity to participate in his own government and destiny. There is little doubt that this conviction has a strong base in Christianity, which, in turn, is indebted to the older ethics and values of the prophets and saints of Israel.

No one profession or group has a monopoly of these objects and purposes. Good health is the objective of medicine, but many sciences and technologies must coöperate for an effective program in individual and public health. Teachers are dedicated to the objective of education, but education can never be restricted to teachers. Provision of material things—"estate," social security, and social opportunities—has been the traditional area for social work, but material things cannot be divorced from the things of the spirit—the personal efforts and gratifications of the human being. It is already recognized that social needs are overlapping. One cannot teach a hungry child successfully, or dig coal productively with an ill or undernourished body. What is being gradually recognized is that the areas of science overlap and that there must be many common endeavors and common tools to reach the common objective of a "health-and-decency" standard of living, not only for subsistence, but in our human relationships.

The assumptions that define helpfulness and coöperation in human welfare must have their base in scientific knowledge and human values, linked in practice. But practice in any profession is itself an art, and there is room for great diversity and many sorts of cultural adaptation. Common needs persist within cultural variations.

Probably the commitment to the objectives of welfare has never been better stated than in the late Franklin D. Roosevelt's Four Freedoms—freedom from want, freedom from fear, freedom of speech, and freedom to worship—and today we must add freedom from hate. The bitterness that arises among men does not seem to be about these desires, but about methods for achieving them. In a long evolutionary struggle the welfare premise gradually coming to be accepted is that the basic human needs of all children, of all persons, irrespective of class and caste, of nation and race, should be met, not ignored or frustrated; and that exploitation, ruthless competition, and armed aggression, as ways of satisfying one's own needs at the expense of others, are inadmissible. Symptoms of an unhealthy society are shown in such trends as a low standard of living, high divorce rates, illegitimacy, truancy, delinquency, large numbers of employable unemployed persons, the prevalence of diseases for which controls are known, inadequate housing, unwholesome or little recreation, and racial, religious, and class discrimination. The purpose of programs of social welfare must be to reduce and, if possible, prevent these ills of society.

There is no evidence to suggest that hunger is better for a black child than for a white child, that it is good for a laborer's child, or for the child of an unmarried mother; and it is known that hunger and many kinds of disease are to a large extent preventable. Society is also coming slowly to believe that under the right sort of educational and general living conditions a great part of delinquency is controllable and also, in part, preventable.

In an illuminating article on "Human Principles," John F. Wharton said,

> If we really want to eliminate war (and don't be too sure that all of us do) our best hope probably lies with small, scattered groups who are not without honor either in their own or other countries. They are people who, with little financial or moral support, are endeavoring to conduct "pure research" into the nature of man. By "pure research" I mean seeking after fundamental *principles*, rather than tangible results.[1]

Unfortunately, I cannot here call on a new principle gained from research which will in its application fundamentally redirect the spiritual energies of man, but I shall attempt to indicate what may be clews to such a principle in examining some of the concepts and methods of one of the oldest and newest of the professions, one that hopes and strives for the application of scientific knowledge and conscience in the task of trying to help one another. This may seem presumptuous, yet my warrant lies in the belief that science and philosophy have come nearer to locating the principle through understanding the personality and the small group rather than the large masses of people. Although man does not yet know how to spread attitudes of brotherhood through the earth, he does know a great deal about the formation of social attitudes in the individual—the dynamics of fear, hate, aggression, and love-security syndromes in the human being.

Social work lies midway between the healing and educational professions and draws on the insights of both. It offers both social treatment and psychological education, depending on human needs. It considers the worth of the individual to be a basic value, and believes that the individual should not be sacrified for the State. Democracy teaches that the more an individual finds him-

[1] *Saturday Review of Literature,* XXX, No. 43 (October 25, 1947), 9.

self, the more he becomes a contributing member of his society. The recognition of human needs leads collectively to programs of established human rights and responsibilities. Human beings are not "equal." The right one must believe in is the right to equal opportunity for the good life and the responsibility of a good society to remove or reduce unnecessary hardships for all.

One of the oldest problems in philosophy, and one of the great discoveries of science, lies in the relationship of mind and body. As medicine has developed, it has tended to incorporate some of the findings of mental health. In modern medicine the lines between physical and mental therapies have tended to grow less distinct. Modern medicine, incorporating psychiatry, becomes psychosomatic in its outlook. Illness is an interaction between organic factors and the total functioning of the body. But science has gone farther than this. It seems clear that the individual responds sensitively to his family and to the intergroup relationships of his culture. Man is not merely a biological organism. The individual and society interact. All problems and remedies can be regarded as psychosocial. These interactions, therefore, become the central points of study. Moreover, when the methods of science are applied to human relations, value judgments enter in. In the human sciences there can be no separation between knowledge and value. Unless high and enlightened values for mankind implement our expanding knowledge, not only is atomic and biological warfare inevitable, but it is difficult to see any purpose in maintaining existence on so sorry an earth.

In its concern with the interactions of the individual and his society, the attention of social work was traditionally given to economic lacks, material deprivations, and environmental strain and pressures; but as social science, like medicine, has assimilated the teachings of mental hygiene, outer pressures are found not to be isolated from internal personality tensions and strains. Many outstanding economists and physical scientists of today appear certain that the resources of the earth are adequate to sustain an efficient standard of living among all people if properly developed, and if political and economic methods are devised from the development and interchange of these resources.[2] Certainly when I began social work few believed that this was possible, even in our own country, still less among less favored nations. Social workers, along with others, assumed that full production was impossible, and that people must continue to live in poverty through no fault of their own but because the American standard of living, high as it was, could not be realistically achieved by all groups. Within a lifetime this concept has been radically changing. Many informed people today believe that it is possible to control recessions and depressions, even though political scientists have not yet agreed on the most effective means. Pioneer social workers, through having convictions as to the importance of economic resources, good housing, and standards of health and assistance, had, in the early days, no very comforting program to offer their clients. Relief, even when kindly, was totally inadequate; slum and shocking sanitation conditions were widespread; disease, delinquency, alcoholism, and misery were everywhere formidable. But the American social worker of today comes into a far from perfect yet certainly a very different picture; he not only finds a more adequate basic structure of health and economic security, but, even more important, he is fortified by a radical change in the philosophy of the leaders of the community and nation; for society is coming to believe that there is no inherent virtue in frustration, deprivation, illness, or any form of the doctrine of lesser eligibility, and that an adequate standard of living can be provided for all.

This, then, leads us to a consideration of the methods of social work which are directed toward the furthering of these newer objectives for a common social welfare. Although the same science and philosophy are basic in the methods of social casework, social group work, and community organization, the specifics in these disciplines vary somewhat, both as to arts of practice and terminology; so for the sake of simplicity, I shall express them in terms of the oldest discipline, and the one with which I am most conversant, namely, social casework. The method of social casework,

[2] K. F. Mather, "Catching Up with Science," *Journal of Social Casework,* XXVIII, No. 5 (May, 1947), 163–67.

which is applied individual by individual and family by family and group by group or intergroup, makes a not insignificant contribution to the progress of social welfare. The method itself cannot be isolated from the democratic frame of reference and culture within which it has developed. Although casework as a technique has developed in Europe and on the other continents to some extent, it has had a distinctive American evolution, and many students of social relations in Europe, Asia, and Latin America come to study it here. Its distinguishing characteristic is the attempt to integrate and implement, through a profession, the complementary principles of human rights and human needs in the growing science of welfare.

We may, therefore, restate, although we shall not re-examine in detail, the key concepts of social casework today. Most of them are not new, and the soundest have been known by the wise of mankind for thousands of years. The formulation of these concepts, however, has been illuminated in recent years by the development of dynamic psychiatry, which has contributed depth and variation to the ways by which psychological knowledge can be translated into realistic means of helping other persons. There is no special priority in the arrangement; one concept hangs upon another.

1. Any ability to help others effectively rests on respect for the human personality—on the person's right to make his own life, to enjoy personal and civil liberties, and to pursue happiness and spiritual goals in his own way.

This means, in application, that social workers do not impose upon the client their own goals or standards of behavior, their own solutions and morals, but respect the client's right to be himself and make his own decisions and plans. They do not scold, or moralize, or threaten. Concrete services and practical assistance are "noncontingent" on conformity in behavior. Goods and services in modern social work, as in modern medicine, are given because the client has need of them, not because he is a "rice Christian." Self-direction, as well as self-dependence, is encouraged, and capacities are released and strengthened.

One sign of respect for others lies in respect for the confidences of the client. It is hard to manage the professional, confidential relationship in solving a social problem which constantly affects and is affected by the behavior of other persons. Social work ethics, however, insists, not only on as much protection of the client's private affairs as possible, but also on sharing our purposes honestly with him and helping him to face those aspects which must be shared for any constructive result. The client's assent or consent is secured for any efforts made on his behalf.

2. Help is most effective if the recipient participates actively and responsibly in the process.

Most people believe that this is the best way to help Europe or China. Few persons are really grateful for a "handout," or for continuous remittances that prolong their dependency. The relation of the benefactor to his client is proverbially uncomfortable and disillusioning. Some are not ready to use help wisely, just as some are not ready to learn. Readiness, however, can be stimulated and educated. Help, as a commodity, often does more harm than good. What most are grateful for in the long run, whether nations or groups or individuals, is a chance to help themselves, to work out their own solution, or at least to have a hand in shaping their destiny. The poor and the less fortunate have this desire just as strongly as do the captains of industry. It is resource, capacity, and opportunity that fail them. Clients are usually satisfied in direct proportion to the degree to which this desire is recognized and respected, and means found to enlist them in their own recovery. Caseworkers have long found pragmatically that self-help is essential in individual rehabilitation and recovery. Low earnings, feelings of inadequacy, difficulty in getting along, neglect of children, and delinquency are explained, in part, from the angle of economic or political or cultural factors, and in part from the personality itself, and few cures can be effective unless the personality is enlisted on its own behalf in the struggle. This is certainly a basic democratic concept. There has been a gradual shift from recognizing the problem, important as that is, to understanding the need, and still further, to motivating the person to use the services to meet his real need.

Caseworkers must have knowledge and skill in all these phases to be effective.

Techniques have been developed to induce the person to move from readiness to ask for help, which is in itself a more constructive step than unwillingness to seek help, toward readiness to use help, or, as we say in our professional jargon, "readiness to involve oneself actively in the treatment process." Working on one's own problem reasserts and mobilizes sources of strength, and helps achieve a better integration of self.

The greatest gift anyone can offer is to enable another to realize his own capacities for change and growth. One cannot, however, release such energies unless the worker himself has been taught systematically how to understand the nature of motivation. Only if the social worker in his professional education has been psychologically well taught can he help the client mobilize his feelings in the direction of change, growth, and adaptation to reality. In social casework the person is stimulated by the worker to participate actively in the study of his situation, in making plans for its solution, in putting active efforts into the solution, using his own and whatever community resources are available and appropriate.

There are several levels or goals in this idea of readiness for change. For the relatively self-directing person, caught in a tangle of external pressures or obvious difficulties, the goal is to enable the person through counseling and practical services to move into changing his own situation. As we have said, he is encouraged so far as possible to do this himself and for himself. If the person is less capable, weakened, or seriously handicapped, the worker must support him more in his efforts and, whenever necessary, actively intervene in the environment to reduce social or personal pressures. It seems to be a well-established hypothesis that change in attitudes or mores can best be effected by creating new conditions within which satisfactions occur which can supply motivation.

The question as to motivation for change is a difficult one, but at least what has always been intuitively known is reinforced by psychological and psychiatric findings. A person is motivated to change because of hope of satisfaction. He can be motivated to efforts to change his situation through an educational process that clarifies a course of action and offers the tools or resources with which to give satisfaction. This may be achieved in "counseling" which—as distinguished from advising—through discussion releases a person's capacity to make more rational choices. But if a person is, in any real sense, to change his attitudes or life direction, this seems not to be achieved on a wholly intellectual basis. Change in feeling can only be brought about through a major experience, such as through a very happy marriage, through great physical or mental suffering, through religious experience, through a significant relationship with one or more persons. It is no accident that the doctor-patient relationship has received so much attention. So far as we know, it is only in a deeply felt experience in relationship that therapy can affect a person's attitudes toward himself and his fellows.

3. Respect for others, acceptance of others, as they are and as potentially they can be, tends to induce between worker and client, between the one who seeks and the one who offers help, a relationship which is not only the medium for educational counseling, but for a therapeutic process.

Without this unique relationship, change is not likely to take place, nor will unconstructive attitudes and patterns of behavior be modified. A great deal is known today about the dynamics of such a relationship. Again, the fact is not new, but the translation of what is known about relationship into counseling and healing efforts is relatively new in professional practice. Love is part of the dynamics of any real healing, but it must be a special sort of love—a disciplined concern, not indulgence for oneself.

The social worker must be a person who has genuine warmth toward others. To be useful to another who is trying to change himself and his attitude the social worker must have a gift for intimacy. He must be willing to enter into the feeling experience of the client, willing to listen to his view of his problem and of his experience, willing to go patiently along with him in his struggles for a solution.

4. Respect for others includes respect for their difference.

Social workers desire neither conformity with their opinions nor uniformity in cultural and individual patterns of behavior. Help is given without regard to race, creed, or color; it is nondiscriminatory. At its best, it accredits and builds positively on the richness of cultural variation, tries to break up meaningless labeling and derogatory stereotyping. This is not a Negro or a Latin who has chanced to become an artist. This is an *artist* who has brought qualities of warmth and creative fantasy to his art from his traditions and racial or national experiences. To us, each one is different, not only as to thumbprints, but as to his unique vision of himself and his world. Each has on him the stamp of his times, his culture, his community, now a blurred impression, now a distinctive one, now adding to his stature and achievement as a human being. Stereotypes about other cultures break down as soon as one gets to know the individuals within that culture.

Fear-hate cycles spring from frustrations of all kinds, of which intolerance is one of the cruelest and most damaging by-products. In a number of experiments to educate children to a greater social and religious magnanimity, it has been convincingly shown that a purely ideological approach has little to offer in combating children's attitudes of prejudice. If, however, warm and friendly associations across color and race and religious lines are provided, then concurrent educational efforts aimed at pointing up ideals of tolerance can have real effect.

Denial of difference is not a constructive approach, but if persons are allowed to share a living experience in a warm and accepting atmosphere and can be made aware of the implications of these satisfactions, tolerant attitudes may be integrated permanently into the personality. It was said of John Winant that his greatness lay in the fact that he really believed in the possibility of the greater "comradeship of man."

5. Self-awareness is essential in understanding others.

There seems to be an important connection between the ability to accept others as they are, with good and bad mixed, and being able to look inside oneself and face the goodness and the badness there. The worker must have a high degree of self-awareness, or his unconscious bias, prejudice, and self-indulgent wishes to please others or to be liked will stand in the way of free movement in the client's use of the relationship.

The motivation for helping others is not always commendable. When we want to help the less fortunate, either our neighbor here or the starving people abroad, we may do so out of a real love of God and our fellow men, or because we feel guilty about our own selfish desires, or to compensate for meanness and ruthlessness in ourselves, or to keep the masses from revolt and Communism "through bread and circuses." The truth is that there are mixed motives in the best and worst of us; so one of the essentials in treating others is understanding and facing ourselves. The social worker, of course, is not free from unlovely motives, but he will not prove really helpful to others unless he has learned to recognize the bad as well as the good impulses in himself—learned to accept them as fact—and in spite of them developed his capacity to "love" many different kinds of person, or at least to refrain from injuring them by being aware of the less admirable feelings which persist within. If the social worker has warmth and a sincere purpose to help, he can in his training learn to control his impulses wisely, but if he lacks concern for others he can never be trained for effective service. It is not true that social workers become "hard-boiled" through professional training. If some are hard, it is because their deepest impulses toward others are not really kind or mature, and they have set up certain defenses against them in the character structure.

To rely on a good heart would not be enough even if the impulses of the heart were more dependable. Nor can one rely on manuals of policy and procedure, no matter how detailed, to guide workers who must reach into the real needs of the person. The merit system under civil service in many states is still at poor educational and training levels for welfare staffs. Much of the work is carried on by persons with little training and even less aptitude for the occupation. Salaries are still appallingly low. Licenses are still unnecessary for this most complex of all the professions. The demand for trained social workers far exceeds the number now available or in prospect. It is estimated that there are somewhere between one hundred thousand and one hundred and seventy-five thousand persons in social work positions in the country; of these, about fifteen thousand have completed the appropriate graduate training, and about thirty thousand more have had only one year of professional training. The group of trained personnel is outnumbered about four to one by the untrained. As both social welfare needs and the number of social work positions are expanding rapidly, due to a growing social consciousness, the gap between demand and supply is widening rather than narrowing.

There are forty-four professional schools of social work in this country, three in Canada, one in Hawaii, and one in Puerto Rico which are members of a national standard-setting association. These schools offer a two-year program toward a Master's degree. A few schools offer a doctorate in social welfare, but funds for this essential but expensive advanced degree are still limited. Under the Federal Mental Health Act a few schools offer a third year, beyond the Master's degree, in psychiatrically based social work. In addition, introductory training programs are being offered by an increasing number of colleges and universities. The need for guidance in the development of progressive curricula appropriate to our times suggests that a great deal more money must be spent on advanced professional education to train teachers and administrative leaders for social work. Much has to be done to improve the general level of professional education so as to insure high quality practice throughout the country. Not only greatly increased educational resources, but research, to determine how to test and screen for the essential aptitudes requisite for practice in social welfare, are urgently called for in this field.

6. The individual has responsibility, not only for himself, but toward the society in which he lives.

Society has responsibility, not only to protect the lives and interests of all its members, but to allow opportunities for creative development, achievement, and contribution for its members. The social worker educates the person to a more realistic sense of his responsibility to his community, tries to encourage in him, not only efforts on his own behalf and in his role in the family, but also as a citizen. Critics of social work say either that social workers are too "moralistic" or not "moralistic" enough. Ideally, one is not "moralistic" at all, but one must have a strong sense of social, moral, and spiritual values for oneself, personally and professionally. One does not seek to impose these, but to help the client strengthen himself as a human being and a citizen through his own normal associations with religious and civic groups.

Social workers are interested in positive programs of welfare, as modern medicine is interested in positive programs of health. Each community has the responsibility to support, from time to time, skilled surveys of its needs, and as resources are created citizens should be awakened to an intelligent use of these resources. Because social needs are interrelated, services should also be interrelated, in a usable, effective pattern. While many cost studies have been made, the over-all cost cannot be once and for all determined. Practically all experts, however, agree that hit-or-miss and inadequate programs cost most in the long run. Mental institutions, hospitals and jails, disease and unemployability, cost more than do strong, well-conceived programs of welfare; a slum, in its own way, is as deadly as the TB bacillus; prejudice and racial intolerance are virulent infections in the whole of society. Only a multidiscipline professional approach can hope to reduce the problems of the complex modern community.

A modern program should include the group fee and low-cost facilities. Social work has suffered somewhat from its association with the generally stigmatized problems of illegitimacy, poverty, delinquency. All these are stigmatized more than are the diseases of the body. A courageous program will tend to remove the stigma both from the problem and from the remedies or services offered to meet them. Social services should be made good enough for anyone to use and, in fact, the spread of fee charging in social work has made these services far more acceptable. The needs of any community determine what a social worker does, but how it is to be done is communicated through responsible professions using common skills and techniques.

The love of one's neighbor has become of increasing social significance. The development of each individual into a good neighbor must, therefore, become the goal of society. All the institutions which can help toward reaching this goal must be revitalized, and of them all the family is the most dynamic source of spiritual energies.

One of the traditional concerns in social work is the central place of the family in Western culture. It is scarcely forty years since the tremendous impact of the announcement from the first White House Conference—that no child should be removed from his family because of poverty alone—shook the complacency of the American community. It took, however, the conscience and will of many hard-working people to apply the principle and thus reduce the tragedy of unnecessary institutionalized childhood. If basic human needs are to be met, good parents are indubitably one of them. Good parents are still the best insurance of a good society.

Called in to aid families with necessary goods and services, social workers, like doctors, priests, and educators, have been forced to look, not only at the economic, but at the affectional and educational basis of family life and family relationships. Not only have social workers become expert in supplying foster parents and substitute relationships for orphans, for illegitimate children, for those from broken homes of one sort or another, but in their role of maintaining homes with social, health, and economic resources they have come to grips with unwholesome marriages, with parents who have little capacity to offer love and to help children to grow up—immature, dependent persons who project their difficulties upon social misfortunes in order to evade looking honestly at their own marital and parent-child relationships. Thus, social workers have moved inevitably from the more external aspects of family maintenance and child placing into the more psychological areas of family guidance and treatment.

At first, clients asked of the family caseworker little except the provision of goods and services, such as money, convalescent and shelter care, job opportunities, vocational guidance, and recreation. Gradually, as the skill of the caseworker has increased, the client, who intuitively knows whether one can help him or not, has begun to ask for marital and parent-child guidance or therapy. The caseworker is in a strategic position to give this guidance—especially in incipient problems—to young persons and adolescents, to couples entering upon marriage, and to parents whose children are beginning to show problems of behavior. Often well within the range of the so-called "normal," this behavior, if not treated in time, is likely to become a permanent character defect and a source of unhappiness to the child and others around him.

The family agency, with its first-hand knowledge of homes, is today a vital force in the community for the stabilizing and strengthening of family life. It is still not enough recognized or used by the average citizen. Far too many marriages end in the divorce court because expert advice was not sought in time. The fundamental character of family casework is just beginning to be acknowledged and accredited. There are, of course, pathological families so bound together, not by love, but in a love-hate relationship, that help, even if sought, will not be used. There are situations that have gone beyond repair because of deterioration or gross social conditions. The modern family agency is unwilling to be pushed into a residual role; rather, it turns its resources toward research, prevention, and social action to attack social pathology at the roots. For the last thirty years social work has proved itself especially hospitable to the incorporation of programs of mental hygiene in its day-by-day practice.

Family casework has, like medicine and education, been giving more and more attention to the well-being of the child in his earliest years. The Children's Charter calls for the right to a good home, a strong body, education, a place to play, social, religious, and ethical teaching. In the developmental process, emotional influences and stimuli, particularly of parental figures, mold to a considerable degree the future life pattern. In early family casework, treatment was sought and given at the parental level, the child rarely being treated directly. In casework today it is recognized that children may be said to have their own problems, and that treatment may be most productive if both parent and child are involved in the treatment experience. This does not detract from parental authority, but helps parents to attain a greater awareness of their role and to take greater responsibility in it.

A great deal is beginning to be known about the types of experience in the first six or seven years of life which tend to influence the character of the growing child. Techniques for his education and training in a wise and ethically mature setting are being more clearly seen for each stage in his development. Successful efforts here should point the way toward changing economic, social, and cultural conditions in larger areas, and with broadening the scope for experiments in living together at peace. The good way of life must be shared to be a good way of life.

The parable of the Good Samaritan takes on new meaning today in its familiar aspects of a philosophy of welfare in which we are constrained not to pass by on the other side, but actively to help one another. But beyond this we see that Samaritan and Levite, Greek and Buddhist, Christian and Mohammedan, nations with divergent cultures and forms of government, must learn how to live creatively together, accepting personal and cultural difference as good neighbors in a world which must be committed to nothing less than goodness and spiritual unity.

The Development of Governmental Responsibility for Human Welfare

KARL DE SCHWEINITZ

NOT LONG AGO I sat at lunch in a Washington cafeteria with two persons, strangers to each other and to me. One of the men, looking at new construction across the street, opened the conversation:

"I like to see buildings going up. It means that we'll have more office room."

"Wouldn't we get the same result," said the other man, "if we fired half the government employees?"

That kind of generalization, which my table companion would not have thought of applying to business or industry, is the measure of the lag between what the public service is today and our knowledge and appreciation of its uses and personnel. Most of us still think of government in the negative terms of the eighteenth and nineteenth centuries, its only function restraint, its existence the penalty man pays for his failure to control himself.

We see the public official through the eyes of our fathers. To them, he was the fellow sitting outside the police station or in the courthouse waiting for something to turn up. They saw him as separate from the main current of American life with its emphasis upon activity. Since they regarded government as an evil of doubtful necessity, they did not want him to be too busy; yet they despised him for his idleness, and themselves for maintaining him in it. The work which he did do and for which they employed him, they did not respect. To them, government required no great amount of knowledge or skill. They believed that any one of its jobs could be done by anybody, at least anybody except the incumbent.

The official perhaps most often cited as an illustration of incompetence was the overseer of the poor. Everybody knew him as the man who managed the almshouse and supplied outdoor relief, as assistance in money or goods was called, to the people who could not support themselves. The inefficiency of his administration was notorious, a combination of neglect and petty despotism.

While his treatment of the persons entrusted to him was usually all that the public thought it to be, and worse, the overseer himself was largely the victim of a society that did not know what it wanted. Its feelings were divided. On the one hand, the necessity of providing for the poor was recognized. That implied a humane administration. On the other hand, people did not like to be bothered by beggars, and they wanted their property protected. As one nineteenth-century writer put it, "It may be considerably cheaper to fill empty stomachs to the point of ready obedience than [by maintaining a larger array of military or police force] to compel starving wretches to respect the roast beef of their more industrious neighbors." [1] From this point of view stern measures were required, and public relief before the twentieth century was administered as a function of the police power of the state.

Always present as a major complication was the fact that not everyone in need was sick and feeble. Some people were able-bodied but did not have jobs. The duties of the overseer included the provision of employment, but at no time did he succeed in finding work for all those who sought help. The difficulty of the problem did not cause the community to be any the more willing to maintain the person for whom there was no work. Such individuals were immediately suspect, and this suspicion extended to the official responsible for determining and relieving their necessity. The community expressed its frustration in contempt for the overseer. He, in turn, vented his exasperation upon his

[1] Charles Babbage, on reverse of title page of Sir George Nicholls, *A History of the English Poor Law* (new ed.; London: P. S. King & Co., 1898).

charges, representing government at its punitive and repressive worst.

With this most despised of public officials, the community deposited its central social problem. It turned over to him its human wastage, the people it wanted to forget, the least appealing among the miserable in body and mind, and those whom it disposed of by calling them "unworthy" and "undeserving." The need which contained the greatest challenge to the social order, which represented life at its significant worst, and thus offered the broadest opportunity for human understanding and constructive statesmanship, was delegated to a personnel so incompetent as to give substance to the traditional concept of the civil service expressed by my companion at lunch when he suggested that we fire half the government employees.

Yet this area of activity, discredited by earlier generations, is today the field in which the most positive expression of the public service will be found. Next to defense against war, it occupies the largest room in government. Whereas in 1848 public expenditures for social welfare were not even recorded, today they are counted in the billions, far exceeding the total combined expenditures of the local, state, and Federal governments of a century ago. Most of this increase has taken place in little more than a generation. The two years for which reasonably comparable figures can be obtained are 1913 and 1940. In 1913 the outlay—local, state, and Federal—for purposes most nearly approaching social security was $21,000,000, or twenty-two cents per inhabitant, one tenth of one percent of the national income. In 1940 it was approximately $4,500,000,000, nearly $34 per capita, almost 6 percent of the national income.[2] Here is an increase that goes beyond a progression in an existing order. It is evidence of an extensive and basic change in our use of government.

While this change has come upon us with almost revolutionary suddenness, we are, in fact, witnessing the fruition of a long development. We can trace its beginning to the ideas about the

[2] *Security, Work, and Relief Policies* (Washington, D.C.: National Resources Planning Board, 1942), Table 63, p. 291.

individual established in the Declaration of Independence and the Bill of Rights and to the humanitarian movement, symbolized and stimulated by the campaign for prison reform which John Howard commenced in England in 1773, by Dr. Philippe Pinel's unchaining of the maniacs in Paris in 1792, and by the founding in 1817 in Philadelphia of the Friends Hospital so that "the insane might see that they were regarded as men and brothers."

Not, however, until the nineteenth century had approached and passed its half-way mark and moved toward our own times did broadly organized, nation-wide social programs develop. Then to the belief in the dignity and the rights of the individual and the urge toward human betterment was added the stimulating influence of the dramatic contrast between wealth and poverty. Our immediate predecessors saw for the first time the problem that through the centuries had been left with the overseer of the poor. That problem had now grown to the point where it was becoming visible to the casual observer. In the rural community there had been nothing dramatic or startling about an occasional tumble-down shack or the fellow whom everybody knew and accepted as a ne'er-do-well. With the growth of cities and the segregation of rich and poor into separate neighborhoods, what, on the one hand, man could make for himself in a desirable environment and what, on the other, life in slums entailed was demonstrated for anyone to see. Urbanization showed us both the power of our wealth and the extent of our misery. We discovered the other half, but we also discovered ourselves.

As the century approached its closing years, came the cumulating influence of the findings of modern science. Increasingly there were becoming available the means of treating, controlling, and preventing disease, physical and mental, and of improving conditions of life and labor. The concatenation of these three influences—the visibility of the social problem, the mounting evidence of enormous material resources, and the opening of the new biological and physical knowledge—had a catapultic impact upon a rising company of citizens imbued with humanitarianism and a concern for the individual.

It was in the forties that widespread manifestations of the effect of this impact became evident. Among the first of these was the beginning of modern philanthropy. In founding the Association for Improving the Condition of the Poor of New York City, Robert Hartley enlisted hundreds of volunteers in a service which cut across race and creed and aimed at covering a whole community. Through its counterparts in other cities it was national in scope and in awareness.

A generation later came charity organization to reinforce the volunteer with the trained worker and the settlement movement and send a new type of pioneer into the congested urban neighborhoods.

The A.I.C.P., the Charity Organization Society, the settlers, represented organized philanthropy. Men and women were now competent by reason of first-hand knowledge to discuss the social problem. To quote one of their leaders: "They who can truly voice the inarticulate woes and pleas of the miserable must ever speak with authority to every humane and candid heart." [3] It was this kind of authority that was to provide a substantial part of the foundation for much of the governmental activity of our times.

The year 1848, the year of the incorporation of the A.I.C.P., was also the year in which Dorothea Dix presented her memorial to the Congress, asking for the appropriation of land from the national domain as an encouragement and help to the states in the development of hospitals for the care and treatment of the mentally ill. She failed in her efforts with the Congress, but she succeeded in her efforts with the states.

Miss Dix did not ask government to assume any new responsibilities. She only urged that it do a better job of what for centuries had been its task. She took the insane from the jailer and the overseer of the poor and placed them in special institutions. Her contribution was a strengthening of the categorical principle and of institutional operation as a function of the state. She took a portion of the social problem and made it clear for

[3] "Hints to Visitors" (Philadelphia: Philadelphia Society for Organizing Charity, 1879).

anyone to see. There had been state care before her time, but she established it as a pattern that was to be increasingly adopted in the years that followed and which is expressed in the hospitals, tuberculosis sanitoriums, and the many different kinds of institutions that are an accepted part of government today.

A third significant development of the forties was the great awakening in the field of sanitation. Here humanitarianism and the emerging scientific spirit combined in a movement to cleanse communities as a means of preventing the spread of disease. This movement was first defined and charted in 1850 in Lemuel Shattuck's report of the Massachusetts Sanitary Commission. He proposed a sanitary police, a program of public education, and local and state departments to carry on these activities. In 1869 Massachusetts followed his recommendations and established the first board of health. In 1872, the American Public Health Association was organized. By the end of the seventies sixteen states had followed the example of Massachusetts. The public health movement had begun.

This combination of regulation and education was increasingly applied to the correction of many social and industrial evils rising in its use to an inspiring climax at the close of the century with the campaign that led in 1900 to the establishment of the New York Tenement House Commission, to the tenement house code of 1901, and the appointment of Robert W. De Forest, president of the Charity Organization Society, as New York City's first tenement house commissioner.

Organized philanthropy, the development of institutional provision for special categories of need, and its use in public health and related fields of government as a regulatory and educational force opened the way during the nineteen hundreds for a wide-fronted drive toward social action. To the growth of scientific knowledge and an increasing awareness of the social problem and of the power of our wealth had been added actual experience in the employment of measures of treatment, control, and prevention. This knowledge, awareness, and experience were now channeled into a succession of campaigns and organizations directed to applying our material and spiritual resources to the improvement of social and living conditions. In discussing the part which Mr. De Forest played in the creation of the Russell Sage Foundation, the authors of the history of that institution have epitomized in a paragraph about him the spirit of the times:

> He shared the fresh enthusiasm of those early years of the Twentieth Century for hunting down the causes of poverty, disease, and crime, and discovering what could be done to eliminate or at least control those causes; the confidence that a large part of the "human wants and ills" in America was preventable, and, therefore, would be prevented if only the facts about conditions and remedies were generally known.[4]

This enthusiasm and this confidence expressed themselves in the formation of a great diversity of national organizations and movements: 1904, the National Association for the Study and Prevention of Tuberculosis and the National Child Labor Committee; 1906, the National Recreation Association, the American Association for Labor Legislation, and the National Probation Association; 1907, the Russell Sage Foundation; 1907–08, the Pittsburgh Survey; 1909, the first American Conference for the Prevention of Infant Mortality, the first White House Conference, and the National Committee for Mental Hygiene; 1911, the National Federation of Settlements and the Family Service Association of America; 1912, the first National Conference on Social Insurance, the Survey Associates, and the National Organization for Public Health Nursing; 1913, the American Cancer Society and the National Vocational Guidance Association; 1914, the American Social Hygiene Association.

These organizations were symptomatic of their times. They were founded in a passionate belief in the possibility of an immediate abolition of poverty. They typified the aggressive initiative of a civic leadership and a missionary secretariat directed to getting the facts and laying them before the public, men and women who aimed at the employment of every appropriate measure, public or philanthropic, that would lead to a more favorable environment and a better life for people.

[4] John M. Glenn, Lilian Brandt, and F. Emerson Andrews, *Russell Sage Foundation, 1907 to 1946* (New York: Russell Sage Foundation, 1947), I, 5.

The field of child welfare provides an interesting illustration of how the opening decades of the twentieth century thus contributed to the development of government as an instrument of human welfare. In 1899 the first juvenile court was founded. Children were separated from the procedure of the criminal trial and given a setting of their own. In 1912 came the United States Children's Bureau.

During the same period the movement for what today we call "aid to dependent children" developed. In 1907 the first publicized attempt had been made to state in dollars the cost to a workingman of maintaining a family of five—himself, his wife, and three children. This estimate, reported by a committee of the New York State Conference of Charities and Correction, was based on a study conducted by Robert Coit Chapin. It inaugurated the use of a device that has greatly influenced the economic programs of industry and government. It also dramatized the woeful inadequacy of relief. Two years later, the first White House Conference called the attention of the nation to the alarming extent to which children were being taken from their homes for no reason other than the poverty of their parents. The response was immediate. Beginning in 1911 the states in amazingly quick succession enacted legislation providing for the administration under local auspices of mothers' assistance.

The responsibility of government for the relief of need had been redefined and re-emphasized. Hitherto, the fear that without the whip of an imminent privation people would not work, the frustration and suspicion caused by the failure of the overseer to solve administratively the problem of determining need, the contempt and hatred engendered for the object of a policy which provided relief as payment of a kind of blackmail, lest property and life be endangered—all these factors together with the low quality of public administration in the years following the Civil War had combined to convince the philanthropists and social reformers of the nineteenth century that "all bodily aid to the poor is a mistake," and most especially that provided under public auspices. Now, out of the needs of children, came a reversal in civic thought and action. The provision of financial aid in the presence of necessity was recognized as having a positive value.

During the twenties this point of view was reinforced by the movement for old age pensions, a modified form of relief, first established in 1923 in Montana. Representatives of the family service societies and other voluntary agencies, their resources inadequate to the need that was pressing upon them even in those prosperous days, now began to urge the extension of governmental responsibility for public assistance.

In the first decade of the century another attack upon the economic problem of the individual led to the adoption of a new form of public service. Beginning in 1908 legislation was enacted to systematize and regularize the discharge of the responsibility of the employer for the employee who was injured while at work. Matching in rapidity the movement for mothers' aid was the quick adoption of laws requiring industry to provide for the compensation of the injured person. To this end a number of the states created their own insurance systems. Here was an innovation. A public service was now offered which individual employers and corporations might use—in some states must use—in making certain that money would be available to compensate injured employees or the families of those who had been killed. In so doing, government was including among its functions that of operating as a social utility.

From this time forward there was persistent advocacy of this principle as a means of promoting human welfare. Small but vigorous groups of civic leaders urged the application of social insurance in dealing with the problems of health and medical care and unemployment. These efforts extended into and through the nineteen twenties.

Appropriately paralleling these various movements was the effort to improve the quality of public welfare administration. The first steps in this direction had been taken in 1863 when Massachusetts created the first state board of charities. New York followed four years later. In 1872 the founding of the New York State Charities Aid Association had marked the beginning of citizen organization directed specifically to the promotion of an effective administration of public health and welfare. The S.C.A.A. was thereafter to exercise an enormous influence, throughout the nation as well as in New York, upon the development and operation of social programs.

By the second decade of the twentieth century, supervision, standard-setting, licensing, and the actual administration of certain welfare activities had been sufficiently established as a function of the states to become part of the executive branch of government. The first state department of welfare was created in 1917. The twenties also saw a mounting campaign for the replacement of the overseer of the poor by county welfare boards and for the employment of the services of representatives of the developing profession of social work. Here and in child welfare and mothers' assistance, in municipal and state welfare departments, social workers began to find increasing opportunity for applying their special knowledge and training. At first they regarded themselves as pioneers in new territory, but by the autumn of 1930 public welfare was a recognized form of social service.

The onset of unemployment that year found us ready for action. Philanthropist and professional social worker soon moved from positions of leadership in the voluntary relief programs to the administration of unemployment assistance under public auspices. In every area of human welfare the concepts and programs that had been evolving since the eighteen forties, and that had expressed themselves with increasing vigor in the opening years of the twentieth century, came into play. The enormous expansion of governmental activity which the last two decades have witnessed was founded upon, and grew out of, ideas and experience that had long been in the making.

Our own times, if we may so describe the period between 1930 and 1948, have added four concepts of special significance. The first is the Federal-state grant in aid. This is an old mechanism, but since 1932 it has been used so largely in public welfare as essentially to represent a new development. It has contributed greatly toward making social services available to the whole nation and toward lessening the inequality of their application in various sections of the country. It has been responsible for a vast extension of the civil service and the merit system in the states. It has raised the whole level of public welfare administration and, incidentally, has largely increased the administrative and supervisory powers of the states, notably in the areas of unemployment insurance, public assistance, child welfare, and related fields.

The second significant concept of our times is the national minimum, the belief that in the United States, with its great material resources, there should be a level of health, welfare, and education below which no one should be permitted to fall. We aim to maintain this level through governmentally provided services and benefits designed to facilitate or to supplement the activities of the individual on his own behalf. In different parts of the country and in the different necessaries of life the definitions of this minimum and its application vary.

The President's Commission on Higher Education advocates setting the national goal in education at junior college, but at the same time it points out that 20.4 percent of children living in rural areas and 11.2 percent of urban children have only five years of grade school or less.[5]

Public assistance bases its minimum for the person in need upon studies of the cost of living, but the moneys appropriated almost always fall below the amount upon which even the most meager existence can be supported.

The Federal Government has made a beginning by insuring private loans for middle-income housing and contributing to the creation of housing for low-income families. New York and two or three other states have begun supplementing what the Federal Government is doing, but the amount of public activity in housing is still small. We have made great progress in the movement for public health, but sickness insurance exists in only two states, and social insurance for medical care not at all. Nevertheless, irrespective of the extent of its application in practice, the prin-

[5] *Higher Education for American Democracy; a Report of the President's Commission on Higher Education* (Washington, D.C.: United States Government Printing Office, 1947), I, 31.

ciple of the national minimum is steadily winning general acceptance.

The third concept is that of universalization. We no longer identify social programs with a submerged group. We apply them to everybody. The psychiatric and child guidance clinics are used by people at every level of income. Under the G.I. Bill of Rights veterans from every group in society are receiving grants for tuition and maintenance as government's contribution toward their education. The American insurance system was one of the first to cover persons of high as well as low income, and the demand of the small businessman and of professional people to be included in the system is significant. They and many others are seeing that government can serve them as a social utility through which they can channel their resources in achieving education, housing, recreation, health, and security against vicissitude.

The fourth concept is expressed in, and influenced by, the first three. Our ideas about the nature and sources of personal initiative are changing. In the unemployment of 1930 we learned that the person who, being out of work, was obliged to seek assistance was no different except for his desperate situation from other people, that he had the same problems and the same strengths. He was in need, not of moral reform, but of opportunity. We have learned that what human beings want, in the main, is a chance to make the most of themselves, that an improved environment can discover unsuspected resources in people, that economic security and hope are greater feeders of enterprise than inadequacy and fear, that the respect one feels for another person influences his feeling of respect for himself, and that his sense of self-respect influences his capacity to do and act.

These beliefs about the individual which have come from the study of human behavior and experience in work with people have been implemented in law. The right of appeal, not only in the insurances, but also in assistance has been found to contribute to the dignity of the individual. The money payment in assistance which gives the recipient the power to use his grant as seems best to him conserves his ability to make his own decisions. All this points to a new quality in the relationship between the citizen and his government. It is the inspiration of Federal grants in aid, of the national minimum, and of the tendency toward a universal use of the public services by citizens at the upper as well as at the lower economic levels.

Correspondingly, these concepts are making increased demands upon the art of public administration. Carl R. Gray, Jr., the head of the Veterans Administration, put the case recently in a talk to a group of executives in that agency:

> The great difficulty in administering and operating an organization such as the Veterans Administration is that the very magnitude of the responsibility forces upon us a mass-production type of operation; but every problem that confronts the Veterans Administration, whether it be insurance, claims or medicine and surgery, is an individual problem involving one human being, and it takes a great deal of serious thought to reconcile these two widely divergent methods of approach.

This provision of a service that while reaching the many must have meaning for the one requires an unusual combination of qualities. The public official who undertakes this work must be able to master a field of substantive knowledge; that is, he must be competent to operate with a specific factual subject matter or in relation to it. The subject matter may be mental disease, tuberculosis, social insurance, employment. Whatever its nature he must be adjusted to its facts. He must be able to translate this field of substantive knowledge into social programs as expressed in law and in the administrative policies which derive from law.

Whether he helps to create law and policy or whether he interprets and applies it, he can only be effective if "he knows what it is all about." He must be capable of developing or appreciating a social philosophy. He must be able to think in terms of the whole community, of the public interest, of the greatest good of the greatest number. At the same time, he must have the practical ability that gets things done. He must be the philosopher in action, and his actions must be carried out with, and in relation to, the actions of others. To work in a large organization in the public interest requires thus a feeling for policy and a competence in associative operations.

Finally, there is the individual who is the object of the service and for whom the service exists. He is the one who forms the many, but he never ceases to be the one. Mass operations cannot eventuate in the public interest without being pointed with regard for the way in which the needs of each person are affected and met.

Curtis Bok describes this necessary relationship between the total and the individual in the words of the principal character in his book *I Too, Nicodemus*. The speaker, like his author, is a judge. He tells how his concern is for "the whole trial, its tones and its overtones, and what everyone in court will take away with him when it's over. The main difference between tyranny and democracy," he continues, "is courtesy—an attitude of affectionate respect for everything that lives because it lives." [6]

The qualities required of those who perform a service which through mass operations is directed to the individual seem to be mutually exclusive: the philosophical and the practical, the factual and the personal, the general and the specific, the intellectual and the emotional. Actually, this combination is precisely what living as a human being involves. Of course, nobody achieves this diversity in perfect, integrated proportions. We are all lopsided; some have more of this, some more of that. Therein is the value of organization. It can bring together all the variety required in a service that, extending to a whole community, is designed in the interest of the individual. Yet to do well any significant part of the job one must in some measure contain in himself these different elements.

Where shall we find such public servants? We already have them—not nearly so many as we need, but in sufficient numbers to give us hope. Knowing what we want and having it here and there shows that our goal is attainable. Defining a job is the beginning of filling it. The problem is, in part, one of education. We must prepare for the public service.

The lawyer who leaves the law school today may be ready for private practice. He is not ready for public administration, certainly not for participation in the social services. The psychiatrist with all his understanding of people only too often comes to gov-

[6] Curtis Bok, *I Too, Nicodemus* (New York: Alfred A. Knopf, 1946), p. 220.

ernment without any preparation for working with others through organization toward a common goal. In social work we are only now discovering that the administration of benefits to individuals requires a discipline of its own, a discipline that is founded in the same knowledge of human behavior but that has a different orientation, a different setting, and involves different emphases in relationship from those required in social treatment or in personal counseling. Our growing use of government and its larger place in the lives of all of us has important implications, not only for the professional school, but also for the undergraduate college and the teaching of the liberal arts, for education for citizenship as well as for careers in the public service.

Most people now in government did not come into it with specific preparation; for even if they could have secured that preparation, they did not know that government was where their careers would be. For a long time to come this will continue to be true. It will be true of people who start in the beginning jobs and it will also be true of the persons who are elected or appointed to the top posts. In the expanding responsibilities of government for human welfare new knowledge and new skill are constantly developing, and even the person who comes with an adequate equipment soon finds that what he once learned no longer applies. On all these counts we need an adult, postentry education. This has long been available in the armed forces; it is familiar in medicine. It is not foreign to other professions or to industry. The three-week seminars which the American Press Institute offers at Columbia University to managing editors and other top newspaper personnel are a case in point. That kind of opportunity should be opened to people in the public service.

But no amount of education will alone provide the best in government. There must also be civic participation and active citizen support. This includes recruitment for the public service of personnel from the boards and staffs of our social agencies. It involves over and above everything else a consistent, discriminating support of public welfare, both program and administration.

In a large part of this field, we are still in the position of the overseer of the poor. We must work for and with a community that is in conflict with itself. It does not want people to suffer, but it does not want to pay the price of alleviating that suffering. It never quite makes up its mind, and so it is quick to see fault in the person who seeks the services of government and in the public official who provides those services. The need is for an informed citizenry able to "voice the inarticulate woes and pleas of the miserable" and at the same time to view individual events in the public service and the actions of public officials in their relation to the whole life and total circumstances of an administration.

Basic to this kind of support is an understanding of the nature of government and of the social services in government. It involves resisting the common desire in all of us to create life in our own image and to evaluate the objectives and activities of others in terms of what we do in our own work. Granted a fundamental community of interest in the goals of the voluntary and public agencies, they are in many other respects different. The difference is deeper even than that implied in the problem of reconciling mass operations with individual need. It inheres in the contrast between a mandate that in the voluntary agency rises from the initiative of a relatively few kindred minds and a mandate that through legislation stems from the total community, but which for that very reason does not represent unanimity and which requires the maintenance of a clear view of the public interest in the presence of perpetual conflict. The Webbs credit the origin of the Royal Poor Law Commission of 1905–1909 in part to the fact that there was as "President of the Local Government Board, a philosopher who recognized the public advantage of a precise discrimination between opposing principles." [7] When one has mastered intellectually and emotionally the meaning of that statement, he will have made a beginning of understanding the nature of government in our democracy.

Nowhere is such conflict more constant than in the public social services. Only slowly is the ideal of government as a positive good winning over the concept of government as repression and

[7] Sidney and Beatrice Webb, *English Poor Law History* (New York: Longman's Green and Co., 1929), II, Part II, 471.

as a negative force. We are only beginning to discover that human initiative has a greater reservoir in economic, social, and personal security than in fear and deprivation. It is these positive concepts that the leadership in private as well as in public welfare must express if we are to solve the social problem. And solve it we shall; because we are strong. Our strength is the same strength that Trevelyan finds in his England, for we also have reconciled "three things that other nations have often found incompatible—executive efficiency, popular control, and personal freedom." [8]

[8] George Macaulay Trevelyan, *A Shortened History of England* (1st ed.; New York: Longman's Green and Co., 1942), p. xi.

The Human Sciences and the Arts of Practice

STUART CHASE

IN COÖPERATION with the Social Science Research Council I have been making an appraisal of the social sciences in the third year of the atomic age. Ever since Hiroshima the idea has been frequently expressed that the natural sciences are way out in front, and that the human sciences are either nonexistent or too feeble ever to catch up with the physicists. Technical invention, the complaint alleges, has run away with mankind.

Before coming to any final conclusions about this matter, we thought it would be a good idea to find out just what the social sciences actually were up to. How rigorous are their methods? What have they found out about man? What dependable knowledge have they put in the storehouse of science? What are they doing to close the gap between the two departments?

What I would like to present is a kind of mountain-peak survey of the field of social science as I have seen it, a list of what seem to be some of its major accomplishments, a list of some of the great unanswered questions, and a brief account of one exciting application of social science that was made during the war.

I will not devote space to definitions of "science," operational or otherwise: enough to make the point that the scientific method can be, and has been, applied to the study of human behavior, just as it has been applied to the study of the human nervous system, and to the behavior of atoms. It is sometimes more difficult to apply to human behavior. New techniques must be invented, and the probability of correct prediction—the unfailing test of science—is likely to be somewhat lower. No one suggests that meteorology is not a science, but its probability factor leaves something to be desired. For my money, the anthropologists can outguess the Weather Bureau any day.

Dr. J. R. Oppenheimer, the great physicist, came to somewhat the same conclusion in his testimony on the National Science Foundation bill. He said:

> I am aware of the difficulty of establishing in these fields rigorous criteria of competence and qualification. Nevertheless, at a time when the whole world realizes that many of its most vital problems depend on an understanding of human behavior . . . and of the regularities which underlie the operations of our varied society, we should recognize the great benefits which may come from attracting men and women of prominence to the study of these questions.

Because we have a long-honored term, "social science," it is natural to believe that out there in the world somewhere is an entity which corresponds to the term. There is no such entity out there, and we must beware of constructing one in our heads. What is to be found in the real space-time world?

A television camera would show a number of professors lecturing to more or less bored students in more or less stuffy classrooms; some experiments being performed in psychological laboratories; a few clinical studies in factories and offices; teams of investigators taking notes in one or two "Middletowns"; social workers making records on their rounds and in clinics; a battery of Hollerith machines clicking away while they sort social security cards and Gallup poll cards; sunburned persons in pith helmets asking questions of slightly puzzled natives in New Guinea. Finally, the camera would focus on shelf after shelf of books. Many of the volumes are famous; many of them contain prose as good as the advice is bad—for instance, Plato's recipe for bringing up children.

Out there in America 145,000,000 people, scattered over 3,000,000 square miles of plain, valley, and hillside, form and reform into numberless groups and organizations, with loyalties and sentiments clustered about each. In Newburyport, Massachusetts, a recent study showed that there were more than 800 organizations among 17,000 people. The camera would indicate the many curious methods by which these citizens earn their livings, or seek to escape from the frequently intolerable boredom of earning a living under machine-age conditions.

Here is the field for the social scientist, watching these people behave, and searching out the laws which govern that behavior. Kurt Lewin believed that the laboratory of the social scientist is living society, that observations had best have a date put on them, for society is always changing, and that a small, controlled change can be made to provide a scale for measurement and comparison.

The consensus of opinion admits five disciplines as the hard core of social science: cultural anthropology; social psychology; sociology; economics; and political science. The order corresponds with their probable grading in the use of the scientific method, anthropologists being the most rigorous and political scientists the least. It corresponds inversely with their age, for anthropology and psychology are the youngest of the disciplines, while political science is the oldest. Aristotle could be nominated as the father of political science. His *Politics* "has furnished the generations with many of the great axioms of political truth," to quote the *Encyclopaedia Britannica.*

Economics, which used to be called, perhaps more accurately, "political economy," became a formal discipline with the work of Adam Smith in the late eighteenth century. Sociology was launched in the nineteenth century with such sponsors as Emile Durkheim, Leonard Trelawney Hobhouse, Franklin H. Giddings, and Lester Frank Ward. A little later, social psychology gathered impetus from William James. Cultural anthropology was born with Lewis Henry Morgan's work on the family pattern among Seneca Indians, and came in strongly after the turn of the century. A landmark was the publication of William Graham Sumner's *Folkways* in 1906. Franz Boas and Bronislaw Malinowski were also founding fathers.

In addition to the above Big Five, various other disciplines have been offered as candidates in the course of my study. History receives almost as many votes as political science, but usually with the proviso that because it deals with events which have gone into limbo, history can never hope to measure living phenomena or use the full scientific method, and must therefore remain a kind of accessory discipline.

Legal science receives a number of votes, and so do educational methods, social work, demography, human geography, semantics, and public administration. There are a few scattering votes for philosophy, comparative religion, and ethics, but without much conviction behind them. Almost universally, now, these studies are being classed, not with social science, but with the humanities, where one sits in an armchair and reads the great books, and where the scientific method has little place. The humanities are noble studies; they elevate the mind and are often productive of great psychological certitude, but they put little in the storehouse of knowledge. The problems they solve do not stay solved. For a statesman to rely on any known system of philosophy as his main guide in meeting the world crisis of 1948 would be somehow unthinkable.

The Big Five of anthropology, psychology, sociology, economics, and political science stand out above the others, with the qualification that the lines between them are beginning to melt. Like railroads, or steel companies, the social disciplines have a tendency to merge. The Social Science Research Council is itself a kind of holding company. Some day we may have only one discipline: the science of man.

Assisting the Big Five are four tools: mathematics, statistics, logic, and semantics. Each of these tools is a formidable discipline in its own right; each is useful if not mandatory wherever problems are to be solved on any front. The scientific method would be stillborn without mathematics and statistics. It could make no hypotheses without logic. Increasingly, we are realizing that human beings often do not know what they are talking about without some functional understanding of language and its pitfalls, which is the domain of the young discipline of semantics.

With the help of questionnaires, interviews, and wide reading, I have accumulated a list of more than 100 outstanding accomplishments in the social sciences. The one with the most votes is what we may call the "culture concept" in anthropology and sociology. This label covers a body of principles derived from field studies, all revolving around the basic idea that an individual cannot be understood apart from the culture which contains him; or, to put it another way, man is a social animal. It is a broad and general concept, something like Darwin's theory of evolution. The anthropologists, by studying living cultures, have worked out some of the laws which govern all human societies everywhere. A ruler, a statesman, a big business executive, a general, a reformer—especially a reformer—who neglects these principles is likely to be beaten before he starts.

The next most favored accomplishment, surprisingly enough, is the new technique of public opinion research. It is so new that no one knows where it belongs, whether in sociology, psychology, political science, or among the tools used by all of them. Hopefully, it will never be pigeonholed, but will stand by itself as a dramatic contribution to the science of man. For it is dramatic! The public opinion polls have vindicated political democracy by proving time and again that the people are ahead of their leaders, and several light years ahead of Congress. They have thrown out of court Alexander Hamilton and his dictum—"Your people, sir, is a great beast!" The polls have proved that Hamilton did not know what he was talking about, and neither does any other pundit who would write off the lower brackets as morons, softheads, and ignoramuses.

Elmo Roper has proposed that the Federal Government itself should maintain a public opinion research agency, whose members would rank in objectivity with Supreme Court justices, constantly to poll Americans on public questions, so that Congress and the Administration really could know how people feel. As it is now, Congressmen rely on their intuition or their mail, the latter being normally the product, not of average citizens, but of angry citizens, or citizens gently stimulated by the Edison Electrical Institute.

Other accomplishments of social science which have received high ratings in my survey include:

Population forecasting, especially the reproduction index of R. R. Kuczynski

Sampling theory as applied to census figures, insurance, and the remarkable techniques of the Social Security Board. It is also the scientific basis of the polls.

The Army Airforce psychological program, a variety of aptitude testing, which picked out pilots from navigators from bombardiers from groundsmen—and probably saved the lives of 20,000 aviators. One of the most brilliant scientific achievements of the war.

Rorschach, Seashore, IQ, and other testing techniques

Dr. Alexander Leighton's extraordinary work on Japanese-Americans interned during the war

The strategic bombing surveys, where teams of social scientists combined with teams of physical scientists figured out how long Germany and Japan could last.

The preparation for dealing with natives on Okinawa, which again saved the lives of thousands of American soldiers and marines

The "Middletown" surveys, especially Lloyd Warner's work in Newburyport

Elton Mayo's revolutionary approach to labor-management relations, in which he and his Harvard Business School group have combined anthropology with psychology, sociology, and economics to find a formula whereby men can work more harmoniously together in the age of mass production

The studies in race relations by Franz Boas, Ruth Benedict, Otto Klineberg, Gunnar Myrdal, Donald Young, and others. There is no scientific proof of racial inequality. The real problem today is how to transmit these scientific findings to a group about to start a lynching, or break up a housing project.

William F. Ogburn's work on social change

Wesley Mitchell's work on business cycles

The development of GNP, the Gross National Product concept, during the war

The Keynesian approach in economics

The study by William Healy and Augusta F. Bronner which revolutionized ideas about juvenile delinquency. Leonard Doob, the Yale psychologist, says the publication of this research in 1936 made four fifths of all the previous literature obsolete!

The Cross-Cultural Index at Yale

The semantic analyses, including the work of Alfred Korzybski, Percy Bridgman, Wendell Johnson, C. K. Ogden and I. A. Richards, and others

Dr. Alfred Kinsey's extraordinary analysis of American sexual behavior

The manpower analysis without which we could not have effectively recruited soldiers or war workers

New techniques in public administration
New light on the psychology of crime and punishment
And so on, and so forth . . .

This is the way the accomplishments have been reported, more or less at random. Some I knew well, some I had heard mentioned, many were a complete surprise. I had had no idea that so much knowledge was already gathered. Most social scientists, I found, have no idea of the richness of the total field.

Can we give the list a more orderly classification? To classify by discipline is almost useless, as many of the achievements embrace two or more disciplines. The strategic bombing surveys and the Okinawa project, for instance, were the work of teams. Perhaps the following classification will do as a starter:

1. *Social science theory.*—Generalizations and "laws" which hold good in any society at any time. Examples: the laws included in the culture concept; the reproductive index in population studies.

2. *Applied social science.*—Techniques based on sound theory, available to anyone—statesman, manager, social worker, labor leader—who can learn to use them. Examples: polls of public opinion; "Middletown" surveys; training-within-industry programs for foremen; aptitude testing; fiscal devices like the techniques for checking inflation.

3. *Techniques or "know how" useful in limited areas, not universally applicable.*—Many studies in this class belong to a kind of no man's land, between the scientific method and common sense. Example: business cycle theory which applies to western civilization only.

As I pursued my studies I asked a number of social scientists this question: Do you recall any regrettable examples where accredited social science knowledge was available and not used? It brought a lively list of grievances, of which the most frequent was against the "high brass" in Army and Navy that refused to let the scientists have enough scope in running the war. Among the complaints were these:

Military Government did not really apply social science.
Army waited too long before using it.

Race data was not sufficiently employed in dealing with Negroes in the armed services.

Social science was not adequately used in psychological warfare.

Army chiefs did not realize that 1942 draftees were a different type of youngster from those of 1917. We tried to tell the chiefs what had happened to America in twenty-five years, but they would not listen.

Not all the generals disregarded social science by any means. Great strides were made in its application during the war; witness Dr. John C. Flanagan's work in picking pilots. If an admiral or a general had his share of intelligence, and the communication line was open, he soon realized that here was a powerful new weapon. So powerful indeed was the cumulative impression on the top echelons that now, long after V-J Day, the services are financing extensive research projects on human relations, still very hush-hush. Among other things, this can lead to a better understanding between the officers and the rank and file.

One can page back through history and find numberless tragic examples where our present knowledge applied at strategic periods would have saved a crushing load of needless suffering. Men persecuted men, not because they were evil, but because they did not understand what they were doing. Consider the Inquisition, the witch burners of Salem, the ferocious doctrines of the Aztecs concerning the effect on crops of human sacrifice. Consider, on another level, the terrible practices of "hardening" workers, and "building character" in children by starving and maltreating them, the dreadful "iron law of wages" propounded by economists of a century ago which held that workers could never hope to improve their condition. Aldous Huxley once defined history as a long succession of gratuitous and unnecessary miseries experienced by the mass of the people at the hands of their leaders.

Social science has now demonstrated the irrelevance of these practices, but there was little or no proof at the time they occurred. How many of our 1948 practices which obviously hurt and bewilder people will some day be found to be based on equally false assumptions? How well founded, for instance, is the case of the American Medical Association against group medicine?

Unsolved questions form the program of any developing science, and my survey has disclosed an impressive parade of them. The scientists who helped me were mostly very honest about the things which they had left undone. Indeed, there was little self-congratulation to be found but rather the contrary: "We have been at it so long, and worked so hard, and produced so little . . ." This is perhaps a better foundation to build on, however, than a mood of serene confidence.

The storehouse of social science has many empty shelves. How to contain atomic energy is, of course, the most immediately ominous problem, but plenty more are crowding right behind it, such as:

Is there any way to make the Russians understand that the Acheson-Lilienthal plan was offered in good faith; that we are really ready to surrender sovereignty?

Under what conditions can a workable world state be set up? This is probably far more of a problem for anthropologists than for political scientists.

What is the nature of patriotism? Can the drive be deflected to serve all mankind?

How big can a society grow before its members lose touch with one another, and so begin to lose their humanity? For man is a social animal.

Where does personality cease and culture begin?

How can we elicit more agreement?

Where can we discover a more dependable psychology? This is a favorite complaint among the experts.

How can leaders be protected from the demoralizing effects of their own power?

What kind of social structure can provide both freedom and economic security? Has Sweden found a formula?

What is the effect of high-energy culture on human beings, especially workers in mass-production industries? Are mental diseases on the increase?

How can workers in Western civilization again find interest in their work? Is this the key to labor-management relations?

What kind of education does a high-energy culture demand? How many child-years per pupil are wasted by present methods?

How can we apply more widely the knowledge already in the storehouse?

Such are the kinds of question which await the social scientist. I asked Dr. Louis Wirth, among others, to give me a list of what he considered the great unanswered questions. He did so, and ended with a statement which was so fine that I would like to quote it:

> The great unanswered questions of the social sciences are the great unanswered questions of mankind. How can we get peace, freedom, order, prosperity and progress under different conditions of existence? How can we establish the conditions of human well-being that have been attained in some parts of the world, or by certain groups, so that they will apply to other groups, and to other parts of the world? How can we achieve consensus in a mass democracy? How can we get the advantages of a rapidly developing technology without destroying the other values which we cherish? I know these are general and cosmic questions, but until the social sciences make a usable answer to the ways and means of achieving such ends, they will be playing a game which may be interesting enough to themselves, but one which they have no right to expect society to support.

Fortunately, many devoted students have taken up Dr. Wirth's challenge. I find them in the universities, in labor-management clinics, in government, even in business. Some signal advances in both application and theory were made during the war. I would like to close my rough and random account with one example of social science at its best.

Probably everyone has heard of how Dr. Alexander Leighton and his small staff of social scientists helped to settle the revolt of the 11,000 Japanese-Americans in their internment camp at Poston in the Arizona desert in 1942. The story is told at length in his book, *The Governing of Men,* which should be a kind of Bible for social workers, and for social scientists generally.

Dr. Leighton had unusual opportunity of studying and measuring a human society created *de novo* and then subjected to intolerable strains and frustrations. It was comparable to any other human society, except that everything developed faster, like a speeded-up movie. As a result of the study, he was able to put his finger on the key points, and to tell the camp managers how to handle the strike before it broke into great violence and bloodshed. The advice was followed, the strike was called off, and the members of the camp regained their dignity as human beings.

It is a dramatic and moving story, and would make a novel in any language. But most significant of all is the list of conclusions and principles which came out of it. Dr. Leighton begins the analysis with two constants:

1. In all the different peoples of the world there are universal basic characteristics inherent in human nature.
2. There are profound differences in belief, sentiment, habit and custom among the various communities, tribes and nations which make up human kind.

He then proceeds with a categorical list of about 100 "assumptions," "principles," and "remedies," which should prove invaluable to any student of social problems. Here are a few of them.

Do not think of people as racial, national or class stereotypes. Get up close and look at them, particularly at the children.

Think of human similarities before you think of human differences.

Never dismiss complaints as trivial; they may be storm signals.

The test of administration is ability to meet the needs of the people in that situation. When needs are not met, tension begins.

Try to control aggression, but never try to stamp it out. You will only make it worse. Get at the roots.

Always keep the communication line open, both down from the top and up from the bottom.

When the strike erupted on a gray November day, Leighton's group were in constant attendance during the critical hours. They did not make the final decision of whether or not to call in the Army—which would probably have meant a massacre with very serious international repercussions—but they put the major characteristics of the situation before the man who had to make it, so when he said "No," it was on the basis of understanding instead of passion or fear or prejudice.

The proof of the pudding is in the eating. The decision worked. It gave the right solution to a very difficult problem. This exact solution will not fit every problem of group tension. But the experiment at Poston reveals a technique, and a body of principles, which no administrator anywhere on earth, whether he runs a continent or corner grocery, can afford to overlook.

Dr. Leighton shows us what social scientists can do when they really roll up their sleeves. He shows us, too, a happy combination of observation, theory, and practical application. Enough work like this and we will begin to know something about controlling the bombs of human nature. Then we need not much fear the bombs the physicists make.

Steps toward Welfare in a Democratic State

EARL HARRISON

IT HAS BEEN SUGGESTED, and I thoroughly agree, that "neither the lay public nor the technical professional folk see social welfare whole to the degree that is desirable if public and private programs (looking toward social welfare), as well as professional and lay citizens, are to find ways of playing their several parts." To the extent that we see only in part, it is manifest that we understand only in part. While we see and understand only in part, it is inevitable that our steps toward welfare will be retarded and made shorter because of conflicts of interests more often imaginary than real.

The steps that have been taken toward social welfare in our democratic state are clearly reflected in the hundred-year history of the Community Service Society of New York. They constitute the story of the evolution, in the main slow but at times comparatively rapid, from individual almsgiving, helping the "poor," then through organized efforts at "charity," finally to the more modern concept of extending "the helping hand to people in all walks of life who need skilled assistance and counsel and intelligent direction in order that they may cope with their problems more effectively."

It is the story that begins with "kind-hearted ladies and gentlemen" and in its later pages deals more with the board member, the trained social worker, the agency, the community chest, the government administrator. The steps were many in number between "pauper" and "client," from the "handout" or "dole" to "service" and "insurance." This story, in its broad outlines, is well known to all of us. The terminology we have used almost in itself tells the story of our steps toward welfare. It is a story characterized throughout by increasing consideration and understanding of the individual, his dignity and his worth in our society; more understanding, too, of the real causes of personal disaster which call for assistance, for counsel, for, in short, the helping hand.

In its daily work the Community Service Society constantly stresses the family. I would stress today another kind of family, a family the three members of which have been responsible for the steps forward that have been taken toward social welfare. This family, like most families, has been marked at times by dissension, by bickering and jealousy, by lack of understanding of the function and importance of the other members of the family. Frequently, there has been more pulling and tugging than marching together. Perhaps that is just typically American: we do not like regimentation. It becomes disturbing only when the members of this social welfare family do not recognize the family relationship and the absolute interdependence of each member upon the others for progress toward the goal of a truer democracy.

Obviously, the family to which I refer, the family which, while working in harmony, has made the greatest strides toward social welfare, is comprised of the individual citizen who years ago worked almost alone in helping his neighbors; the private organization, which developed in order to make more effective and scientific the efforts of many individuals; and finally government, which as our young country has grown more complex has had to assume its large share of social responsibility.

It is clear to many, but unfortunately not to all of us, that the task of improving and insuring the social welfare requires the understanding, the participation, the coöperation, of all three members of the family. It seems to me that is the truly American way of tackling the problem. It represents the complete "all-out" effort. Yet there has been a curious tendency, as a new member has been added to the family, for those who theretofore comprised it to suppose that somehow their social responsibilities lessened or indeed even vanished. Unfortunately, the task of moving forward on the social welfare front is too vast to permit of that. Sometimes, too, there has been resistance to adding new members to the family of those seeking to improve the human lot. Progress will be retarded, the forward steps shortened, so long as people in our communities even think, much less say, such things as: "Why should I support the community chest—or this or that agency or hospital—when the government gives relief, social security, and the rest?" Or, "These government programs of public assistance, aid to this group or that, are just bound to destroy the initiative, the self-reliance, the independence of the people and make them weak and irresponsible." Or even, "I support the community chest and pay my taxes—don't ask me to do anything else in this so-called 'social welfare' field."

Such remarks flow from the mistaken belief that responsibility for social welfare belongs to one or two but less than the threesome mentioned. Our principal problem, it seems to me, is to continue to demonstrate, as past experience has, that social welfare in the days ahead is indeed a tripartite business.

It has been largely this uncertainty, I think, as to whose business social welfare is (plus, perhaps, a feeling that each individual should and must look after himself or else depend upon benevolent private industry) that has caused us as a nation to lag behind in our steps toward welfare. Modern law students are astonished to learn how comparatively late we were in adopting workmen's compensation legislation; they read with amazement, in a course I give, the exhaustive opinion of the highest court of this state of New York in 1911 which held invalid the first such statute passed in this country, as inconsistent with our constitutional form of government. The idea of distributing risks and losses from accident, sickness, unemployment, old age, or death spread very slowly here, nearly one quarter of a century after the start of the British governmental system of insurances and nearly half a century after the commencement of the German program. It took a national disaster finally to spike the widely prevalent notion that "every man could establish his own provision against disaster."

It is manifest, as we look back over the evolution of social security legislation in this country, that vast progress was made in a single decade. Yet that able public servant and sound administrator Commissioner Arthur J. Altmeyer is still obliged to remind us that "the greatest inadequacy of our present social insurance system is, of course, the failure to provide protection against the economic hazards of ill health" and that "except in periods of deep and prolonged depression, ill health is the leading cause of destitution in this and other industrial nations." In spite of the enormous gains in the number of persons covered by voluntary plans for the prepayment of medical or hospital services and for health insurance, there is considerable reason to believe that one of our next steps for the common welfare must be to decide, in the interests of all, the issues raised by the Wagner-Murray-Dingell bill and the Taft health bill. It does not redound to our credit as a nation that a recent survey based on a number of significant health factors, including sanitation, recreation, housing, economic conditions, and hygienic practices, should classify half the states of the Union as either poor or bad.

Our furtherance of the social welfare was strengthened and made more sure when the organization, whether it was a voluntary social agency or a business enterprise, joined with the individual in planning and executing programs for assisting those in need. Again a long step forward was taken when government joined in recognizing the obligation to assist in the solution of human problems. The steps we will find it possible to take in the future will depend in large measure, in my opinion, upon the continued interest, participation, and coöperation of the lay citizen, the private organization, and the public institution of government.

Few of us any longer hold the view once vociferated that it is a reflection upon the capitalistic system, upon free enterprise, that government should be looked to for any form of individual security even in times of distress and hardship. At the same time, if we are to preserve, as we must, the spirit of personal initiative, incentive, and industry, we must guard against too ready acceptance of the notion of "let the government do it." The interest, the concern, the efforts, of the other two members of my mythical social welfare family must be retained. I like to think of it as the American approach to the problem of furthering the social welfare. As individuals, we are concerned with people and their well-being—they may be our relatives, they may be our neighbors. To the extent that we may be in a position to do so, we lend a helping hand here and there, we share. Then, because we know that this business is full time and frequently requires great skill, we set up organizations which can do a better job than we as individuals acting separately can do. Finally, we recognize that in some situations so many of our neighbors need assistance of one kind or another in spite of their best efforts that we call upon and make it possible for government to join in the business of human welfare.

There are encouraging signs that greater teamwork is developing. This is due in no small measure to another development of which I would make special mention.

I am constantly amazed at the general lack of comprehension of the desirability, nay the necessity, of professional training for social work. I suppose that many still hold the opinion expressed some years ago by a prominent political figure that "all it takes for relief work is a good heart and common sense." That point of view over the years has cost us plenty of money and many a broken spirit. Some of those who were supposed to possess both a good heart and common sense had neither; instead, they had political friends.

Several years ago, I delivered the commencement address at the graduation ceremonies of the Pennsylvania School of Social Work, the first of such occasions following the affiliation of that School with the University of Pennsylvania—a relationship which, I am happy to say, recently ripened into a merger. I selected as the topic of my talk, "Professional Training for Social Work." A member of the law faculty, destined later to be a senior colleague of mine, said to me immediately before the exercises, in a tone that was not too reassuring, "I shall be glad to hear your argument."

I knew that his skepticism was shared by others and I was ready for them. Rather aggressively, I stated the difficulty I had in understanding why professional people and others should so completely accept the fact that law students could acquire skills through the study of case histories, and medical students through the clinical method, and yet should wonder whether one planning a social work career would benefit or could acquire skills through precisely the same techniques and methods. I was rewarded after the ceremony by admissions from several listeners that they had never thought of the School of Social Work in that light.

Gradually, the performance of the professionally trained social worker is demonstrating itself. Graduate schools of social work, like other professional schools, are flooded with applications. The demand for their graduates is much greater than the supply. It has been the competence and ever increasing skill of the trained social worker together with the maintained interest of the lay board member and volunteer that has brought our private agency to such a high state of efficiency and our public services to sounder, more effective, more economical operation.

For years, as a result of my experience with many social agencies and with some government programs, the trained, career worker has been included in my social welfare family as an indispensable part of private organization and of government in its welfare responsibilities. While there has been a tendency in parts of government to disparage the importance of professionally trained social workers (as well as lawyers), it is clear that the steps which we must take toward welfare will require the skills and competence of those specially trained for the tasks. Karl de Schweinitz makes this eminently clear in his recent book *People and Process in Social Security*.

A recent writer, in discussing the American way, referred to "the weapons of the world's most dynamic ideology," and then wrote: "For what are the two most dynamic motivations in the world? One is individual opportunity for profit; the other is dedication to the service of humanity." The steps we take in future will determine perhaps more than those taken in the past whether dedication to the service of humanity is one of the most dynamic motivations of our democratic state.

The Unique Place of Voluntary Welfare Agencies in American Culture

HAL H. GRISWOLD

THIS TOPIC is a challenging one. It is one on which I have very strong convictions, convictions that are not grounded on any profound study of social phenomena nor implemented with any professional training as a social worker. They are strictly the reflections of the man on the street. They are the thoughts of an ordinary citizen who has been close enough to the social problems of one of our great cities to have some intelligent comprehension of how much there is he does not know, and yet far enough away to view the situation in perspective.

Whether right or wrong, the thoughts of the man on the street are of vital importance. He is the raw material out of which our culture must be fashioned; to a large extent, he is the tool with which the work must be done; he is the source from which must come the motive power to drive the tools. It may prove to be more important that the experts and professionals in social work should know what it is that the layman does not know, how much of what he thinks he knows is not true, than it is for him to know how much the professional worker knows.

The terms "democracy" and "social welfare" are dangerously vague. We may yield to the temptation of being satisfied to accept them as slogans without too critical consideration of their realities. In the Introduction to his volume of American writings which he calls *The Democratic Spirit,* Bernard Smith says, "The words men fight and die for are the coins of politics where by much usage they are soiled and by much manipulation debased. They have come to mean whatever anyone wants them to mean."

The same might be said of the term "social welfare." Both the limitations of space and a lawyer-like sense of caution forbid me to attempt a definition of either, but I think we can agree that two concepts are included in both.

Democracy must produce an environment in which the individual can express his inner urge for something better, in which he can grow and feel that there is a purpose in life for him. It must also cultivate in the individual a capacity for adjustment to the conditions of his environment which he cannot change. This is an important part of a social welfare program.

The first essential in projecting a social welfare program that will meet the needs of a democratic society in the fast-moving complex world of today is to arouse in the mind of every thinking citizen an awareness of the extent and nature of the social needs in such a world. It is not enough that the social worker should know. It is not enough that the man on the street should give merely abstract intellectual assent. He must have convictions. He pays the taxes, he makes the contributions. When his methods of operation in business give rise to conditions that interfere with the social welfare, he is forced to submit to many forms of regulation that limit the freedom of his enterprise. Furthermore, he votes. That is important in a democracy. He is likely to vote "no" on what he does not understand.

He must be brought to see the social welfare program as something more than merely giving food and shelter to the poor in the spirit of sweet charity. He must see it as a project in social engineering, as a means of conditioning and preparing the raw human materials of our society to stand up under the stresses and strains of life in an age of power and speed. He must see it as a program that will parallel, in its intelligent approach and scientific method and in its money cost, the processes of conditioning the raw materials of modern industry and the development of the economic and industrial system that has made America the most powerful country in the world.

The man on the street is ready for that concept of an approach to the solution of social problems. For the most part, he is himself an expert in some more or less limited activity, whether in adjusting automobile motors, raising red hogs or black and white cows, or writing ads for cosmetics. He knows the value of special training, and how to use expert service. He knows that poor tools are expensive.

But the man on the street does not now understand what a social welfare program is. He does not grasp the urgency of the need for such a program and he does not understand why it will cost so much. This is not because he is a fool. It is not because he is indifferent to human welfare. It is because he is engaged in what seems to him a tremendous struggle for his own economic survival in the intense competition of the business world today. To him, the idea of a planned social program—as distinguished from merely helping someone in trouble—lies on the outer fringes of his consciousness. He knows such ideas exist, but their outlines are blurred and distorted. That picture must be brought sharply into the foreground of his vision. There is no instrument at hand which can be as effective as a well-organized private social agency in bringing before the eyes of the intelligent citizen the picture of the social problems that arise out of our amazing material progress. Give him a place on the governing board or on an active committee and the chance to feel that he has a real contribution to make, allow him to get the "feel" of dealing with a social problem, and we will find that we have tapped unsuspected resources of power. The service that the man on the street is asked to do, must be made real, not merely perfunctory—and it usually can be, with proper planning and proper appreciation of his potentialities.

The history of every large community is rich with examples of men who acquired their first glimpse of social planning by perfunctory acceptance of a place on an agency board and who then, sensing the larger possibilities, have brought their keen vision and organizing genius to bear, not only on that agency, but on the problem of so shaping economic and business practices as to correct conditions out of which social maladjustments grow.

This is true not only with respect to the big men of business and professional life whose names are familiar in the headlines; it is true of countless others in many walks of life, from the work-bench or the counter to the executive's chair. Here is a great storehouse of latent social power to which voluntary social agencies hold the key. Wayne McMillen in a chapter on private social agencies has said that there is a tendency to overemphasize case-work and underemphasize basic community conditions in which problems of maladjustment will not arise. Business and professional men and women who can be induced to serve on agency boards are in a strategic position to influence such conditions, and history proves that they have done so.

The second essential for building a social program is to get some measure of its probable magnitude.

In the lifetime of a few generations we have seen three historic revolutions. The political revolution in Western Europe, of which the formation of our democracy was a part, uprooted age-old concepts of human relations as expressed by the law and made necessary the scrapping of many cherished traditions. We are now struggling with the burden of trying to make democracy work.

The Industrial Revolution made more change in the conditions in which man lives than had occurred in any period of a thousand years before. If all progress were to stop today, if not a single invention, discovery, or improvement were made for a century, the impact of what has already happened would be felt for many generations. But material and scientific advance will go on and at an accelerated pace.

We are now in the midst of a revolution in international relations that brings our American culture and ideologies into close proximity to other cultures and ideologies. Like the attraction or repulsion of magnetic poles, the influence of one on the other probably increases inversely as the square of the diminishing distance between them. The social effects of these rapid changes are superimposed upon each other. Each of them has components that are transmitted through the social system and are eventually brought to bear on the individual. Finding himself the focal point of social forces, rapidly changing in intensity and direction, the individual faces, indeed, a stupendous task of adjustment.

Social effects usually lag behind the causes that produce them, and they do not lag to the same degree in any two cases. A change in educational methods may require ten years to reach its peak effect. A change in tenor of radio advertising may reach its maximum in two. If some mathematical genius with a social work attachment could derive a mathematical constant which we could call a power coefficient of social complexity and which would tell us how much social complexity increases with each increase of horsepower per capita, available to mankind, it might help us estimate the growing difficulties of social adjustment that confront mankind. Of course, such a thought is fanciful, but the need for some method of measurement is real.

I have no idea what such a coefficient might be, but it would be staggering. The thousands of men and women who are serving on voluntary agency boards today furnish the nucleus around which to build an understanding of the magnitude of the task we face and an acceptance of the truth that the effort must be commensurate in terms of money and time with the cost of building the economic structure. They know that they cannot lubricate their high-compression motors with the ten-cent box of mica axle grease I used on the old farm wagon. They are intelligent enough to draw the parallel.

To illustrate, rather than to enumerate some of the questions which the future may pose for us, I mention a few, picked at random from the talk of the man on the street:

"What is all this talk of social security going to do to the ambition of mankind? How can you expect him to plan, to strive, and to save if he knows he is going to be cared for anyway?"

"What are we doing to the mind of mankind by high-pressure selling, and lurid, strident, discordant advertising appeals for selling gadgets? Are we not creating desires that have no relation to real needs and preparing the individual for frustration because no day is long enough and no stomach big enough even to try out all the things that are made to seem so alluring and desirable?"

Perhaps the advertising man would answer that second one by another question, "Does not this process build up a power of discriminating choice and thus benefit instead of frustrate mankind?" My answer is a qualified "yes." Yours might not be. The real point is that neither of us knows.

We could multiply these questions by the hundreds. Each one has his own list. I do not know that any of the conditions will present real hazards for the future, but I do know that in our high-speed organization we cannot afford to assume without some scientific study that such questions have no meaning. Some of these conditions, moreover, may prove to be real hazards, and unless we have a means of quick detection of such new social effects, many a dangerous social condition will develop which it is difficult or even impossible to check in the advance stages.

The private social agency has historically been the means by which weak spots in our social fabric have been brought to public attention. Some individual who has suffered or who has seen others suffer from a specific social condition which is not generally sensed, has organized an effort to provide a remedy. Sometimes the efforts have been foolish and fruitless. Sometimes the sponsors have been fanatics. Nevertheless, when the need has been real, it has eventually drawn the attention of others who have the balance and vision to do something effective. In the turbulent days that surely lie ahead of us the private social agencies can and must, to an even greater degree than in the past, be the sensitized organs of our social system to detect and report the points of social friction.

The third essential is the adoption of the scientific method. The bewildering complex of social forces, created by the three revolutionary movements, and their cumulative effect on human thought and human action present to mankind history's greatest challenge. Has man created a Frankenstein which will destroy him?

This age of miracles in which we live, this age of power and speed and size, could only come when man ceased to guess and began to measure. He then began his mastery of physical power,

Seven hundred odd years ago, the philosopher Bacon made the classical statement of the scientific method of investigation of all phenomena. It was not until 200 years ago that the full value of this method of thought was put to work in creating mankind's age of power. It is only within a half century that anyone but the few pioneers has recognized that the same sequence of steps in thinking can help create a social system to accompany the modern era of power, speed, and gadgets. At each one of the steps in the classical scientific method, the voluntary social agency has a unique and valuable contribution to offer.

The strength of the scientific method lies in the order of sequence of its operations. The true scientist tries to keep them separate in his thinking. The first step is observation and experimentation. Find out what are the facts. That search is sometimes spectacular. More often it is a slow and painful process. It is typified by the physicists' measuring of the electrical charge of an ion. For countless hours they sat with eye glued to the ocular of a little telescope, timing the passage of minute charged particles of oil between two electrically charged plates. Thousands of observations were necessary. And when they finally had the answer the number was so small that it required some twenty-eight ciphers before the first significant figure in order to express it. Out of such searching for the infinitesimal came electronics. Many of the researches needed by social science are like that. The primary unit of social science is the individual. It is the play of the complex of forces on the individual which we must analyze if social health and welfare are preserved. These forces acting on the individual and interacting with his own inherent powers are, in turn, the power that operates democracy.

The physicists tell us that we can completely define any force by stating its direction, its intensity, and its point of application, and, given the intensity and direction of each of the forces playing on a given point of application, the physicist can determine the direction and speed with which the point will move. No such precision has been achieved in social science, but the principle is the same. For the study of the individual case the private agency is ideally equipped. The agency can limit its intake, choose its cases, and pursue its quest of facts. It is not confronted to the same degree as the tax-supported agency with the necessity of "treating everybody alike." It can keep more complete and significant case records without fear of being accused of creating political jobs for stenographers. This can be helpful in revealing defects in community organization or in public agency work.

The second step in the method is classification of data. Facts must be arranged and classified so that all forces which bear on a single point are brought together. If facts are missing, this process reveals the gaps. The private agency which is a member of an organized group and has access to a social service exchange is in a strategic position in this process. The agency function in classifying and assembling factual material is made more important because many social facts are such that they cannot be revealed by the artificial process of experimentation to the same degree as in physical science. They must be found in the field. With a board which understands the value of the scientific approach, an executive devoted to the search for truth even when truth hurts, and a chance to receive from other agencies and give to other agencies the results of its observations—and insulated from the clamor of pressure groups that might seek to influence results—the private agency can correlate and classify its facts and organize its materials in the scientific method of study.

The third step is the most important—generalization. From the facts assembled and classified, conclusions are drawn as to the general principles governing the subject under study. The private agency with a board composed of persons who know the value of research in industry, and who have a more flexible control of funds, can attract a grade of scientific talent not available otherwise. Many outstanding research projects have been carried out by public agencies, but for quick adjustment to new needs or long and expensive pursuit of principles that may for the time seem unimportant, the voluntary agency has a flexibility that is invaluable.

When conclusions are drawn and stated there comes the fourth step—the acid test of application to the practice of every day. Few great industrial discoveries are tried out on a mass-production basis. Pilot plants are set up where mistakes can be freely made without too great a cost. The private agency is often the pilot plant of the social service system. Its flexibility and freedom are particularly suited to this task. The price of progress is usually a multitude of mistakes. The private agency can make them faster and more cheaply than one which feels an obligation to try to serve all alike. In such a setting, creative imagination has a chance to play.

The last step of the scientific method is verification. No true scientist ever accepts even the severe test of practical application as final. He always seeks new situations, new combinations of his basic facts, to test the soundness of his conclusions. As in the stage of experimentation, the voluntary agency, alert to the importance of keeping step with progress, can make itself indispensable. The intensive methods of social casework reveal many human situations which no scientist could foresee. Only a critical check-testing by personnel professionally qualified is likely to do an effective job.

The fourth essential for sound building is the recognition of the kind of material with which we are dealing. In this age of speed we are accustomed to quick results. We want the architect's preliminary sketches today, his basic drawings Saturday, the working drawings a week from Thursday, and the grand opening in sixty days. We have speeded up mechanical processes unbelievably. We may make the mistake of trying to do the same thing with our social system. But we must recognize that human society is an organism, not a mechanism. As an eminent biologist has said, "There is no such thing as a state of rest in the organic world. An organism either grows and matures or atrophies and decays." And each organization carries within itself certain limitations on the rate of its change, and these limits cannot be violated with impunity. We must not be too impatient with the slowness of social change.

A social agency is an organism too, but it may not and probably will not change at the same rate nor in the same direction as the society which it serves. In the words of the physicist, it is in a different frame of reference. It may require a sociological

Einstein to keep a social agency properly related to the society in which it works. And therein lies one strength of a voluntary social agency, its power of organic adaptation. A social agency created by law and governed by detailed regulations is an element of stability in the social organization and an indispensable part of a democratic system. But it is likely to have weaknesses that are inherent in the manner of its creation. Close association of public and private agencies is a source of strength for both.

In discussing the characteristics of private agencies which give them a distinctive place in our culture there is no intention to imply that such agencies are better than public agencies nor that they are the exclusive possessors of the virtues discussed. Each has its points of strength developed in process of organic adjustment to the needs of the general social organism. The thought should be not *Private* vs. *Public,* but private and public agencies working in harmony as parts of the organism of society.

As the extent of public welfare services increases, the role of the voluntary agency as a complementary instrument becomes more vital. Private agencies and private agency groups have much to learn in the art of influencing legislation concerning, and administration of, public social welfare services. There may be times when it is necessary for such agencies to institute a group pressure movement. Telegrams may sometimes succeed. But the better contributions of voluntary agencies have been made when a confidential, personal relation has been created between the board members and the staff of the agency and the public authorities in charge of welfare services.

Improvement of welfare services may sometimes be obtained by creating fear of losing votes. Such victories are likely to be short-lived. A more effective contribution can be made when an earnest citizen, identified with a voluntary agency, and with no ax to grind, is able to sit across the table from a public official and talk to him as "Jim" or "Charlie" and show that he has an intelligent understanding of the difficulties under which that official works. The ideal that the social worker shall be entirely aloof from politics seems attractive, but it is seldom practical.

Politics is the lifeblood of a democracy. We cannot purify the stream by avoiding it.

In the business world today the intensely practical consideration of profits has forced a realization that there is usually one best way of doing any operation. An attempt is made to adopt the best, and out of these attempts grow standards of performance. Sometimes in business they take the form of standard specifications. Standards of doing social work are no less vital to success, but the value is seldom quite so obvious and the acceptance of standards not so general. There is no balance sheet and no profit and loss account to prove it. The voluntary agency, again, is peculiarly adapted to developing standards and demonstrating their value when they are adopted. This is one way in which the private agency can be helpful to the public official.

The role of private social agencies in our culture should be studied, not only with respect to what they have done in the past, but, more important, with relation to what their unique characteristics may enable them to do for the social welfare of tomorrow. There can be little doubt that if American culture meets the challenge of the hour, every instrumentality will need to be used to its utmost efficiency. The workman must know his tools. He must be ready to redesign them if conditions require.

The private social agency system is undergoing change and growth. The possibilities of further growth and adaptation are unlimited. The process may consist of new agencies or modification of programs of existing agencies or both.

The suggestion that formation of more private agencies may be called for is not a pleasing one to a community chest officer. With limitations on the sources of funds for private philanthropy becoming more marked, the problem of budgeting is already complex enough. The answer lies, however, not in a consideration of the quantity of social service to be financed from private contributions, but in the character of the service. To a greater degree than ever the private agency will perform the function of revealing the needs and demonstrating the methods than in carrying the mass load of service.

Two safeguards must be maintained against undue multiplication of private social agencies in any community and undue burdens on the relatively limited supply of private funds. The first lies in recognition of the organic nature of the community. No agency today can make any effective contribution to the community which does not bear a close relation to other agencies, both public and private. Councils of social agencies, if carefully organized, can provide a screening process to form a sound judgment as to whether a new agency is needed and to arrive at a logical definition of its functions. There must also be a means whereby agencies which have outlived the need which created them can be absorbed or eliminated. This must not be a process of arbitrary decision but of slow, organic adaptation.

The second safeguard is to recognize more fully that a social agency is not necessarily a charitable agency in the conventional sense of the word. Many of the social needs of modern society arise out of other causes than poverty. The services the agencies have to offer are such that the recipient will be better served if he pays for them. Character-building agencies, hospitals, and family service agencies have gone far in this direction, and the principle is susceptible to even broader application.

The shorter work week and the shorter day, the longer vacations, and the longer life expectancy after retirement age have made available a great quantity of leisure time. Students of social phenomena have recognized that this presents a social danger. Such time not used constructively might prove to be a serious danger. But we must see in it an opportunity too. Many thousands of men and women are finding that ordinary kill-time recreations pall. They feel the need of something to do that gives them a sense of doing something worth while. Here is a social force of almost unlimited latent power. Volunteer workers carefully trained in nonprofessional activities can supply much of the manpower for the expanded social program, and thus the agencies can avoid too great a reliance on governmental programs.

Democracy will be stronger if not all its processes are channeled through government. The processes that gave rise to the concept of democracy are still going on. The spirit of democracy must find means of expression far broader than mere civil government. The temptation to regiment the conduct of our fellow man by governmental mandate is strong. But it is dangerous, even when used for desirable social ends.

To the extent that voluntary group action can produce the same result by demonstrating the soundness of an idea rather than the strength of a mandate, democracy will be strengthened. Voluntary social agencies can exert a power out of all proportion to the numbers of their membership or the amount of money spent. They are one of the finest types of expression of the democratic spirit.

A Group Educational Approach to Child Development

MARIANNE KRIS, M.D.

THERE HAS BEEN in social work a transition from the field of welfare in the traditional sense of charitable interest to the modern conception of welfare as assistance in social adjustment. This change in scope contains an implication: charity aims at relieving an actual hardship mainly by economic support, whereas help in readjustment—both economic and psychological—aims at creating conditions in which we hope to protect the individual so far as possible from the recurrence of hardship due to external or internal pressures. It implies, therefore, a step in prevention.

In every field in which we, as psychiatrists, study human beings, we have made and are making similar steps. Our interest is shifting from therapeutic to prophylactic techniques. Empirical data and theoretical considerations have suggested this shift. During the last half century we have learned, in our clinical work, to understand the importance of earliest experiences for the growth of personality; in our theoretical considerations we have come to think in terms of dynamic and genetic connections. Both the therapeutic and the theoretical sides are based, largely if not exclusively, on Freud's work.

I shall suggest in merest outline, and probably in as yet unpracticable form, some steps that social work or psychiatric welfare might find useful in the future, starting from the fact that in the majority of cases, psychiatric social work is likely to lead to the point where the conscientious worker or the client (and especially the client who profits from the agency's work) complains that the contact with the agency has been established "so late"; in some instances, that the contact has been established "too late."

Let me illustrate:

In the McCallum family the mother and father are working, both in clerical jobs. There are four children. All the members of the family have become the agency's clients except the father, who cannot be seen regularly because he is too severely handicapped. A number of years ago he had a serious accident from which he retained a permanent impediment; three years ago he developed epileptic attacks which have imposed some limitations on his working capacity. Shortly before his first epileptic attack Mrs. McCallum had returned to work since the living expenses of the growing family made it necessary to increase the family income. In reality, it seems that the children had already become an emotional liability to her, and she was attracted by the possibility of being absent from home for the major part of the day.

Twelve-year-old Elizabeth shares her mother's problems. She is able and efficient in the care of her younger siblings but shows the effects of the strain this identification imposes upon her; she worries about her younger brothers and participates in her mother's likes and dislikes for them. The worker who treats her finds that Elizabeth needs help in order to make the transition from being an infantile matron into being an adolescent.

Elizabeth's dislike of nine-year-old Tommy, the sibling next to her in age, is marked. He is a ruffian and has joined a gang. All that is known about him seems to indicate that he is on his way to delinquency; one might say that he is predelinquent. The mother expresses great concern, since she feels that her oldest boy has slipped away from her. Little help can be expected from the father, who, especially since the development of his epileptic condition, tends either to be overirritable or to withdraw from his family when he returns from work. The agency is trying to make plans for Tommy's readjustment by establishing more favorable social contacts for him after school. Little can be said as to the probable success of these attempts.

The two younger boys pose different problems, although both are to some extent identified with their wayward older brother.

Charles, aged seven, is not only prone to be a fire-setter, as Tommy is, and to steal and indulge in occasional spells of truancy, but he has other, even more disturbing behavior patterns: hyperactivity and destructive impulses, which he seems unable to control and which lead to outbreaks of what his mother calls "devilish laughter." At other times he suddenly gives up motility and lies motionless on the floor. It seems that he impersonates either Tommy or his father. Both impersonations are unbearable to the mother, who frankly admits that she feels so unable to cope with Charles, and especially with his demands on her attention, that she prefers her work to her home. And yet Charles is the main object of her concern.

Matthew, aged five, shows many features that remind one of Charles. The arsonic proclivities of his brothers are alive in him, and he throws stones at windows in the street. He is difficult to control and as hyperactive as Charles, but alternatively he sucks his thumb and displays baby manners. The nursery school which he attends found that Matthew could not without help adjust to a normal school environment and insisted that the mother establish contact with the agency.

When Mrs. McCallum discussed Matthew's problems and was shown that he could be helped, she at once stated that he was not the only one in the family in need of treatment—and to her mind not even the one whose need was most urgent. She considered Charles the most severely threatened child.

I shall not enter into a further discussion of the McCallum family, which has profited considerably from the agency's intervention, but shall draw attention to the inadequacy of the referral. Only the circumstance that an understanding nursery teacher sent Matthew for treatment set the ball rolling. So far as the agency is concerned it will roll for a good many years. Had the agency had an opportunity to intervene when the family was first exposed to a traumatic situation—when the father had his severe accident, shortly after Elizabeth's birth—all subsequent developments could have been more easily guided, and the effect of the father's behavior on the children and on his wife might have been favorably influenced. We can see further potentialities in early referral. From the history of the case we find that it took Mr. McCallum nine years to decide to use appropriate help in relation to one of the consequences of his accident, not because medical advice was lacking, but because he was psychologically unprepared to accept this advice. A psychiatric social worker might have been able to accelerate the solution of this problem.

Let me turn to a second and even clearer example:

When Mrs. Johnson died, her husband, a workman, was left with two children, Peter, aged five, and Alice, aged two and a half. We know little about the mother, but it seems that her death, caused by an accident, might have occurred when she was in a state of intoxication. Mr. Johnson took a serious view of his responsibilities. He wanted to maintain a home for his children and replace the lost maternal attention. From the agency's later experience with Mr. Johnson it appears that his intentions were, at the time, sincere, and with appropriate guidance he might have succeeded in living up to his intentions in spite of his rather rough approach toward the children. However, he did not establish contact with the agency, and the course of the developments in his family can only be reconstructed from data collected four years later. By that time Peter had had several encounters with the law, and the minister of Mr. Johnson's church advised him to approach the agency.

After the death of his mother, Peter apparently showed grief and withdrew into himself, while Alice enjoyed the full attention and possession of the father. The attraction seemed to have been mutual. All three had to sleep in one room, and Alice slept in Mrs. Johnson's bed. Alice and the father became close companions, and Peter felt excluded. He joined a street gang and gradually adjusted to the behavior of the older boys. His father reacted with severity, criticism, and continual scolding. The boy reinforced his rebellious waywardness. He soon was adept in throwing stones, breaking windows, and stealing, thus proving his virile adequacy in terms of the gang's ideals. Unlike other members of the gang, he managed to expose himself both to physical danger and to the danger of getting caught; we may suspect that the identification with his mother was here at work.

Peter has greatly profited by the treatment the agency offered. The dramatic story of the battle of good and evil in him need not be told here; it is one of the cases in which the therapeutic skill and devotion of a psychiatric social worker have saved a child. One aspect of this case deserves our attention. If contact with the agency had been established immediately after Mrs. Johnson's death, or even earlier, not only would Peter have been able to avoid his delinquent career, but Alice also could have been protected. Now, at eleven, she is in a boarding school. Reports from the school indicate that she has developed into a sexually endangered pre-adolescent, undoubtedly as a consequence of the early stimulation of her sexual fantasies through the closeness to her well-intentioned father—to whose love she was exposed without the protection of a mother figure.

The social worker also gave guiding help to Mr. Johnson during her treatment of Peter. The father showed so much coöperation and developed so much understanding of the boy's needs and the implications of the triangular situation existing after his wife's death that we are justified in assuming that guidance at that time might have helped him to avoid many mistakes and their consequences and possibly have facilitated his own readjustment. His closeness to Alice seems to have prevented him from finding a wife for himself and a mother for his children.

These are the types of case where the help that psychiatric social work is able to give came late and possibly too late.

Let us turn now to a positive example, a case in which the agency's intervention came just in time, although it seemed at first as if the agency were once more too late.

Agatha, aged nineteen, was sent to the agency by the court. She had been picked up in a house of prostitution on the day that she had reluctantly entered it. The pretty and intelligent girl told a story that sounded fantastic but proved to be literally true. She was married and pregnant, and had done what she did in order to obtain money for an abortion. Her husband was a college student who had kept his marriage a secret from his family, mainly from his mother, who fully controlled him psychologically and only partly supported him economically.

The situation seemed oddly complicated until its psychological dynamics became apparent in Agatha's treatment. Her mother had died when Agatha was nine years of age. The father had placed her in various foster homes and institutions. At fifteen, she left the last of these placements on her own decision, started to work, and attended high school at night. She then lived with friends, and her life seemed to be on an even keel. Three years later, her father remarried. Agatha suddenly felt the urge to live with him and his wife. She intruded into their home and found a series of disappointments. Her father demanded most of what she earned but pursued her with unceasing criticism; he described her as a failure in every respect until she could no longer bear his nagging. She left her father's home, half determined to become the failure he saw in her.

As a first step in this career of debauchery she entered into a sexual relationship with John, a school friend, with whom she had been going steadily. As a next step she became pregnant. John at once consented to marry her, but after their marriage he could not bring himself to inform his family or to accept the role of father. At this point Agatha became desperate and with great reluctance let herself be induced to enter the house of prostitution from which she was fortunately rescued in time.

The social worker who saw Agatha was soon in a position to uncover the motivation for her unusual career: she was engaged in a bout of vengeful rebellion directed against her father and displaced onto her husband. When she had been made aware of this, and the unconscious tendency to aggression against the male had, in part, been worked through, the agency could intensify its contact with John, which had been established previously. He was assisted in his attempts to resist his mother's domination. Both Agatha and John were soon ready to look forward to living together with their child. This result was partly achieved by additional clarification of their economic situation. When John was helped to understand that his life with Agatha and the child would not necessarily interfere with his studies and plans for his career, he became determined and even enthusiastic to achieve it.

Reports of their life that have reached the agency almost encourage us to say, "and so they lived happily ever after." Or, let us say with some circumspection that these reports encourage the hope that John and Agatha will bring any later difficulties to the agency before it is "too late."

Let us survey these examples. In the first two cases we raised the question of how soon the agency's contact with the client should have started. That question was answered in the third example. The contact should start before the birth of the child. This is in full agreement with some of the clinical findings of psychiatry which, during the last two decades, have gained in precision, incomplete and fragmentary as they still are. We have come to learn a good deal more about the types and phases of crucial experiences in the child's life, and have extended our knowledge to the toddler and to the infant. The various contributions of Anna Freud to our knowledge of early child development are the kind of data that I have in mind. Her reports of systematic observation in Vienna over several years before the war, and, during the war, in the Hampstead Nursery in London,[1] have not only added here and there to our knowledge, they have linked the impressions of the clinical work of the psychoanalyst concerning the childhood experiences of his adult patients to direct observations of children. We know now better than before how the event—which in retrospect appears important or traumatic—looks to those who observe the child while the event is taking place.

The studies of Anna Freud and Dorothy Burlingham[2] and those of a large number of other workers have also suggested how artificial it is at any point in the child's early history to draw a sharp division between child and mother. The studies of Dr. Margaret A. Ribble,[3] René A. Spitz,[4] and Margaret E. Fries[5]

1 Anna Freud and Dorothy T. Burlingham, *Infants without Families* (New York: International Universities Press, 1944).

2 *Ibid.*

3 Margaret A. Ribble, "Infantile Experience in Relation to Personality Development," *Personality and Behavior Disorders,* ed. J. McV. Hunt (New York: Ronald Press, 1944), Vol. II.

4 René A. Spitz, "Hospitalism; an Inquiry into the Genesis of Psychiatric Conditions in Early Childhood," in *The Psychoanalytic Study of the Child* (New York: International Universities Press, 1945), I, 53.

5 Margaret E. Fries, "The Child's Ego Development and the Training of Adults in His Environment," in *The Psychoanalytic Study of the Child* (New York: International Universities Press, 1947), II, 85.

have, partly under experimental conditions, elaborated on this point and demonstrated that even in the earliest phases of the infant's development physical contact is of decisive importance. It not only reaches into the first days of the child's existence—as, particularly, Dr. Merell P. Middlemore [6] has shown—but is dependent on the mother's experience during birth and pregnancy. May I here remind you of the work of Phyllis Greenacre [7] on the influence which the process of birth has, and that of Helene Deutsch [8] on the relation between the fantasies of pregnant women and their attitude to the newborn.

Some of this knowledge is being widely used and is finding its way to the general public, partly through books and pamphlets and lectures on mental health and related subjects, partly through clinics and hospitals, where the training of some of the younger medical and nursing personnel has brought them an understanding of these problems. I should not like to minimize these efforts but I do believe that the lack of trained specialists has been an impediment to any large-scale program, and that the use of printed material is not the most effective means for communicating knowledge of the type involved to large numbers of men and women.

The following suggestions aim at filling this gap, by establishing a person-to-person contact between the parents and the agency before the birth of the child. The agency should act as a channel through which our current socio-psychological knowledge reaches the family. Our first step, however, must naturally be a modest one. We have to refine the methods of our psychological family counseling services.

In speaking of face-to-face contact I do not think of the relation between an individual worker and an individual client. I definitely envisage group contacts, which will be more impressive to the participants because they permit the discussion of a greater variety of situations. In addition, parents are likely at first to gain

[6] Merell P. Middlemore, *The Nursing Couple* (London: Hamilton, 1944).

[7] Phyllis Greenacre, "The Biological Economy of Birth," in *The Psychoanalytic Study of the Child,* I, 31.

[8] Helene Deutsch, *The Psychology of Women* (New York: Grune and Stratton, 1944, 1945), Vols. I and II.

an understanding more easily in discussing problems related to their own difficulties but with which they are not directly emotionally involved than in the discussion of problems that concern themselves and their families. Moreover, the shortage of personnel would in itself suggest the use of group work for reasons of economy of time.

Much attention has to be given to the selection of the participants of such groups. My inclination to aim at the greatest possible homogeneity needs hardly to be justified. Homogeneity should be considered in terms of socio-economic and educational status; if possible, one should select members of one close community.

Justification, however, will be required, so far as one other point is concerned. I feel that groups should, whenever possible, include fathers. While it might not in practice be easy to achieve the regular attendance of fathers, I think that they should be included. At any step in our counseling, the whole family group is concerned, and even during the pregnancy the attitude of each future parent is or should be related to that of the other. The pregnancy presents not only the wife, but also the husband with a set of emotional problems. During the development of the child the father's role becomes increasingly important. His influence is not only desirable, but essential, at least during certain phases of the child's development. A special problem that we frequently meet concerns the inconsistency of the parents' educational attitudes. While they ought to supplement each other, the danger that they contradict each other is considerable. This may well be avoided by early guidance.

I do not envisage the groups as linked to the prenatal period only. I should like to consider this parent counseling service as one that extends throughout childhood into the time when the child has passed adolescence.

I should suggest that we initially select two or three mothers pregnant for the first time and their husbands; after the delivery of the children we may add to this same group some mothers in an advanced state of pregnancy, and after their delivery another few. Proceeding in this way we shall gradually reach the most suitable size for a group; I am inclined to think in terms of ten to twenty families.

This method of group selection permits the members of the group to discuss their experiences with each other. It offers to new members the additional advantage of learning ahead of time about problems with which they are likely to be faced some time later. If we succeed in keeping the group together, the increment in problems would take the group through all the vicissitudes of parenthood and child rearing and all problems of intrafamilial relations. The frequency of the meeting, or of participation in meetings, would be to some extent dependent on the age of the children in the family; parents of children of latency age or of adolescents will less frequently feel the need for contact than those of infants, toddlers, or young children. The nature of the contact between the group and its leaders is not thought of as therapeutic. We are not dealing with problems of group therapy, since we are not dealing with pathology. The aspect of group guidance seems more appropriate.

We know from experience that there will be participants who will require more than guidance; their treatment can then either be entrusted to the individual therapy of psychiatrists, to treatment by psychiatric social workers, or to work in special therapeutic groups. I envisage that what might begin on the smallest possible scale for our own education—as procedure to establish procedures—would later rapidly spread and become an institution of community life.

The institution of the family doctor was once a new one and was introduced when medicine had something to offer; the institution of the family guidance worker should be introduced at a time when psychology has new insights to offer that can be communicated to people at large. At our stage of social organization, however, not the private practitioner in this field but rather the representative of a social agency may introduce this new specialty. Moreover, institutions in the field of medical care have taken on similar functions. Pregnant women are somewhat accustomed to visiting prenatal clinics; babies are seen regularly at many well-baby institutions. All we suggest here is to supplement the physical care with psychological care, or, in other words, supplement one field of preventive medicine with another. In this new field, however, we aim, not at temporary, but at permanent contact. Our aim is not to give help during a period of danger or hardship, but to provide a guidance service meant to maintain healthy family life. Hence the particular role that I see for family agencies and for social casework. The existing hospital organizations devoted to prenatal care may well be called upon to coöperate with the agencies.

At this point my suggestions require a wider framework, for we trespass upon the field of community planning. We can, however, see such a plan already in action in the Rochester Child Health Project of the Mayo Clinic in Minnesota or in the project initiated several years ago by Margaret E. Fries which pursued similar goals.

One of the crucial problems that confronts us is that of personnel: who is to be the representative of this new specialty—the family doctor, the family psychologist, or the family guidance worker?

In the setup of an institution such as the Community Service Society, conditions seem to exist which promise to approach the problem of training specialists with a minimum of effort, or at least with less effort than any comparable setup. Moreover, from my experience as a psychiatric consultant of the Society, I am impressed with its growing concern with the role that the child, particularly the disturbed child, plays in the family. The project that I have outlined fits into this framework, since it aims at preventing some of the typical and most frequent disturbances in the child's development before they affect the family as a whole. An intimate knowledge of, and a day-to-day familiarity with, this setup is therefore a prerequisite for any worker who may act as group leader in this field. Hence the psychological guidance worker should be fully trained in psychiatric casework in a family agency. But his training cannot stop at that point. Social work, like any other field, cannot avoid the progress from work in a general field of experience to other more specialized areas, cannot avoid the participation in the differentiation of skills and techniques that characterize the development of professional work in modern society.

The training in child development which I have in mind should naturally not only embrace a thorough familiarity with problems of maturation and development of the child, but should relate these data to the dynamics of the child's psychological life history; it will therefore be necessary not to draw too sharp a line between child psychiatry and child psychology. In these areas, however, mere theoretical knowledge is particularly empty. A good and most natural training is motherhood. But it would not be fair to expect that every worker in this field will have had this experience. Nor will the experience of motherhood, however desirable, suffice in itself. I believe, therefore, in the necessity of practical work, if possible both in institutions and in families. In working out detailed plans, it will not be enough to provide facilities for field work in nursery schools only; I should like to stress the necessity that the workers' training should comprehend practical experience with every essential phase in the child's development.

Briefly, what I suggest for those who wish to specialize is a detailed and comprehensive program of theoretical courses and field work in child development and child care, not to replace the training of the psychiatric social worker in a family agency, but to supplement it.

All our knowledge concerning the psychological dynamics of the child indicates to what extent the growing up of the child is dependent on the adults in his environment. In our theoretical presentations, when we speak of "the love object" we mean the mother and the father; when we speak of identifications, we refer again to the daily contact between child and parents; when we speak of frustration and gratification in the child's life, we refer to the relations between members of a family—their mutual dependency, their irritations with each other, and the infinite number of vicissitudes that the course of the day brings to mother, father, and child. To put it concretely, in studying an individual child we find that we frequently cannot come to an understanding of the type of behavior displayed by the child without a very detailed acquaintance with his parents. The child borrows from his parents the types of defense he will use, sometimes before other manifestations of identifications strike us.

The child's denial of danger, for instance, may reproduce the mother's denial, or his overexcitement and aggressiveness that of one of his parents. By the same token, the child's sublimations are frequently directly dependent on the parents' capacity to sublimate. The observer who knows the child only does not even know the child.

The main reason, however, for recommending the family caseworker for the position I envisage, lies in the technique of guidance that I have in mind. It is not one that approaches the child directly. The child does not appear on the stage. What is attempted, is to influence the child through the parents. The child will, in fact, appear only on a screen, as it were, in the parents' report. While this type of relationship tends to become anonymous or abstract, this anonymity might be reduced through the relationship of the agency to the family. Ideally speaking, I should envisage a condition in which the group leader is at the same time, as a social worker, acquainted with the families she has assembled for guidance; she may have visited their homes and is therefore aware of the particular problems of each family group.

While the project here developed seems at first to impose an additional burden on the agency's work, I feel that in terms of long-range perspectives, the procedure may prove, not only more efficient, but also more economical than those procedures followed up to now. Two types of economy are likely to become apparent, one earlier and one in due course. First, through the group discussions some problems may be eliminated which workers would otherwise have to discuss with each client individually. Secondly, the preventive effect would, we hope, lead to improved conditions of family life, so that some families that might otherwise become dependent on the agency's help may never appear as clients in need of therapy or support in crisis. While I am not inclined to believe that such favorable results will occur soon, I feel that even during the experimental stages the type of project

I have outlined would be of value; it would sharpen our understanding of the psychological problems of family life and supply further data of observation in a field in which our knowledge, however rapidly growing, is still far too limited.

Science and Practice in Human Relations

STANLEY P. DAVIES

TO HELP PEOPLE wisely and constructively is one of the most difficult tasks in the world. We come to the end of the first 100 years of community service with a deepened awareness of the knowledge and skills that must be brought to this task, with a chastening sense of how much there is still to learn. One thing is clear: the greater our insight into the motivations of individual and social behavior, the greater the chances of really helping.

Social work has been referred to as applied social science. That is at least the right idea. So imperative is the need to improve human relations—today more than ever before—that it would be a high crime against society not to apply as effectively and widely as we know how any tested knowledge from social science that would serve this end. Specifically, social work practitioners feel obligated to learn and apply everything available from the life sciences that will enable them better to serve people. Yet actually, with the exception of dynamic psychology and psychiatry, which have become closely related to our practice, there has been a conspicuous lack of planned and purposeful collaboration between social science and social work.

In this respect social science and social practice stand in marked contrast with medical science and practice. In the latter field, the practitioners and many of the leading scientists who contribute the research that improves practice are found within the same profession. Not infrequently, the scientist is also practitioner, and practice contributes to science as well as science to practice. The Rockefeller Institute, for example, is a noted research center, but it is also a hospital and treatment center. To it are admitted the types of cases needed for research, which are given the latest and best forms of treatment.

Pendleton Herring, executive associate of the Carnegie Corporation and a director of the Social Science Research Council, has stressed as one of the greatest needs of the social sciences the development of skilled practitioners who can use social data for the cure of social ills as doctors use scientific data to cure bodily ills. He mentions social workers, clinical psychologists, and trained administrators as the clearest counterparts in the social field of technicians in other fields.

In our field there is much too wide a gulf between social scientists and social practitioners. The social scientists belong largely to the academic world, where they have had little or no contact with the human material flowing through our social agencies. Social agencies, on the other hand, have with rare exceptions been devoid of social scientists. Social work practitioners have to a greater or less degree kept up with the social sciences but largely through the literature rather than through personal contacts and working relationships.

One consequence of this, in my opinion, is a loss to social research. Even our most highly qualified social workers have for the most part lacked the technical know-how for basic research and thus have failed to make use of the rich material at their command for this purpose. At the same time, social scientists have been detached from the life experiences available to the social workers, and somehow it has not proved useful for research to try to transmit it to them by merely turning over agency case records. Our brief and all too limited experience in the Institute of Welfare Research of the Community Service Society of New York seems to point to one fact: the utilization of social agency material for basic research calls for a merging of the knowledge and technical skills of the research scientist with the knowledge and technical skills of the social work practitioner. The Community Service Society has made an auspicious beginning, at least, in research in human relations through this kind of collaboration. In our research director and his assistant we have brought to our staff on a full-time basis from the academic world two men of scientific attainments and high research competence who, as it happens, have specialized in the field of psychology. In the research project that relates to casework, for example, they are closely collaborating with the social casework practitioners through a joint research committee. Here we have brought science and practice together within the same organization, and a number of promising leads are being pursued.

In this age of specialization in science and practice social work stands in a unique place. When it undertakes to help a person who is in some kind of trouble, it must face practical realities. There is nothing theoretical or academic about the person there before us seeking help. He stands out sharply as an individual in his distress. We cannot fit him and his problems into some preconceived pigeonhole because that particular combination of this man and his troubles has not presented itself before. Nor can we sort out his internal and external problems into neat compartments classified according to our scientific and professional specialties. No, we have just one man before us and this man, his health, his emotions, his behavior, his ideas and intentions are all interrelated each with the other and with the situation in his family, his neighborhood, his circle of friends, his job, his boss and co-workers, the church and the clubs to which he belongs, his previous life experiences, and so on indefinitely. So of practical necessity the social worker has to try to see how all these things combine in their total effect upon a single personality in order to understand what the man is up against, the resources he has for meeting his situation, and the way in which he can be best aided to marshal those resources. Thus in the interest of serving the indivisible unity that is the individual human being, the social worker in a pragmatic way seeks to achieve a kind of synthesis of the sciences and practices that are geared to man. In this down-to-earth way, social work becomes a kind of common meeting ground for the economic, social, and cultural factors of the social sciences with the psychosomatic considerations of medicine and psychiatry merging within the essential unity of the human being. Perhaps the stern reality which brings social work to deal with the wholeness and oneness of the individual as he actually is and does in his life setting puts it in a unique position to contribute to a real working science of man.

The physical sciences have lifted many burdens from the back of man, have made possible "better things for better living" and longer living. They have steadily increased man's mastery of his physical universe. Have they now, at long last, overreached themselves by unleashing forces that point to man's own self-destruction? Can we hope to develop through social science the measures of social self-control that will channel these terrifying forces into comparably tremendous benefactions for mankind?

The way ahead is pretty clearly pointed. Unless we succumb to complete defeatism in our hopes of saving the world, pursuit of the human and social sciences must proceed vigorously and unfalteringly. A knowledge of what will work in harmonizing human relations and the use of all possible ways and means in applying that knowledge are the price of salvation in this complex world of today.

In this matter of ways and means we face a dilemma. It is the old paradox: Each person is unique, and therefore treatment should be individualized; yet time and resources permit meeting only a fraction of the need on an individualized basis. Modern psychology and social work have illumined for us the tremendous variations in the inherent makeup, culture, and particular life experiences of different people that come together in such an infinite number of different combinations that no two individuals are alike. Generalizations can be misleading if not dangerous.

Social science, both in its theoretical and its applied aspects, faces the very practical question: To what extent is it necessary to individualize; to what extent is it safe to generalize with respect to this social animal that is the human being? The very term "social science" assumes that beneath individual differences there are broad likenesses in human nature upon the basis of which certain laws of human behavior can be discovered and stated.

The answer for social work, it seems to me, is that we must

embrace both approaches, proceeding like the inductive method of science, from the particular to the general. As in medicine or psychiatry so in social work, individualized counseling, treatment and therapy (within its own area of competence) are basic. Let there be not the slightest negative implication as to that. It is basic in more ways than one. The problems of certain individuals and families are such that they can be reached only by this direct, personalized approach. Direct casework that goes searchingly into the study and treatment of personal and family problems is the clinical base which enriches our understanding of, and skill in, human relations. Moreover, it provides the necessary material for teaching and research. We need more rather than less skilled individual casework.

And yet there are limits to therapy. This is as true in social casework as it is in medicine or psychiatry. Therapy, even in its early treatment aspects, operates *after* some sign of trouble appears. With the best of skills it may or may not be successful. Therapy is time consuming and costly. Available resources do not permit its extension to any large proportion of the population.

Is not this distinction valid in our field as well as in medicine: that once real trouble has begun, therapy based on individual diagnosis is indicated; that, however, preventive and constructive measures to ward off trouble before it occurs can be generalized and thus call for the methods of mass immunization, or, in our field, group and large-scale educational programs? Therefore, without relinquishing its direct and individualized services, it seems clear that social work has the further obligation and opportunity to develop and prosecute broad, generalized programs of a constructive, educational nature designed to bring to people whatever knowledge we have gained as to how they can fortify themselves and their families in avoiding the pitfalls that lead to personal and social maladjustment. The fact that, in contrast, for example, with the toxin-antitoxin protection against diphtheria, immunization in the field of human relations is vastly more complicated and uncertain, lacking the clear-cut scientific concepts and definite formulae of public health measures, does not mean that we have any less obligation to develop and pursue such a broad preventive program in our field.

Review of its 100 years shows plainly that the program of the Community Service Society in its concepts and practices has not been static. Reaching out for and applying new knowledge to the better understanding and treatment of human needs, the Society has sought also to adapt its program to changing times and circumstances. One example of the latter is the changing emphasis in our own service in the light of the development of the public assistance and social security programs which the Society has supported. The Society's present program embracing direct services to families and individuals of all ages and economic groups in the preservation of their health and the achievement of satisfying and effective human relations, and including also importantly professional training, research, and community leadership, represents the evolution of a process of learning and adaptation over the years. Equally, as we face the new century before us we are taking a fresh look at ourselves and the world about us, prepared at any point to set new directions if need be in order to make our own best contribution in the further service of the community.

Inevitably in the background or foreground of our thinking in these days is the critical state of world affairs. As a basic fact we recognize that early conditioning in childhood will largely determine the kind of citizenship and leadership upon which the fate of the world hangs. Can we in childhood find ways of avoiding or moderating the frustration and other factors that build up into hostility and aggression? Even though we are far from having an adequate science of child rearing and of parent-child and family relationships, there can be no doubt that we are today in possession of knowledge which, if purposefully and adequately applied, would result in important advances in preparing children for the demands of a democratic social order and world citizenship.

A great overriding question, however, stares us in the face. Is there time? Before August, 1945, we perhaps could feel that there was. Now we all wonder. Dr. Brock Chisholm, Director

General of the World Health Organization, was quoted in the New York *Times* as saying that in view of the potency of methods of warfare known today there was grave doubt "whether the major part of the human race will survive the next few years." Yet the process of social education and preparation through the family, where it must basically occur, even if it could be inaugurated on a sound basis universally right now, would take many years to show results.

Nevertheless, we cannot falter in this work of human relations. I think we can take courage as we look back over 100 years in the progress that has been made in the comparatively brief span of one century as time goes. Indeed, I believe it is a safe generalization that more progress has been made in man's humanity to man in the last century than in all the centuries of human life preceding it. To believe that we have come a long way in the last ten decades, one needs only to glimpse the picture of social and living conditions as they were 100 years ago in New York City. Our own anniversary booklet, *Frontiers in Human Welfare,* states what the early visitors of this Society found: widespread begging becoming a profession wherein even the children were sent to solicit leftovers at the back doors of the wealthy; families crowded in basement rooms without light, ventilation, or heat, where a pile of rags passed for a bed; sewage disposal left to the individual; even the most primitive cleanliness made impossible owing to the lack of running water; an infant death rate of 275 per 1,000 compared with 28 today; 10 percent of the city's children roaming the streets in vagabond bands, many of them, completely homeless, sleeping under stairways and bridges; epidemic and virulent fever attacking 50 percent and killing 25 percent of the people living in the cellars of the affected neighborhood; distribution of polluted milk from diseased cattle stabled in the city and spoiled meat from the slaughterhouses. Trained nursing was still far in the future; many of the so-called "nurses" were women of the streets under detention on Blackwells Island and assigned to do all the nursing there was in the pesthouses that passed for public hospitals in those days; families broken up for reasons of poverty alone; children sent to almshouses where they were indiscriminately herded together with all other types of unfortunates of all ages, tramps and vagrants, the physically ill, the insane, the feeble-minded, and the epileptic.

We have made great and tangible progress in health and welfare in these hundred years. We have, above all, developed and put into practice new and enlightened attitudes toward those in need, treating them as the fellow human beings that they are. Nevertheless, we still have a long way to go in this country in righting wrongs, in improving the conditions of living for all and the lot of many classes and groups of people. Above all, we have a long way to go in our human relations one to another. Looking out beyond the borders of our own country, we can be still less complacent over the comparative well-being of America as we realize the needs of the peoples of the world and the interdependence of these peoples.

So, taking renewed courage from the great humanitarian progress of 100 years, we cannot and must not despair. David Lilienthal, who, as he says, lives with the atomic weapon day and night, stated vigorously in the New York *Times Magazine* that "scaring the daylights out of everyone, inducing hysteria and increasing fear is not going to get us anywhere. Atomic energy," he continued, "has not changed the fundamental principles of democracy which are founded squarely upon faith in the ultimate wisdom of the people when they have been truthfully and clearly informed of the essential facts."

Disdaining the paralysis of fear, then, we need to be reinvigorated in our social efforts by the call from peoples everywhere to find the good life. For new knowledge with which to improve its understanding and skill and for the means of testing the effectiveness of its programs, social work looks to science. For its dynamic concept and motivating force, social work now as always looks to those warm and generous impulses, those ideals of service and obligation to one's fellows that prompt contributors, board and committee members, staff workers, and people as plain citizens to give of themselves and their substance in this humanitarian cause. Social work is solidly grounded in a set of values springing from the highest religious motivations and aspirations of mankind. These values, time-tested in the experience of the race, hold what we regard as basic truths—that the insights coming from science serve but to enable us more fully to understand and apply. These values which animate social work are the same values which sustain our firm belief in real democracy. In its efforts to remove the blot of discrimination, in its demand for human rights, in its jealous guarding of individual liberty, in its support of full opportunity for self-realization, social work is part and parcel of democracy. It has faith in people, in their ultimate wisdom, and in their inherent desire and capacity to live and work together so as to achieve the fullest and richest life for all.

Part II: Professional Training

Contribution of the Humanities and the Professional Schools

IRWIN EDMAN

TO MANY TRADITIONAL-MINDED, HUMANISTIC SCHOLARS, there is still something strange and, if the truth be told, something illicit, about the incorporation into American universities of professional schools. The university, in the phrase that the late Nicholas Murray Butler used to use so often, is a society of scholars, and scholarship, in the minds of the conventional scholar, is by definition a disinterested pursuit of truth for its own sake. Its fruit is theory, in the sense of speculation and vision, not training in skills or discipline in narrow techniques for limited and provincial purposes. Most humanists have inherited and hugged close the distinction between wisdom and prudence, and the special vocation of universities has been held to be that of the pursuit of wisdom, not training in the prudential and practical arts. The toast of the mathematicians, "Here's to the higher mathematics, may they never be of any use," has been echoed until recently (that is, until the atomic bomb made the situation clear among mathematical physicists too) by the literary scholars and the philosophers despite the close, clear, and often sinister consequences of the most remote speculation in mathematical theory.

Education from the humanistic point of view has been designed ideally to educate the soul of man, to turn the eye of the mind from the sordid and the practical to the elevated and the eternal, to give to students in the liberal arts colleges a vision of disinterested science, the free delight of art, the discipline and clarification of pure and unfettered philosophical ideas. On the postgraduate level, the traditional concept of scholarship has been that of expert contributions to specific fields of knowledge, the extension of the empire of knowledge and of the realm of scrupulously verified truth. Somewhere in European education, about the time of the Renaissance, the ideal of the scholar and the ideal of the gentleman were fused; by the end of the nineteenth century, "scholar" and "scientist" became almost identical terms. The training of the gentleman was the ideal of undergraduate scholarship; that of the scientifically precise scholar, that of the graduate school. There was room for both in a university.

The invasion of the university by the professional school was naturally greeted with considerable suspicion both by the humanist and by the physical scientist. Medicine had long won itself an established place, though the degree of Doctor of Medicine is several hundred years younger than that of Doctor of Philosophy. Law, on its more philosophical levels, had long been a part of university education, and so had theological studies. But by the end of the nineteenth century in America, there was a proliferation of professional schools that seemed to the more conservative among university teachers and scholars a matter, to put it mildly, for raised eyebrows. To this day, schools of education are treated with something like condescension by many in the university community, and schools of business, journalism, forestry, agriculture, architecture, and household arts are regarded as necessary though not quite respectable adjuncts of a university. Even where the need of training is clearly recognized, it has been held that these schools do not quite belong in a university, that they offer training in craft skills rather than education in those primary ends and ultimate values which are the high concern of a university. I do not say that this attitude toward these schools is widespread in the university community, but it has by no means vanished. Its sources lie in the historical connection of higher education both with the upper social classes and with the classical notion of a knowledge somehow above that of practice, knowledge concerned with loftier, translunar things, with the ends of life rather than with necessary but essentially inferior means. One may say, indeed, that the traditional conception of a university is a blend of the Platonic theory of knowledge as the purely intellectual contemplation of pure ideas, the Renaissance notion of the gentleman, and the nineteenth-century notion of the exact scientist.

Whatever the traditional humanists have invidiously thought about professional schools in the past, they have been increasingly led to recognize two facts. One is that, for better or for worse, more and more professional schools have become integral parts of the great universities of this country; secondly, the condescension and suspicion have proved to be mutual. The newcomers in the university families have looked askance at the older members. The universities have long ceased to be concerned with a small, leisure-class group, or, within that group, with a still smaller group destined to be literary scholars or pure researchers in the sciences. Our universities have, within the last two or three generations, come to recognize their position and their obligation in a wide and sprawling democratic society, inevitably industrial and inextricably international in its relations. The spread of high schools and the increasing demand for technically trained men and women have brought to our universities a vast population which wishes, along with as much general education and liberal arts study as can be crowded into a limited time, to have, above all, preparation for a professional career. The phenomenal growth of our population has indeed made it incumbent on our advanced institutions to provide professional education, and in the interest of high standards of technical preparation, as well as in the interest of providing such a humane context as is available at a university, the functions of professional schools and even the schools themselves have been taken over by the universities and integrated, more or less, with their more familiar and age-old functions.

Even humanists have (though sometimes reluctantly) recognized the obligation of higher education to minister to the demands of their students for professional training and to the social needs of the society which requires an increasing number of technically trained professionals in a civilization that depends, not only for its growth, but for its survival from day to day on ever expanding technologies. The Sanskrit scholar has come to accustom himself to the school of business only a stone's throw from Philosophy Hall, and professors in the graduate school of English literature have learned to lecture without squeamishness in lecture halls generally devoted to exposition of the techniques of journalism or home economics.

Humanists have learned to recognize, also, that the note of suspicion and condescension has come from the enterprising new professional schools, evoked by the bland and sometimes blind assumptions and superiorities of conventional humanists. Teachers in the relatively new professional schools have observed with impatience and often with justice the ivory tower attitude in some of the more classically established parts of the university. Leaders of professional education have realized how unaware are some of their colleagues in the more traditional disciplines of the changing needs in their own society, how irresponsible as to the bearing for good or ill of humanistic studies themselves upon the conscience and imagination of a democratic society. Teachers in the field of professional education have noted the elements of preciousness and insectivorousness in the study of literature and the unhumaneness of much of the scholarship in art that is mere unenlightened cataloguing, the verbalism and jargon-mongering of much alleged philosophy. Moreover, with the pressures of time and economic necessity that impinge upon their students, administrators in professional schools cannot help accenting what seem to be the essentials and basic requisites in their professional programs. In the early years of medical education in universities, for example, the training was almost completely and narrowly medical, and only such other disciplines were required as were absolutely indispensable: chemistry and physics and biology. Even when first two and then three and even four years of college were required as prerequisite for medical school, the premedical program was crowded, as it is to this day, by such elaborate technical requirements that there was almost no room left for grounding in the traditional liberal arts.

In the same way, there was for a long time, and still endures to a certain extent, the feeling among those responsible for education in journalism and business and law, and even in education, that while the humanities cannot exactly harm a student, they are less necessary than certain other disciplines which their own schools provide. In most schools of education, for example, the philosophy of education is regarded as much more urgent than philosophy; and a school of business would, on the whole, I suspect, prefer to see on a student's preliminary record a course in statistics rather than one in Spinoza, in economic geography rather than in Plato. Obviously, somewhere between the extreme positions I have cited, educational wisdom lies. They patently err who regard the university as an institution educating an elite for speculation about eternal things utterly removed from social and economic and political origins and social and political and economic consequences. To study the great books or great ideas without reference to the life which generated them or the contemporary life which they can illuminate is to miss the human purpose of liberal education, the understanding of life both present and past. To regard a university as if it were the private preserve of a specially privileged class of aesthetes playing with arts and ideas is to miss and to misread the facts of education in a democratic society. A university exists, on the other hand, as always, to maintain the pure flame of truth and to extend the empire of knowledge. If the ends of pure scholarship and the interests of humane learning were to be brushed aside, the university would indeed be betraying a century-old trust.

In our contemporary society in America the university has acquired new obligations. It is committed willy-nilly to the education of unprecedented numbers and to combine with the discipline of the mind and imagination over the whole human patrimony of arts and ideas a training of large numbers for the varied tasks and vocations of a complex technical civilization.

It is in this connection that I come at long last to the contribution that the humanities can make to professional education. A professional school belongs by right in a university just to the extent that education in and for the professions is something more than a training in a skill and a craft and that education in a profession, in the most serious sense, is a vocation. The doctor, the teacher, the social worker, the journalist, the lawyer, is not a mere technician and cannot be such; so closely interrelated are the various arts and sciences that none of these can even be a good technician unless he is a good deal more, unless he is, that is to say, an educated man.

Each profession has its own techniques and its own special ends as well as techniques, but those ends are formed and fixed in relation to the larger purposes of our society and conditioned by the general presumptions of our culture. There are, of course, certain professional considerations and technical disciplines that are the special province of professional schools. But in so far as a profession is conducted on a humane and responsible level, it demands practitioners who have some conception of the relation of their work and their field to the general interests and values of their society. They need to understand the conditions in which their profession operates to understand how they may best employ their talents, their training, and their capacities. The field of social work and community service is an excellent instance. No one knows better than the members of this difficult and devoted profession how the problems arising from poverty, social maladjustment, and underprivilege force a reconsideration of all the values implicit in, or enforced by, our economic and political organization, our social mores, our religious traditions, our moral attitudes, and our spiritual opaquenesses and failures, as well as our generosities and achievements.

The social worker is dealing with the consequences of malaise and disease in our society, with misfortunes that are the functions of misarrangements in our ways of life. He is dealing also with psychological distortions that bring about public ills. In trying to rehabilitate individuals and families he is led to consider more urgently, perhaps, than anyone save a physician (to whom he is analogous) the ends which our institutions serve or fail to serve, the values of the norms which he assumes in trying to bring people back to norms. No one knows more than the social worker how closely the private ills, the private hopes, and the private triumphs of individual life under difficulties are a function of the public hopes, the public ills, and the moral failures, on occasion even the moral successes, of a democratic civilization.

To be an adequately imaginative social worker demands more than training in casework, in medical psychiatry, in legal and social jurisprudence, in the anthropology of sexual codes and sexual practices, in the problems of psychosomatic medicine and psychosocial maladjustments. It demands some consideration of the same ultimate issues with which moral philosophers have been concerned from Plato to the present time: the relation of justice and law, of the individual and society, of private desires and the public good. I think that any member of the faculty of a school of social work or any alumnus of it would agree that a man or woman who came to his professional studies with the clarified context of these issues in his mind would be the better even technically for such clarification. Ultimately, the social worker is working at those crucial points in our society where democratic institutions have not so far been successful. His own work is a disciplined attempt to make those institutions function more adequately, and it is a testament of faith, also, in the paramount worth of the individual, in or out of difficulties—and faith, too, in the possibility of secular salvation.

If philosophy helps the professional man in law, social work, medicine, and education to consider the ends of his profession, the wider social purposes they serve, other humanistic studies help him to realize, in the imaginative sense, the significance of those individuals who might otherwise become for him mere statistics on a chart, or terms in a formula. The function of literature as a humane discipline is not to provide an escape from professional duties. It is rather to remind those given over professionally to the abstractions of the social sciences of the qualities and color of life as lived by individuals. Chekhov was both a doctor and a man of letters, and the better doctor for having the point of view of the compassionate poet. The function of the humanities in general is to provide the professional schools with students who bring to bear on their work, especially with human beings, those realizations of human values that are warmly communicated by the creative arts. Especially in social work, the humanities contribute the gift of insight, of generosity, of human sympathy necessary if social work is to be genuinely and humanly fruitful, not pointlessly and deceptively efficient. The social worker trained in the humanities will never fall into regarding his work as a meaningless or sterile routine. He will regard the individuals with whom he works as individuals, not as mere cases. He will come almost instinctively to regard himself as one among many varied professional workers whose job it is to use the resources of the social and physical sciences to render life more richly human in all the colors and dimensions that philosophy and the arts have made vivid in the past 2,500 years of civilization. The humanities may contribute to the professional schools the tenacious habit of remaining richly aware of what is being done, why and to whom and for what, while the professional schools themselves find every last resource of skill in doing it well.

Preparing Professional Leaders for America's Welfare Program

ARLIEN JOHNSON

THE GROWTH OF PROFESSIONALISM has been said to be one of the hopeful features of the times; for inherent in the meaning of a profession is the tradition of a skilled service rendered in the public interest. This combination of special competence and of a spirit of devotion to objectives whose social significance outweighs the personal distinguishes the profession from the trade. A genuinely professional person selects his field primarily because of the satisfaction he anticipates in the work to be done; earning a living is a secondary reason for his choice. "I hold," said Bacon, "every man a debtor to his profession from the which as men do of course seek to receive countenance and profit so ought they of duty to endeavor themselves by way of amends to be a help and an ornament thereunto." Implicit in the meaning of a profession is the potentiality for leadership in bridging the gap between the world of knowledge and the application of it for the general welfare.

Social work as a profession has emerged during the twentieth century. It arose out of the needs of people, as have all professions. Its expansion has been rapid as a result of depression and wars in the past twenty-five years. Such widespread suffering and hardship resulted from these national crises that the disciplined approach to helping people with personal and environmental problems which we call social work has been in great demand. In the light of such accelerated development, social work as a profession has many problems. Its philosophy often lacks clarity and unity; its methods are imperfect. Preparation for practice is limited to a fraction of those who occupy positions in social welfare programs. Yet, in spite of these limitations, great vitality resides in the body of knowledge and skills that have been identified as belonging distinctively to social work; and underlying all its activities is the purpose of providing a service that improves human relationships.

Unlike such professions as law and medicine where private practice predominates, social work usually operates through organizations. In fact, it owes its origin to experience in the administration of the services of social welfare agencies. When Mary Richmond entered the field, the chief difference between the social worker and the friendly visitor was the pay check. The exciting history of the Community Service Society's 100 years of growth represents the history of social welfare and social work. The vision and devotion of such leaders as Robert Hartley and Josephine Shaw Lowell took form in uniting like-minded citizens into organized groups who were able to translate social understanding into social action for better human relations. This they did by pioneering in both programs and methods. At their best, such voluntary groups moved from a concern about individual welfare to a concern about mass welfare. Voluntary programs that affect relatively few people have led the way for governmental programs that reach all the people. Equally significant has been the contribution that the voluntary agencies have made to the development of methods of helping people to utilize their services. Here, again, we find an illustration in the history of the Community Service Society. The origin of the New York School of Social Work fifty years ago was in the search for better ways of making the agency's services effective. It was not enough to alleviate social problems; the people affected by them needed treatment that came from the services that a skilled and disciplined worker could offer.

In the troubled times in which we live there is again great need for pioneers in social understanding. Ignorance, poverty, and sickness are still with us, but they are no longer the concern primarily of individual leaders. Society as a whole, through tax-supported programs, has begun to grapple with these problems.

New dangers loom, however. Conflicting ideologies are fighting for supremacy in the world, loosed by the succession of shocks that depression and wars have brought. On the one hand, the physical sciences fill us with awe at the possibilities for human annihilation or for human betterment; and on the other hand, the ethical values which should guide us in the use of such knowledge are weak, antiquated, and unequal to the task. Knowledge about human nature and social institutions is not lacking; in fact, social work and social welfare programs depend heavily upon well-established principles derived from the social sciences. It is for this reason that leadership is sorely needed now to extend the services which new concepts of human relationships and forms of social organization can offer in this period.

Social work along with other professions has a contribution to make in the evolution of strong social values which will be equal to withstanding the stress of today. Essential premises for social work are belief in the dignity and worth of human life, in the potentialities of the individual for growth, in the family as the training ground for democracy, in the right of minority groups to equal opportunity with others. These beliefs are fundamental values in a democratic society. Combined with these convictions about interpersonal relationships there is emerging in many groups, of which social work is one, the conviction that new alignments between institutional relationships—social, political, economic—must also be considered. We might describe the latter as national minimum standards for collective security. It is not enough to help an unemployed man to meet the situation with courage and resourcefulness; we must also help to create a society in which those who are able to work can find jobs. It is not enough to help a family ease the tensions and misunderstanding among its members; we must help to remove obstacles to decent, healthful living. Without such a philosophy which preserves our treasured concepts of the importance of individual development and combines with it the emerging concepts about social responsibility, we shall not have ethical values equal to the period in which we live. It is leadership in the furtherance of such a philosophy that we need today. The era of the great individual leader seems to have passed. We must look to organized groups, including the professions, to be the pioneers in social understanding.

How, then, shall we prepare personnel for the voluntary and governmental welfare services? How can we help students in professional schools to acquire a philosophy equal to the times, knowledge of individual behavior and of societal structure, and skill in working with both kinds of material? This is no small task in itself. The urgency of the need for preparing leaders and not mere practitioners becomes evident when we realize that the number of positions in social welfare agencies increased from 40,000 in 1930 to an estimated 100,000 in 1948. In 1947 there were 26,000 persons administering public assistance alone, most of them in local communities throughout the nation. At the same time, a generous estimate of those social workers who have qualified for professional status by education, experience, and membership in one of the cognate professional associations would not exceed 25,000, or one-quarter as many as occupy positions in social welfare agencies. Education for the field is unequal to the demand for personnel. The forty-seven accredited schools of social work have a combined annual enrollment of about 10,000 students, slightly less than one half of whom are enrolled for full-time study. So much is expected of the graduates of schools of social work, under these conditions, that great responsibility rests upon the schools and the profession to make the preparation as adequate as possible.

There are two requisites which are not unique for the person who would become a social worker. They are common to all kinds of education. One of these requisites is personal qualities for learning and leadership, and the other is a good general education. What one brings with him to a learning experience is extremely important for professional training. His personality will have been affected by his relationships in family, school, church, and other contacts. Good intelligence, imagination, integrity, and steadiness of purpose are desired. For social work, another quality is essential. This is motivation that enables the student to give of himself impersonally. Charlotte Towle describes this quality as "capacity for object love as differentiated from self-love," or "subordination of personal self to a larger identity." [1] This capacity implies a high degree of socialization and maturity. Too often, persons who are seeking escape from their own problems or who have hostile and aggressive tendencies hope to find a solution of their frustrations in social work. At present, there are no reliable tests to weed out the educable from those with negative character traits. Most schools of social work rely upon references, the personal interview, and the applicant's self-analysis, for evaluation of personal qualifications. There is genuine interest among the schools in the careful selection of applicants, and it is to be hoped that eventually aptitude tests will be developed as aids.

The second requisite, a good general education, is easily described but not so easily encountered. We recognize the educated man by the breadth of his knowledge, by the universality of his sympathies and interests, by his acquaintance with the cultural past, and by his curiosity about the unknown. Some of these evidences of education arise out of knowledge, but more of them depend upon the cultivation of certain habits of mind. In essence, education is learning how to learn. Ability to think logically and independently is more than knowledge; it enables one to relate facts to facts, to bring the history of the past to bear upon the present. If one thinks clearly he will probably be able to express his ideas effectively. Cultivation of communication, however, is extremely important in preparation for social work. Language, oral or written, is our chief tool. Without thermometer or statute to help in diagnosis, the social worker must be able to make nice distinctions with words, to perceive differences in meanings, to organize ideas and put them on paper in good form.

Because general education too infrequently produces a person with the kind of habits of mind and orientation that I have described, we are beginning to discuss the importance of continuity of education for social work from undergraduate through graduate years. Committees have been at work for several years in the

[1] Charlotte Towle, "The Emotional Element in Learning in Professional Education for Social Work," in *Professional Education* (New York: American Association of Schools of Social Work, 1948), pp. 20, 21.

American Association of Schools of Social Work, analyzing the content of preprofessional education. Most of the emphasis has been upon the knowledge content, especially from the social sciences, at the undergraduate level. When he is ready for admission to the professional school, a candidate's educational achievement can be fairly well gauged through such tests as the Graduate Record Examination. The habits of mind which we have described as characteristic of the educated person are not so readily tested, however. And because their inculcation depends largely upon good teaching, example, and practice, we find that the graduates of some colleges and universities are superior to others in these respects. Karl de Schweinitz in his recent study, *People and Process in Social Security,* has made an excellent analysis of undergraduate education in preparation for employment in the social security programs. He sums up his conclusions in this way:

> Social security wants the undergraduate curriculum in general and the social sciences in particular to provide a medium through which the future careerist can develop perspective, imagination, and a broad social background along with the capacity to deal with facts, to learn new things, and to make effective application of what he learns. . . . The best undergraduate education for social security will be found in the tradition of the liberal arts.[2]

The importance of general education of this kind is very great. The undergraduate years must lay the foundation for an undertaking of the problems with which social work deals. Furthermore, with an estimated three fourths of those in social work positions without benefit of professional education, it will be necessary for many years for liberal arts graduates to be recruited into positions, and to be given in-service training. A steadily growing program of educational leave with stipends, so that promising employees may acquire professional education, is a hopeful development. It should be noted, however, that the greatest number of positions, and therefore the greatest number of untrained personnel, are in the public agencies. The voluntary agencies, on the whole, have a minimum requirement of one

[2] Karl de Schweinitz, *People and Process in Social Security* (Washington D.C.: American Council on Education, 1948), p. 122.

year of study in a professional school, and many of them require the Master's degree.

Professional education as defined by the American Association of Schools of Social Work continues after the liberal arts degree through two academic years of graduate study to the degree of Master of Social Work. Even to the student with a good general education the transition to professional education is a profoundly stirring experience. His concentration of interest and activity shifts from knowledge about people and social institutions to intimate, first-hand acquaintance with them. His success is no longer to be measured by his intellectual mastery of materials but by his ability to transmute intellectual understanding into service to people with whom he enters into a responsible relationship. He must develop a discipline of his own feelings as well as of intellect; in other words, he learns as a whole person, and to learn he must experience growth. Furthermore, he no longer learns as an individual. He has allied himself with a profession which has bonds between the practitioners. Their obligations as represented by a common philosophy and defined function must become his obligations. Through a balanced combination of classroom discussion on the university campus and field instruction in social agencies in the community, the professional school tries to help the student develop into a professional person. This means surrounding him with conditions needed for personal growth that enable him to take independent action, while at the same time helping him to make his own the discipline of working within the limits set by the agency and the profession of which he has become a part. He must achieve a balance between self-direction and group direction. Social work more than most professions has stressed both the necessity of the student's understanding himself and the significance of that understanding when applied to others with whom he enters into a learning or working relationship. Such learning is usually painful to the student and requires skillful teachers both in the classroom and in the field work agency. It is also exhilarating and satisfying, in the long run, to those who accomplish it successfully.

The professional discipline just described has been well developed with respect to social casework services and, to some extent, for social group work. The welfare programs require more than this, however, if professional leadership is to be adequate to the demands of this critical period and if social work is to be worthy of its heritage. I would like to propose two areas in which the professional schools, the practitioners, and interested citizens should work together to improve the preparation of professional personnel, and therefore of the services to be rendered to people by social welfare programs.

First of all, we must clarify our common philosophy and reorient the curriculum of the professional schools accordingly. I have noted earlier in this paper the need for a philosophy suited to the times in which we live and I have expressed my conviction that social work, with other professions, can help to further new ethical values that are tentatively emerging in the United States. The rapid growth of the public social services, and especially the influence of the Social Security Act of 1935, has begun to formulate for us what we might call national minimum standards for collective security. The recognition that the categorical public assistance programs, for example, must be administered as a right, in money payments, with freedom of the recipient to spend his grant in the way he deems best, means that assistance has moved from private beneficence to community responsibility; that there is a social institution arising which may eventually take its place with public education, protection of persons and property, and similar services considered necessary for the general public welfare. In schools of social work we teach courses about public assistance, the administration of public welfare, social insurance, and other forms of social legislation, but it seems to me that we do not at the same time always put them in the broad, conceptual framework which enables the student to understand the dynamics of societal process and how to help guide and direct it. As in general education, knowledge is not enough. It is the meaning of such knowledge in its application to these "irreducible and stubborn facts" of first-hand observation in daily practice which the genuinely professional man must possess. The philosophical base of the profession helps to illuminate knowledge.

Social work, to be sure, has not lacked a philosophy, a sense of social responsibility. What I want to point out is that our philosophy reflects the confusion of the times. Leaders in social work are aware of this, and statements of the problem as it relates to professional education have appeared frequently.[3] The American Association of Social Workers has had a series of articles on the subject in the *Compass* (now the *Social Work Journal*). The problem is how to give cohesion and unity to this growing concern about preparation for social responsibility so that it can be a part of the curriculum in the professional school.

It is not surprising that the curriculum of the professional school has grown by accretion and compromise, for professional education grows out of professional development and practice. Historically, the attack on social problems has been segmental. As we clarify our common philosophy we can improve the curriculum. Already, significant developments are under way. One of these is the movement toward integration of the methods courses, a step that was recommended in a recent report of the curriculum committee of the American Association of Schools of Social Work. To give unity to the curriculum, further study is needed of the similarities between the social casework specialties and work with individuals and with groups. We need to accept the fact that social work is work with people, whether as individuals, groups, or communities, and that this provides a common core around which basic knowledge of behavior and skills is developing.

The other major aspect of curriculum development, needed to give unity and meaning to professional education, as I see it, must be around the broad, conceptual framework that gives perspective and purpose to the professional activity. I conceive of

[3] See, for example, Sue Spencer, "Issues in Professional Education," *Survey Midmonthly*, LXXXIII (June, 1947), 167–69; Benjamin Youngdahl, "Social Workers: Stand Up and Be Counted," *Compass*, XXVIII (March, 1947), 21–24; Marion Hathway, "Preparation for Social Responsibility," in *Professional Education*, pp. 39–46.

this as education in understanding the dynamics of societal process and in developing skill in working with social situations, social institutions, and their modification. The student should develop the same kind of insight into this material as we can now help him to develop with respect to individual behavior. He should learn how to apply the same disciplined helpfulness with community groups that he can now offer to individuals and primary groups. He must know how to distinguish between his activity and responsibility as a citizen and his activity and responsibility as a professional person working with the complex milieu of social change. At present, there is much confusion between citizen responsibility and professional responsibility in this area.[4] I see considerable difference between a professional group signing petitions of protest about current injustices, and the professional activity of members of the group in helping to modify causative factors.

The world will not be changed by social workers alone. We are one of many professions and many organized groups who are aware of social injustices and social trends. As a profession, however, we have potentialities for disciplined service to these groups in applying measures to hasten and guide social change. Such tools as opinion polls, selective use of propaganda techniques, analysis of relative strengths of the diverse forces that create public opinion—these we have scarcely begun to examine for use in social work. The kind of knowledge and skill which I have in mind would also enable us to diagnose readiness for change, to distinguish between those situations which are untreatable and those which are ready for modification. When I studied social casework many years ago at the New York School of Social Work we really believed that social casework could bring about change in anyone, if only the caseworker had mastered the skills needed. The scientific findings that social caseworkers have utilized in developing their method has long since helped them to know that persons vary greatly in their capacity to change and that the ex-

[4] See, for example, Eveline Burns, "Social Action and the Professional Social Worker," *Compass*, XXVIII (May, 1947), 37–40; and "Compass Exchange," letter from Celia S. Deschin, in reply, *Compass*, XXVIII (July, 1947), 21–22.

tent to which casework service can help a person varies according to what the person brings to the situation as well as with what the caseworker has to offer. In time, I believe, we may learn to work with social situations with some of the same discrimination with which we now work with individuals.

This emphasis upon preparation for a broad area of professional activity has led some social workers to propose that the schools educate "generalists" and "specialists." It is true that the social casework specialties have become increasingly demanding of the student's time, if he is to master what is now available for him to learn. Nevertheless, it seems to me that the problem of balance between general education and specialized training is a problem of all education and is not peculiar to social work. The report of the Harvard Committee, *General Education in a Free Society,* provides ample evidence of this assertion. The relationship is described in this way:

> General and special education are not, and must not be placed, in competition with each other. . . . Specialization can only realize its major purposes within a larger general context, with which it can never afford to sever organic connection. General education is an organism, whole and integrated; special education is an organ, a member designed to fulfill a particular function within the whole.[5]

If we accept this interpretation we must apply ourselves to research and curriculum planning along the lines previously discussed. A measure of success would result in the production of social workers who would have both specialized skills and preparation for work in the broad field of policy making. In a word, we would have professional leaders.

The second area in which we need to strengthen professional education, if we are to produce better professional leaders, is relating our special competence as a profession to those groups with whom we have interdependent relationships. Among these I would mention citizen groups, the great body of untrained workers who fill most of the positions in social agencies, and the members of other professions with whom we are often associated.

[5] Report of the Harvard Committee, *General Education in a Free Society* (Cambridge: Harvard University Press, 1946), p. 195.

In other words, we must learn how to do teamwork that makes maximum use of the contribution of each member of the team.

Both governmental and voluntary agencies need to keep close to citizens' interest in social welfare programs and to sustain their participation. As we noted earlier, social work is an outgrowth of voluntary service. The treatment of social problems led to the growth of a method of doing this most effectively. The fact that social work is practiced in social agencies means that the services of the expert must be continuously related to the will of the citizens who organized and who support the agency, if it is a voluntary one, or to the understanding and approval of the voters, if the agency is supported from tax funds. We must prepare students who have a clear orientation to their own function in society, and who understand its relationship to informed citizen interest and participation at appropriate places. The roles of the layman and of the expert are different. Neither takes the place of the other. As the public services have expanded we have found that too few social workers have had the skill required for working with citizen advisory boards. While the individual worker could understand hostility in a client and help him find release of feelings, he could not understand the negative attitudes in a community toward a new public program. Yet we can teach students how to work with community groups toward social goals which they jointly help to formulate. This needs increased emphasis in the curriculum of some schools.

The relationship of the social worker to the many colleagues who enter agencies without professional education is another aspect of the problem of effective teamwork. Because of the heavy responsibility that rests upon those who have had the benefit of professional education, more attention needs to be given by the schools to the sharing and imparting of what the social worker does. For those who are mature and who have had some previous experience—as is true of many students in schools of social work today—we should offer opportunity to learn how to teach, how to supervise others, how to interpret their own knowledge. Another problem for exploration and study is analysis of what types of position in the large agencies require the services of a social worker. This is the kind of self-study which the medical social workers have done so profitably to the advancement of their own skills as well as status. I believe that we have rushed into some of the new programs, assuming responsibility for the total operation without sufficient analysis of which positions required social work skills. Together, the field and the schools might study the distribution of social work services in terms of function. Such critical analysis would enable the schools better to prepare personnel for the public services.

Finally, social workers are more and more frequently finding themselves in positions that require coöperation with lawyers, physicians, psychologists, accountants, and members of other professions. Each profession has its own body of attitudes as well as its own body of knowledge. It is the awareness of the approach of the other profession, and a willingness to give and take in relating the specialized services to the clientele, that we need to help students acquire. As representatives of a fledgling profession, social workers have tended to be defensive and protective of their own knowledge. We do not need to teach the other groups what we do; but we can share with them some of our skills in terms of their service to clients or patients. I recently heard a psychiatric social worker describe the teamwork in one of the big hospitals of the Veterans Administration. She said that the chief psychologist requested the social service department to help their internes learn interviewing and asked that the social worker teach them how to take case histories. After two hours of discussion, the psychologist and social worker were able to agree that it was not the taking of social case histories that the psychologists should learn; if they needed some of the skills in interviewing which the social workers had, they should learn them in application to their own function. A plan was worked out whereby the psychologists would keep records of their interviews with patients, on the basis of which the social worker would teach them something of her approach and technique.

I believe that if we succeed in professional education in teaching the student as a whole person, then the attitudes, understanding, and ways of working with people which become his will constitute a discipline that can be applied to any of the materials with which he works. By this I mean that in work with people certain processes and methods have general application. Also, the student needs to have a rich array of knowledge courses if his discipline is to have orientation. Unless he understands why the public programs differ from those of the voluntary agencies in purpose and direction, he cannot transfer easily from one to the other. Unless he understands the bearing of the larger social issues of the day upon social welfare programs, he will be a worker without vision. This necessity to combine a highly skilled service with broad social perspective has been well stated by the President's Commission on Higher Education:

> All the professions are urgently in need of leadership, of professional statesmanship. They need men who possess disciplined imagination, social awareness, and elasticity of judgment, men who can see beyond the details of their own jobs to recognize professional problems and obligations and take constructive and farsighted action about them. Professional men must deal with matters of public policy.[6]

To prepare professional leaders for social welfare programs will require, as I have pointed out, the selection of persons educable for the profession and equipped with a broad general education that has given them, not only information, but habits of mind that will enable them to continue to learn throughout their lives. Given such students, the professional school helps them to achieve personal growth for independent action while disciplining them to work within the purposes of social agencies and within the obligations that belong to the whole profession. The areas in which the professional schools need to strengthen their preparation are, first, in stating more clearly than at present the broadening philosophy of social work and giving it a conceptual framework by means of which new kinds of skill can be developed. In many ways this represents a union of the pioneer efforts of the leaders in the field with the later refinement of methods and techniques that produced social work. Such a union of concern about social problems and about ways of dealing with

[6] United States President's Commission on Higher Education, *Higher Education for American Democracy: a Report* (Washington, D.C.: United States Government Printing Office, 1947), I, 83.

them must be applied to the current social milieu. The second area in which the curriculum of the professional school can be improved is in training for better teamwork. The person who can turn specialists into a group working for the common goal is, indeed, a leader and in demand.

For the kind of professional education I have presented as desirable, hard work and resources will be required. Although there is a shortage of personnel in our profession we must turn our attention to advanced study beyond the Master's degree. Some of the developments I have pictured will require time and scholarship. Research should be undertaken in relation to the contribution that social work can make to the tasks of today. Most of all, we need advanced study to produce more and better teachers. Without them, the growth of the profession in the directions described will be long delayed. One of the greatest problems of the profession lies in the fact that so many practitioners have been only partially educated by the schools from which they have been graduated. Specialist-minded, they are fearful of losing the fine skill that social work has developed if they turn it to generalized use. But the balance between the general and the special is not a problem unique to social work; it is common to all education. Teachers who have both breadth and depth of knowledge and purposive skill constitute the keystone for the future. To produce them will require new vistas of education and new resources for the support of the professional schools. But with these social work should, indeed, be able to demonstrate that professionalism is one of the hopeful features of the times.

Criteria for an Integrated Curriculum

BENJAMIN E. YOUNGDAHL

A FUNDAMENTAL FACT must be recognized before one can proceed to evaluate the needs for professional training for social work: the profession has developed broadly, and it attempts to cover a wide range of services and functions. The services of a social worker are needed and find their way into widespread public and private programs, local, national, and international, and urban and rural. These services can be found in institutions and agencies and are under the sponsorship of religious, secular, governmental, and even intergovernmental auspices. The whole gamut of human needs, from the more simple but important ones of food, shelter, and clothing to the more complicated emotional needs, is accepted as within the province of the profession. The graduates of our schools deal with individuals and with groups and are expected to be quite as much at home in approaching broad, preventive measures in the public forum as in giving treatment to an individual. Social workers are at one and the same time handmaidens to medicine, to education, to religion, to labor, and to law; and they form an entity by themselves, they give and they receive. Even casual study of the biennial *Social Work Year Book* indicates the tremendous scope and breadth of the activities commonly encompassed by the term "social work." It is not surprising, then, that any attempt to train for this ever enlarging scope and function becomes increasingly difficult.

There are three major phases of professional education for social work as it is now arranged: course work, field work, and research. One of the difficult problems for a school faculty to solve is how to determine the proportion of time which a student should spend or use on each of these three elements or vehicles of learning. When each one is considered separately, the conclusion is almost invariably reached that not enough time is spent by the student on that particular phase. There is constant clamor from many sources for an increase in the number of individual courses which a student "ought to have," and from other quarters the urgency of expanding the amount of time a student spends in supervised practice in an agency is argued just as strongly. Still others press the viewpoint that if a profession is going to mature and advance, it must be infused with research, which ought to be an important element in the training of a social worker. All three approaches to learning have contributions to make in the training of a professional worker, and it should not be impossible to dovetail the three elements in such a way as to bring about the desired goal.

I should like to discuss the goals of professional education for social work in a broad way and without reference to specific methods, such as casework, group work, and community organization, and without consideration as to whether the goals can be achieved in courses, in practice work in an agency, or in research. Neither will there be reference to where or at what level in the educational framework a person would secure the items of knowledge enumerated. It may be that in many instances it would be proper for him to acquire some of the knowledge and background in his preprofessional education, but most of it would, of course, come in the period of graduate professional training.

In other words, without reference to current courses or to the hierarchy of sequences now established in the schools, the specific question which is posed is this: What should any professional social worker be, and have, and know? If we can agree on this much, we are then ready to decide how we can reach the desired objective most economically and effectively and what arrangements of courses, field work, and research are most appropriate.

Much of the material which follows is an adaptation of some tentative studies which are being made by the faculty of the George Warren Brown School of Social Work in an effort to factor out the elements which should be a part of the equipment of any professional social worker. Any emphasis in statement or errors in logic belong to the writer, but if by chance this analysis turns out to be helpful, the credit belongs to the faculty of the George Warren Brown School of Social Work. Inasmuch as the faculty has not agreed completely on certain aspects of Area 4, the writer assumes complete responsibility for the conclusions drawn. It should be said that the examples and details are meant to be illustrative and not inclusive.

Actually, the criterion for an integrated curriculum is an integrated student. What should a student get and have and be by the time he reaches the status of a professional social worker? It is possible to set down four broad goals (or yardsticks, if you please) for professional status. Perhaps these are more properly called areas of knowledge, and they will be referred to as such.

1. The first area is self-awareness, knowledge of self. A professional social worker will appreciate that factors inherent in himself will affect his professional practice and that he has a responsibility to control and direct his subjectivity so that these factors do not adversely affect his personal operations. This implies a recognition and control of prejudices, a willingness to handle reaction to misfortunes of others with sufficient facility to be of help, and a recognition and understanding of the meaning of the role he has in the minds of those he helps. It means, moreover, that he should accept the fact that as a professional worker he must assume responsibility for action and self-discipline, oriented to the welfare of others rather than to purely personal need. More specifically, this includes such things as responsibility for helping when one has undertaken to do so, fulfillment of promises and agreements, willingness to assume responsibility for needed action and to assume authority required by any position accepted by the worker in the profession.

To become a professional worker, a student must demonstrate attitudes which are conducive to continued personal growth and which contribute to the development of a profession. Realistic self-criticism, a critical frame of mind, receptivity to new learning, and a realization that competence comes from knowledge and experience in practice are all important.

Equally important is a devotion to, and the use of, a code of ethics which will guide professional conduct in relation to clients, colleagues, and community. Such a code would include, among other things, a respect for the contribution of other professions; a regard for the confidential nature of social work relationships, and avoidance of the misuse of positions or of skills against the best welfare of client, agency, or community; a respect for the time of others; a loyalty to the principles of sound personnel practices; and a willingness to promote the development of others for the sake of the effectiveness of agency and field.

Included in this area of self-awareness and knowledge of self are certain philosophical concepts that form the basis of professional activity. Belief in the dignity of man and the worth of the individual, in democratic principles, in the right of self-determination of people for their way of life, unless the rights of others are infringed, are well-known basic concepts. A non-judgmental attitude and an acceptance of the fundamental rights of people to an opportunity for full realization of capacity and for services which promote well-being and prevent social ills are likewise included. There is also acceptance of planning for, and application of, social services based on understanding of cause and effect within the total environment with recognition of physical, emotional, and cultural factors.

This self-awareness and the capacity for personal growth are fundamental to the practice of social work in any setting. A person is not a professional worker unless he can direct his own feelings and reactions without impeding his helpfulness to others. Likewise, his attitudes, beliefs, and professional standards are important in his own personal growth and in his ability to give effective service. The underlying contention is that self-awareness is contingent upon a sensitive recognition of the influence of the community and of other people on the self, which in turn has its influence on others and on society.

2. The second area of knowledge, which should be a part of the equipment of any professional social worker, is knowledge of

the "community." This would include such broad aspects as materialism, the pattern of our culture, and the increased role of government and of broad planning. It would encompass the broad background of the many social changes which began in the nineteenth century and have been accelerated in the twentieth: changes in the function of the family, growth of big business, recurrence of financial depressions, increase of technology and scientific knowledge, mechanization of industry and specialization of occupations, improvement in methods of communication and transportation, growth of labor organizations, centralization of economic power, our aging population, international rivalry, etc. Such knowledge would encompass the philosophical and historical foundations of democracy and the steps which society has taken to meet the changing social and economic forces and to control them or divert them. It would include not only such efforts toward palliation of their ill effects as tenement regulations, employers' liability, etc., but also the struggle to get more preventive measures, such as the income tax, various governmental controls, collective bargaining, the control and development of water power, and public health measures.

In the long run, democracy is dependent upon the capacity of individuals for self-determination and for voluntary significant group participation, which include both obligations and privileges. Democracy is not the inevitable result of natural forces, but is the achievement of struggle; it does not perpetuate itself automatically, but is maintained by allegiance, application, and hard work. The meaning, faith, attitude, and habits inherent in democracy, the recognition of the inherent right to work, the freedom of individual growth, the capacity of individuals to develop loyalty, interest, experience, and to find security in developing society in the midst of conflict—all these must be acquired in learning of various kinds and are included in this second area of knowledge.

We are faced with specific problems: putting together the democratic ideal and our cultural ideal in an environment of economic materialism; making political democracy effective in the economic sphere; the trend toward specialization and the use of specialists; the confusion of values; the problem of how to induce the individual to participate with satisfaction in a highly centralized and increasingly managed social and economic order and government; and the accelerations in our common life, resulting in a neurotic pattern of progress with all its compulsion. Knowledge concerning these problems will make the social worker more effective in his helpfulness.

To know the community means to know the programs that are in operation and their background. Of equal importance are the mechanics of organization and methods of administration, and the philosophy which underlies ways in which services are given. Variants in philosophy and approach result in certain structural formations and a complicated network of associations, boards, and committees, financed by both public and private auspices and occasionally merged into autonomous units or federations. A social worker should know something about how social work is financed and administered in all its aspects and should know how to interpret programs to the public and to promote social legislation in order to widen the sphere of influence and service.

Research and planning are important parts of knowledge in this area, as are, of course, the rise of education for social work and the status of the profession itself and its associations.

Social work is a servant of a democratic society and responds to the needs and demands of the community. Knowledge of that community and the functions of leadership as a part of the servant role are essentials for a professional worker.

3. The third area of knowledge which any social worker should have as a part of his equipment concerns the growth and change of any individual. This includes the understanding of the individual as a whole, physically, emotionally, intellectually, culturally, and socially, and likewise includes both the normal individual and significant deviations from the normal. Sometimes called the dynamics of human behavior, this area would include the methods of prevention and treatment of deviations.

In an article of this kind, one can only illustrate the nature of the content which would be included under this area which encompasses behavior of an individual from birth to death. In the prenatal and natal period, such segments of knowledge as heredity, constitutional factors considered in relation to intellectual, physical, and emotional equipment, parental health, emotional factors in pregnancy, prenatal delivery and postnatal care, causes of mental defectiveness, types of care, maternal and infant mortality rates in relation to facilities for care, etc., would be important.

In the period of infancy, there are the factors of physical care and feeding of the infant; psychological factors in nursing, weaning, and toilet training; emotional factors in the separation from parents; and the normal physical, emotional, social, and intellectual development of an infant.

Included in the period of childhood are such important elements as norms of physical growth; psychosexual development, social relationships, and meaning of group experience; intellectual development and the use of tests; communicable diseases of childhood, orthopedics, the meaning of handicapping conditions, and the resources for illness prevention, immunization, and treatment.

Adolescence would cover such things as physical changes and their significance, emotional growth and change, changing relationships with parents, conflicts relating to dependence and independence, attitudes toward authority, intellectual development and interest, social relationships and the importance of interaction with groups.

In the adult years we would have the same norms of physical, social, and intellectual growth, but would also include such things as marriage, the physiology of sex, normal sex life, emotional aspects of marriage, sexual deviations, emotional factors in structural change or damage, menopause, unmarried parenthood, and the meaning of cultural factors in work and achievement.

Then, finally, in old age there should be included knowledge of physical, emotional, and intellectual changes which accompany that period of life, together with the common illnesses of the period, and the social needs and community planning for the care of the aged.

Included in all these age periods would be the various common illnesses, mental and physical, the social aspects of disease, methods of diagnosis and treatment, including physical and psychiatric treatment, diet, and psychosomatic aspects of illness.

Fundamental to the professional practice of social work is knowledge of the growth and change of the individual. And throughout is the effort to see the individual whole; moreover, it is to see that whole as it is affected by the environment and culture covered in Area 2.

Perhaps there will be little disagreement with the analysis thus far. The following material, however, presents a point of view as to "method" which is a controversial one, and undoubtedly most faculties will find difficulty in getting complete agreement on a definitive statement.

4. Area 4 deals with "method" and states that method is really a synthesis of the first three areas. It is the part of social work that deals with action and it is a combination and use of the first three areas, rarely combined in equal measure: knowledge of self and awareness thereof; knowledge of the broad community and its forces; and knowledge of how any person develops. This combination becomes a synthesis, and to the degree that it becomes a new knowledge, it creates a motivation or philosophy and an interested dynamic detachment that permits the social worker, faced with a situation requiring action, to be enabling or helpful by adding to the situation the catalyst of his special knowledge. The how, when, and why a certain action is taken are dependent on a host of factors arising out of each situation, and the more background the worker has in the three areas of knowledge, the more skilled is his performance likely to be. In a sense, the method is knowing when to do what.

The accumulation of knowledge alone will not in itself make a person a good worker. The knowledge must be integrated into a tool and guide for action. Some plan of carefully controlled practice work is necessary and economical in the learning process. Errors in human relations are costly, and, frequently, once made they cannot be undone nor can the results be changed. Area 4, therefore, must be given emphasis, not wholly, but largely in supervised field work. It represents a skill in combining and using the various elements of the first three areas.

In field work, as in theory courses, a student is given a range of cases or situations, typical and atypical, sampling the important and common problems. He learns under supervision how to use the elements of knowledge in the first three areas while at the same time he is expanding his understanding of those areas through application. Skill in method is based on knowledge gained and absorbed through experience; skill through repetition without an increase of knowledge happens only when the skill is mechanical. It is not likely that a single case or situation with which a worker will deal in the future will exactly duplicate the situations of his field work experience. However, he has learned some patterns and a way of approach and has developed an ease that makes his knowledge increasingly more usable. The specific method he uses in each case, group, or community situation will depend upon the numerous variable factors present and the way they impinge upon one another and himself.

It is possible, however, in a broad way to state the several functions and tools included in this area.

First, it includes the analysis, diagnosis, or evaluation of data of all kinds bearing on the client, community, staff, or self. A worker projects abstraction into the specific situation and gives it reality. For example, he takes available medical information, sees what it means in the given situation, and evaluates medical records in terms of the client's feelings, economic situation, family setting, and community. In this identification of the need and evaluation of the data, it is important to consider the stage of development at all times and realistically to limit the scope of the plans and to time the actions as well as the where and how of the action and its degree. In all of this, he must be aware of himself, of the community and its forces, and of the way in which people develop.

Secondly, Area 4 includes the interview and other communication on a planned basis with purpose and movement toward tentatively set goals. With the establishment of constructive relationships, there is the application of knowledge of the behavior and understanding of personality to the individual interviewed. Interviewing includes the obtaining of information and the giving of information and a purposeful direction toward the desired end. It also involves effective listening.

The third function is to lead, guide, facilitate, and enable. A professional worker takes responsibility when appropriate, makes an effort to change the ideas of other professional people, willingly faces great disagreement or lack of acceptance, has skill in condensing material in recognition of salient facts in a wide range of recorded situations, secures support, interprets, and makes decisions. The ability to initiate and to make decisions is essential.

Finally, this action area includes the organization of work, functions, responsibilities, or area of activity and self, with purpose and dispatch. Resources are used in such a way as to find out what exists and how it is best used; work is organized in relation to self in such a way as to be most effective; other people and agencies are drawn in so as to offer the most effective contribution toward achieving the goal; delegated responsibility is carried out; and working relationships with colleagues, other agencies, and community groups are developed.

In performing these functions, the worker uses the knowledge gained in the first three areas and does the job of enabling and facilitating, of leading, guiding, and organizing, and of analyzing and evaluating.

Social work, then, is an art based on the sciences; an art which by dictionary definition means "skill in performance acquired by experience, study or observation." It is an art based on a foundation of knowledge including knowledge and awareness of self. knowledge of the broad community, and knowledge of how any person develops. A balanced synthesis of these three areas of knowledge makes possible the action which in a broad sense is referred to as "social work method" or "function" but which in each case or situation varies with the milieu.

With the accumulation of knowledge in the three areas and with the development of skill in the synthesis and use of this learning, a person has arrived at the level of professional status and with some limitations should be able to work with individuals, groups, or communities. This status, then, forms a generic base from which may stem specialization on the job or in the school. If we agree with these goals and can center our attention on them rather than on arbitrary or traditional administrative courses or divisions, the task of integration between field practice and course work becomes less difficult.

Agreement on these goals does not solve our problem but is only a beginning. There remains the formidable task of spelling out the detail, dividing the material into segments or courses, making the important decision as to where in the academic structure the various elements should be placed, and deciding how long it will take an average student to acquire the minimum training needed for professional status. Once having answered that, the currently realistic problem of subprofessional or quasi-professional status can be resolved more easily.

The real problem in this matter of integration of knowledge is to liberate the student to become a free, professional social worker. It is to help him, both in classes and in field work, to free himself so that he can integrate knowledge, think independently, compensate for bias, prejudice, and taboos, and acquire confidence. The criterion for an integrated curriculum is an integrated person—a person who knows himself, who knows the dynamics of human behavior, who knows the broad community in which people live and have their being, and who knows when and where to apply the pertinent aspect of his knowledge to any individual situation or set of circumstances. Such a focus, rather than one on traditional courses, will prove helpful in planning for the progressive development of our professional training programs.

The Field Supervisor as Educator

ELEANOR NEUSTAEDTER

THE PRACTITIONER who becomes a field supervisor becomes an educator. And the heart of her educational problem is this: information, knowledge, opportunities, do not add up to casework practice. The student may be a superb passer of examinations and, nevertheless, be unable to help a troubled person take heart and move toward a solution of his difficulty. Therefore, the task of the supervisor is not only to offer the student opportunities for learning, not only to help him transform information into knowledge. The task of the field supervisor is to help the student use his opportunities, his knowledge, and himself in his contacts with people and in his efforts on their behalf.

In this endeavor the supervisor has three kinds of responsibility: the development of a field curriculum; the integration of casework theory and field practice; and the creation for the student of an environment in which he can learn. This last is a basic educational activity of the field guide: if he is to learn, the student must feel that in the agency setting he can be sure of something, of somebody, yet he must gradually develop a sense of freedom. He must feel that his supervisor is dependable and that she understands his need to depend. But he must also feel that in conference with her he dares to "speak out," to say what he thinks, perceiving that she recognizes and accepts his need and his struggles to stand on his own feet.

The student must find in this busy agency where he is so earnestly trying to become a "professional person" that feelings are important, his feelings as well as his clients. Here and now, he, who so early learned to conceal his feelings, may begin to dare to feel. Only as he finds it possible to relax, and, in this new setting, to be himself, will the pieces of his experience begin to merge, become interrelated, form a pattern, and make sense. Only as the student's life experiences become integrated will he be able to move into new situations and activities with ability spontaneously to use knowledge and experience, what he has learned and what he is. When he can so use all of himself, freely, in his contacts with troubled people, we can then say that he has become a professionally mature practitioner of casework.

In the years past, methods and concepts of supervision and emphases in training have changed in spiral fashion. There was the catch-as-catch-can era when students spent their working day in a whirl of vigorous activity, learned by doing, and from time to time had a word with the supervisor. There was the era when we were absorbed in the effort to understand the dynamics of human behavior, our own as well as our clients'. From this stemmed the era of so-called "passivity," when no unnecessary word passed the lips of the field guide. All suggestions for meeting a new situation were drawn from the student. His experiences might have been meager and his ideas few, but "What do you think?" was the unfailing supervisory response to the groping student. In this period the supervisor showed confusion as to what her role in training should be. She earnestly tried to find an answer to the question, "Is there a difference between casework practice and student training?" Was she a therapist or was she a teacher? For a time, some of the "best people" leaned heavily toward therapy, and many a bewildered and, shall we say, resentful student coming to be taught, remained to be treated.

More recently, we have been, and still are, very aware of the student in his relationships to people, supervisor, and clients. We have realized that no amount of knowledge or skill in assembling data of themselves equips a student to help troubled people. He must be able to relate himself to them in such a way that they feel and respond to his wish to help. We have realized that the student who experiences a good relationship with his supervisor is more free to use and learn from the opportunities for practice that she offers. Indeed, so "relationship"-conscious have we become, that the word is becoming a cliché, although to many a student its meaning still remains nebulous and elusive.

However broadly and vaguely we may use the term, the importance of relationship in practice and in training we do understand. From each phase of supervisory experience we have learned. Today we note a lag between the understanding of behavior and relationship that we have gained and our clarity concerning the broad content of field training and our pedagogical method. This is the era when we need to do more thinking about what we teach and how we teach it.

The schools are working out criteria by which to gauge the student's knowledge and performance at the end of his period of training. We field supervisors should have something to say about the part of his training that the student can be expected to absorb in the limited period of time he spends in our agency. We should know what experience in our agency can contribute to his knowledge and skill. We must perceive the methods we are using or can use to help the student learn.

The first task of the field supervisor is to develop a training program or curriculum in the field. She must devise a series of experiences that can be offered to all students who train in the agency. She knows that basic casework can be learned by experience in any casework setting. She also knows that settings are not identical: agencies differ in what they do and what they have to do with. Moreover, the communities which form the setting for agency practice vary in what they have to offer for student training. One community is richer or poorer than another in community spirit, in the number and type of agency resources, in the attitudes toward training for social work of citizens, officials, and even of social workers themselves.

Therefore, each supervisor should look at her agency and at her community to see what learning experiences they offer. She then devises a series of related experiences that will tap the reservoir of agency and community resources and offer the student a well-balanced field program. It is not enough to give the student a group of cases that happen to be available, from which it is hoped he will learn something. He will learn something, but he should and will learn more if his experiences are broad in scope, varied in content, and well balanced. He needs experiences with different kinds of people with different kinds of trouble; with different kinds of agencies and community resources.

So the supervisor looks at her community. She sees it as the setting in which those whom the agency serves live their lives, as the environment which either contributes to their difficulties or offers solutions. She sees it as the setting for agency practice. She asks herself: "What learning opportunities does this community offer the student who for a time will be part of it and who will learn to practice his profession in it?" The supervisor thinks. She thinks about the ways in which people in this community earn their living, where they live and recreate and worship. She asks herself what problems this community creates for the clients. What organizations are influential, what individuals? What social agencies does the community include? Is there a visiting nurse service, a neighborhood house? What people and what agencies are resources for training? And how can the supervisor help the student to come in contact with them?

Of course, case assignments may offer a natural and easy opportunity for meeting, but if not, the supervisor does not leave to chance the student's contact with key personnel and agencies. She uses initiative and imagination in acquainting the student with the setting in which he is working. Joint staff meetings with the staff of another agency and participation in agency conferences with another worker are but two familiar ways of developing opportunities for contact when unhappily the student's case load is meager or ill balanced.

Over the period of the student's placement in the agency the supervisor includes in his training program as broad an experience as is appropriate in the community in which he is practicing. Thus he is helped to relate to the field the idea of "community" as it is discussed in the classroom. He begins to perceive who "the community" is. He experiences working together. He sees himself as part of the community, a resource for colleagues in other agencies as they, in turn, are resources for his clients and for him. The student experiences community life and integrates with practice a concept with which he has become familiar in the classroom.

Having surveyed the community from the viewpoint of student learning, the supervisor looks at her agency. What is it organized to do? What services does it offer? Is it a hospital, a court, a welfare department, an institution? Thinking broadly, through what experiences in this agency can the student apply knowledge to practice and develop skill through doing?

At this point the supervisor has a problem: intake. She knows the experiences that she wants included in this field curriculum. She also knows that it is not easy to have available a group of cases that will afford these experiences. Nevertheless, she plans. It is better to plan even if the plans miscarry. Then, at least, the supervisor knows where, in relation to curriculum, she needs to put her effort. So she makes it her business to try to assemble a group of cases that over the training period will offer experiences that are typical of agency practice, and that as fully as possible use agency resources. In a family agency she can include cases that offer experience with broken families, whole families, people alone, old people and children; people with problems of housing and finances, health and family relationship; people needing social services; people needing help with feelings of unhappiness arising from stresses without or within.

In curriculum planning the sequence of student experience is quite as important as content because no one learns anything at all unless the new idea is related to what has been experienced and is known. Therefore, the first principle in field training is, "Begin where the student is"; and the supervisor's first question is, "Where is the student?"

At this point the supervisor is helped by the material sent by the school to the agency in advance of the student's arrival: data concerning his past experiences; what he has done, and when and where. These data may not be accurate, but they include information that the student and his friends have given the school. They are what we have to use at the beginning of training; and they can be used in planning first assignments and bridging the gap between the student's past and the present. Therefore, the supervisor assigns to her new student a case, an activity, something to do that will represent something old and something new. She gives him a task within his scope that he can take hold of with the feeling, "I can do it."

However, a word of warning is in order. It concerns the possibility of misusing the record of the student's past and beginning where the student is not. It is possible to assume that a previous experience was a rich and positive one for the student, and on a wrong inference to assign tasks for which he is unprepared. The supervisor gauges the student's readiness for an assignment, not alone from a record, but from discussion with him. And the sequence of training experiences continues to be built up through discussion and observation of the student's performance and again through discussion.

A very practical and concrete illustration of this principle is the way in which in a case involving financial difficulty, an agency service can be used for training. The service can be used in three ways: to meet a client's need, to teach the student how to do his job, and to integrate classwork and fieldwork. I cite budgeting. I cite it as one way of paying attention to what is important to the client and dealing with it. And since it is of concern to the client, the caseworker's concern with budgeting may well serve to establish or maintain a positive worker-client relationship.

In many casework settings discussion of finances has a place. People come with problems of insufficient income or inadequate management. They come to a clinic with requests for medical appliances. They come to various agencies with requests for a camp for their children, to hospitals for free care, to family agencies for special grants, to public departments for maintenance. When they approach a fee-charging agency, they must discuss finances in order to relate fee to income. Money and budgets are part of the life of each of us. They are problems to many client groups. Feelings about money are usually strong and often conflicting. The schools know this and give courses in financial planning as part of casework training.

The supervisor then, in many an agency, irrespective of whether the agency has a "relief budget," will do well to include in her student's training, experiences that will help him to relate to the client's financial problem what the student has learned in life or in class about financial management and budgeting. The student, groping for light on the elusive client-worker relationship, may find to his surprise a good relationship beginning to develop as he takes up the client's problem of money, discusses it, and by practical figuring, demonstrates in black and white that he is both interested and understanding. It must be understood that a discussion of ways and means does not obligate a student to meet a budget deficit. But, it has been said, "People have finances as well as emotions." And certainly we know from experience that the emotions in connection with finances must be perceived by the student and understood whether he gives help or is unable to meet the need.

Of course, the point in training at which a particular case will be available for assignment cannot be determined in advance; nor can the supervisor know in advance when such a case will appropriately fit into the sequence of training experiences designed for an individual student. But she misses an opportunity if, when money and management are problems, she fails to help the student experience a practical discussion of income and of spending.

A good worker-client relationship develops when the caseworker finds ways to show to the person in trouble that she grasps the meaning to him of the difficulty and that she is prepared, not necessarily to meet the request, but to give serious consideration to the problem.

Now, what of the setting in which the student's activities take place? For it is the immediate environment which largely determines whether student activities are learning experiences or sterile bustlings, meaningless alike to student and to client. The basic ingredient in a good setting for student training is the supervisor herself. Supervisors should be sound practitioners, sure of what they have to teach, disciplined people. Beneath and above all, they should be people of controlled but warm and kindly feelings, so truly professional that they dare to be natural. The supervisor's contacts with her student should be a demonstration of how good and how helpful a human relationship can be. This is important because through identification with the supervisor, a professional person who can accept his dependency as it shows itself and who at the same time treats him as an adult, the student learns and is himself helped to become professionally mature. He comes to the training agency wanting to help. He uses trial-and-error methods. He is uneasy with his clients. He is blocked and frightened, or possibly carried away by his own feelings and those of the troubled people who look to him for help. He leaves the agency able to be helpful. The tested methods that he uses are becoming his very own. He is not afraid to recognize and express his own feelings. He catches the feeling of the client, deals with it, and accepts him as he accepts himself.

Since the supervisor represents to the student a figure of authority, he gains in self-assurance when eventually he begins to perceive her as a person to whom he can express his thoughts and feelings. It is easy for us to forget how fearful of feeling we were in our first field setting. Yet only as the student dares to put into words his "gripes," his likes, his antipathies; only when he can freely say, "I don't like this," or, "I do like you," will he be able to hear the client's expression of feelings or respond to it.

So the supervisor creates a permissive setting in which the student is free to feel, to "say it," to act, to experiment, to make mistakes and retrieve them. But she does not mistake a permissive setting for one that is nebulous. The supervisor knows that the student needs something on which to depend and learns more readily when he can see the limits and form and shape of the setting in which to operate. From his first day to his last day in the agency, the student should know what is expected of him —at first in relation to the office, gradually in relation to the client and the agency.

The student starts with so small a prop as knowing where in the office to hang his hat; where to sign in and out. He has a little manual of office practice. He knows something about the agency. He has tasks related to his setting and within his ability to perform. He is given enough to do so that his time is filled with activities geared to his experience and competence. Crippling insecurity and self-doubt are not likely to develop and flourish in an environment where the student is daily finding what he can do.

Gradually, the number and scope of his responsibilities are increased. The supervisor is aware that one test of the student's ability to meet reality is his performance in relation to the requirements of work within the agency. In the past we have, at times, tended to overprotect the student, feeling that the realities of the job might be too threatening. We now know that usually it is the unknown rather than reality that undermines self-confidence. As he accepts and meets the demands of the job, the student gains in self-assurance and moves toward professional and personal maturity.

The need to be both realistic and permissive challenges the supervisor to adapt her teaching methods to the individual student. She therefore studies the learning patterns of her students through observation of their performance. How does the student learn? Is his tempo fast or slow? Must he find out things for himself? Does he look for a blueprint? Can he use a suggestion? Has he what John Dewey calls "the fund of relevant knowledge and the experience that produces ideas and suggestions"? Do ideas come slowly, and, if so, is it because the student has a meager background, poor endowment, emotional blocking? Or has the supervisor, perchance, failed to give information that would guide the student to the knowledge which produces ideas?

As the supervisor perceives the ways in which the student most easily takes on new ideas and moves into new experiences, she varies her methods to meet his needs. No training problem is new to the experienced supervisor. The same learning problems arise again and again in different forms with different students. As they arise the supervisor recognizes them and adapts her teaching method and content flexibly to the need of the individual.

She lets him experiment and "find out." She trusts him and controls her anxiety. She helps him with a too difficult situation. She shares experience and responsibility. She demonstrates ways of approaching an individual. She gives information. She refers him to a source from which he can secure information. She gives him a reading reference. She says what she thinks. And she still says, "What do you think?" She uses this question, not as a supervisory cliché, but as a means of helping the student understand that he must be an active participant in his own training; for it is a basic principle that supervisor and student together share responsibility, and both are active in the teaching-learning process. The supervisor does not seek to make the student in her image. He learns with her and moves on to make his own application in practice of things learned in training.

There is one basic educational problem in every setting, for every student and for every supervisor. That is the problem of integration—specifically, the integration of classroom teaching, reading, and field practice. This aspect of student learning is fundamental in training, and yet casework teachers and field work supervisors give too little attention to it. In the classroom, teachers emphasize the importance of concepts and skills that are minimized or neglected in the field. Conversely, the field emphasizes the importance of concepts and methods realistic in practice that are not stressed in the classroom.

The field supplies superb illustrations of concepts taught in every class. But there are supervisors who may not know what courses the student is taking, what he thinks about their content, and how he sees course content in relation to his daily activities in the field. This should not be. Class and field are the warp and woof of what has been called the fabric of professional education. The field supervisor can help to move the shuttle. How?

The supervisor has a list of courses taken by the student before he goes to the field. There is variation in the extent to which individual supervisors use this list. At the beginning of each quarter or semester the supervisor should make it her business to find out what grades and comments the student received in his last period of class work, and for what courses he is registered in the period to come.

For her own orientation and for use with the student in the field, the supervisor should have a syllabus of the casework courses. Failing this, she can at least ask the student "what goes on" in his classes. Some students move their own shuttle, continuously relating field experience to class and other life experiences. Some students need help to see in problems, personalities, and situations, illustrations of concepts discussed in class. They must be helped to see how a concept, dry and theoretical, looks when personified by Mrs. X. Conversely, they must be helped to see that while the behavior of Mrs. Y. may be extremely puzzling to them, the psychiatrist "has a word for it."

Reading references, the supervisor's own as well as bibliographies used in class, help along the integrative process. The school bibliographies are comprehensive and may appear somewhat formidable to a student who is discovering that he needs a longer rather than a shorter working day. If copies of the bibliographies in use at school are available to the supervisor (and if she has time in which to peruse them), she is able to relate some of the reading assignments to the student's current problems of practice, or to suggest additional pertinent references. The reading list becomes more vital when it is perceived as important in practice as well as in class work.

A final word on integration has to do with the written evaluation of the student's field work and its use in agency and school. To be sure, where the relationship is a good one, the formal quarterly evaluation conference is a recapitulation of matters previously discussed, because the basis of a good relationship is a frank exchange of opinion and a realization on the part of student and supervisor that each is a "trustworthy other person." Nevertheless, the formulation of a written evaluation of the student's field practice can be a superb teaching device. There is an opportunity for supervisor and student to compare and integrate their thinking, and for practical application of the principle that student and supervisor are jointly responsible for the teaching-learning process. The student should participate in a planned quarterly discussion of his work and in the writing of a statement concerning his progress. Moreover, in the putting into words of the thinking of supervisor and student concerning the latter's field practice, there is opportunity for the integration of class work and other life experience with performance in the field. Time, enough time, should be given to evaluative conference and discussion so that the student comes through with the feeling of "Now I know what I can do; now I know what I should do." For the purpose of the evaluation is exactly that: to show what the student can do and where he should put his effort during the next learning period. Vague generalizations are no substitute for clean-cut statements about the student's knowledge and performance, backed by facts.

Now the school has a stake in this evaluation. The student, like Noah's dove, goes out from the school into the vast spaces of agency work. What kind of an olive branch, in the shape of performance, does he bring back? The school needs to know, should know, what application the student is making of knowledge gained in and around the classroom. Student advising, planning of courses, references, are geared to what is known of the student's ability to integrate theory and practice. School and agency together have a question: "What kind of practitioner for the field of social casework are we preparing?" The well-prepared and clearly written field evaluation should be an answer.

Why do the agencies collaborate with the schools in training students, and how do they train their supervisors? Student supervision takes staff time and, therefore, costs the agency money, a great deal of money. Agencies give the services of their staff to student training because staff members want the experience, but this is not the primary reason for agency investment in professional education. Agencies train students because students become new practitioners, and new practitioners are the life and hope of the field. The therapist of tomorrow is the well-trained student of the well-trained supervisor of today.

Supervisors are recruited from among capable, young practitioners who want the experience and who are interested in teaching. They have some initial help from the school, and for the safeguarding of students many agencies offer their young supervisors opportunities for consultation with another staff member who is experienced in supervision. Because they too are young, and enthusiastic, and not too far removed from their own student days they have a special contribution to make to the student. They usually start by having assigned to them one or two beginners. In general, they learn by doing, and usually supervisors have too much to do.

This picture needs retouching. In the first place, the most difficult kind of supervision is supervision of the young beginner. Ideally, it is the supervisor who has already demonstrated competence in supervisory practice who should have responsibility for inducting into the field the young student of casework. The competence and security of the supervisor should support the student and compensate for his own inexpertness and self-doubt. Some of us are raising a question as to whether beginning supervisors and their supervisees might not do better when the student either has had agency experience or is a young staff member who already has made his adjustment to practice. Here and there this plan is being tried out; the idea merits experimentation.

But more fundamental than consideration of the students with whom the young supervisor should start practice is this: before any supervisory experience whatsoever the young supervisor needs more preparation for teaching; her work with students or with the younger staff members should be in the nature of supervised field training. And field practice in supervision should be correlated with school courses in supervision. The art of teaching requires aptitude, but it also requires teaching and training in pedagogical method. There is a lag between our training of students and our training of the supervisors whose responsibility they are.

These comments suggest the need for further collaboration between school and agency; for an additional expenditure of money, time, and thought; for the working out of supervisory courses and supervision. It is a joint responsibility and a serious one because on supervisory education depends the quality of student training, of practitioner competence, of the usefulness of the field of casework in the profession of social work. Supervisory education is tremendously important in the world today, at a time of upheaval and great need when without exaggeration or metaphorical flight it can truly be said that the "field is the world."

The Classroom Teacher as Practitioner

CHARLOTTE TOWLE

THE AIM OF PROFESSIONAL EDUCATION is to convey knowledge in such a way that the student may not merely possess it, but use it. Furthermore, its aim is to train for tomorrow's practice. From its very nature, social work education operates under fast-changing conditions which continuously challenge its content and its processes. It follows, therefore, that students in a school of social work are not to be regarded as so many jugs to be filled with a content that is to be preserved for all time. Instead, they must learn to use certain knowledge in an ongoing way. Hence the educator's constant concern is that students develop the emotional as well as intellectual capacity for remotivation and reintegration as later they experience the impact of a field of work which ever must be oriented to social change.

A profession must have leaders. Hence, one aim of professional education is to develop capacity for leadership. In the field of social work, with a large membership of untrained practitioners, its professionally educated members long will continue to be conscripted, often prematurely, into administrative, supervisory, and teaching positions. Therefore, social work education, to an extent beyond education in certain other professions, must produce people qualified for leadership. It is recognized that patterns for leadership are formed in early family and school life. Therefore, they are brought—or are not brought—into adult education, so that selection of students is a matter of decisive import. It is possible, however, to use leadership potentialities so that they are strengthened or to inhibit them in this decisive period when the student is undergoing considerable reorganization of the personality. This paper is concerned with the place of the classroom, and more particularly with the practitioner in the classroom, in an educational process concerned to develop leaders for tomorrow's practice.

It is important, first, to consider the student in relation to the general nature of the experience which he will make a part of himself when and if he gives himself to a wholehearted pursuit of a profession. It is recognized, at least in the field of social work, that normally professional education is not merely an intellectual pursuit. It is a vital life experience, one which engages the emotions profoundly.[1] One's life work always is serving certain basic purposes in maintaining the equilibrium of the personality. Furthermore, the educational experience represents the individual's preparation for survival in a competitive world. His professional choice involves his concept of himself as an adequate adult, a concept which will be a composite of his wishes, strivings, basic aims, often bearing also the imprint of deeply influential relationships. Thus this endeavor may represent a culmination of all that he has been growing toward, at an age when he has not yet found a firm footing in the adult world.

There is much at stake emotionally in success or failure in terms of the development of the ego. By reason of the fact that professional education is a means in the maturing process, it can be a source of deep gratification, an inspired pursuit. The decisive factor here is that given intellectual capacity, aptitude for the endeavor and capacity for growth, the student will bring a natural bent for learning, a serious intent to learn as part and parcel of his growth impulses. This frequently has enabled him to learn in spite of conditions unfavorable for learning. When, however, the latter are overwhelmingly adverse, a profound reaction can be expected, as occurs inevitably when basically growth is obstructed. In these instances the student may deal with the anxiety provoked through projection of responsibility for learn-

[1] For full discussion see Charlotte Towle, "The Emotional Element in Learning" in *Professional Education* (New York: American Association of Schools of Social Work, 1948).

ing, through marked resistances, and through the formation of defenses against it. In such defenses, which represent his struggle for adaptation, he resists the change implicit in learning, an experience essential for the development of tensile strength with which to meet stanchly but flexibly the requirements of changing conditions. If conditions are reasonably favorable for learning, the natural urge to learn which the student brings to education for his life work makes for an inspired response which is ever challenging to the educator to improve content and method. The dynamics for the attainment of our highest aims are here. We have but to understand them and to orient our educational systems to them. We have but to use in the educational situation that basic knowledge and understanding of human behavior which have served the social worker well in helping people make maximum use of their capacities and resources in meeting and solving their problems.

Consider some of the demands of a profession which the student experiences during his preparation for practice. A profession is a field of service established to serve the common good rather than the commonweal of its practitioners. It has a philosophy, an ethical system by which its practitioners are guided to the extent that they are not free agents. There is a recognized body of knowledge and skill to be attained for competent practice, and its members must give evidence of capacity to use it. A profession has a defined scope and function even though it merges with other fields of knowledge and skill. Its practitioners in using borrowed content must not lose identity with their own field. These several characteristics exert a multiple demand on the learner; notably, there is small place for self-aggrandizement. There is a high demand for social conscience; there is an enduring demand for subordination of personal self to a larger identity. There is a continuous problem of working within limits and yet remaining free and creative rather than worshipful of those limits. The educable student, therefore, will be one who enters the field with a readiness to grow into carrying the responsibilities of a mature adult; in fact, this educational situation immediately exerts pressure that he mature rapidly. He must act beyond his years. Furthermore, in social work he must meet the dependency needs of people in trouble, individuals whose years and experience of life's realities are beyond his own years and experience. He must meet the impact of their emotions, objectively and helpfully. He must subordinate, against the day when he truly outgrows them, the many biases, prejudices, and emotional convictions which still have great values for him personally. He must seem to feel and to think and to act in ways appropriate to social work, before he can work through his feelings and actually experience basic change. Thus he must repress and deny his own impulses, a demand which may cause considerable tension and anxiety.

The significant conclusions of all this are: The student in this field is having to undergo basic change in his feeling and thinking at rapid tempo against heavy demands and frequently at a vulnerable age. In that his life work is implicated there will be a great deal at stake in making good. Learning will involve the fundamental growth process. Hence, there will be a larger element of disorganization than in many learning situations, and reorganization that is reintegration will occur at a slower tempo. It means, also, that there may be some lag in integration of the various components in learning. Educators in this field note and decry the slowness with which integration occurs. Perhaps we are making an unrealistic demand when we expect a nice integration of content within a two-year period. Perhaps this manifestation is, in part, a commentary on our present educational schemes. It may be that they have impeded rather than facilitated integration, a question which will be considered further as my discussion proceeds. It is clear, however, that the integrative function of the ego is being worked at a maximum, so that there are periods in given individuals when it is functioning below par. It is also clear today that sound professional education should help the student keep his ego intact. The experienced social work practitioner has helped many people under stress at times of drastic change when some disorganization of the personality is occurring through their very struggle for adaptation. He knows ways of helping individuals to conserve and to use their strengths, ways which with some translation are applicable to the educational situation.

It has been said that in order to teach arithmetic, a teacher desirably should know, not merely arithmetic and sound methods for imparting it, but also Johnny and, finally, himself. Whether or not this is true for instruction in arithmetic, it is eminently true in a profession which engages the total personality in learning as does social work. It is obvious that an instructor cannot know a student intimately as an individual. He can, however, know him as a learner in terms of his response to a particular educational content and in the light of a basic understanding of the ego, its needs, its defenses, its adjustive mechanisms as it operates in the learning process. The latter orientation will not only give meaning to the responses and learning problems of particular students, but it could well throw light on the teacher himself, his teaching methods, his relationship to his classes, the soundness for these students of the content conveyed; in short, on the nature of the demand which his total instruction exerts. When the faculties of schools of social work individually and collectively from this standpoint look intently to see and listen intently to hear what the total educational systems which they are administering are doing to students in terms of their maturation for the demands of the profession, then we may learn what will facilitate rather than impede learning in social work, its nature being what it is and its stresses what they are. If the stresses are what I have depicted, and if one problem confronting us is that of helping the student maintain an emotional equilibrium so that defenses and the struggle for adjustment may not inhibit or devitalize learning, then it is clear that sound educational practice will be governed continuously by four working principles that are basic in social work practice:

1. The instructor will meet freely and adequately the valid dependency which the student brings into professional learning. This is the dependency implicit in the teacher-pupil relationship and the dependency inevitable in a situation in which a student begins practice before he knows its what, why and the how. This implies that the educator recognize that even at the level of adult

education, the learner has dependence on the teacher for acceptance of his limitations, understanding of his failures, and for help to become competent, given in accordance with needs which fall within established norms.

2. The instructor will use and affirm the strengths which the student brings. This implies teaching methods which actively engage the student in learning, which place responsibility in him for class preparation, for participation in class discussion, and for seeking help as he needs it. The most basic impulse is the impulse to survive. The need to feel secure, that is, safe, is fundamental as an assurance of survival. Fear emerges quickly when survival is threatened. The impulse to learn is the basic means to survival. Activity in learning eases anxiety and affords security. In the educational situation, the adult will not be satisfied with marginal learning which permits him bare survival in his professional group. He will both need and want to strive for mastery of knowledge and skills which will make it possible for him to contribute through leadership. In professional education, activity in learning is so important that faculties could well scrutinize their curricula to determine what proportion is taught didactically.

3. The instructor will avoid making unrealistic demands. He should begin where students normally should be at the start of a course, and proceed with an orderly progression from the simple to the complex. The instructor will avoid assignments and examination questions which demand application and integration of knowledge beyond that step or so ahead which stimulates the student to learn on his own. The instructor will avoid imposing his standards of performance and his tempo through leaping from crag to crag. He will realize that in repetitive descending and ascending the student's learning proceeds soundly, by reason of the fact that the simple fundamentals of the bottom lands can well be trod again and again. There inevitably will be certain unavoidable, unrealistic demands, as often is the case when, for example, classroom content and field experience cannot be nicely timed in terms of pressures or in terms of essential knowledge and skill imparted. At such times a

student may need help in bridging the gap. While instructors individually may not violate this principle of "not making unrealistic demands," it is possible for this to occur in the student's total program. The entire regime, composed as frequently it is of several courses, much library work, many written assignments, course examinations, comprehensive examinations, thesis requirements, and field work, constitutes an incessant barrage which the student must meet within rigid time limits. When this occurs to excess, the student may not have a productive learning period, and we may note anxiety and defenses, one of which may be temporary regression evidenced in projection of responsibility and increased dependency. In the interest of survival, students will acquire ways of "getting by." They will have had an experience in submission, in pretension, "in seeming to be rather than in being," which is not conducive to the development of professional integrity. This matter of unrealistic demand implied in overcrowded programs calls for careful observation and revision if the aims of professional education are to be attained.

4. The instructor will firmly insist that the student meet the reality demands of his field of instruction. In so far as these demands verge on the unrealistic in terms of constituting a big step ahead for a given student, the instructor will help him meet them rather than overlook or waive them. The amount of help that it is realistic to give is sometimes a difficult determination, but always it is an important one if the student is to accept and incorporate professional discipline.

We have now a picture of the nature of the experience which professional education for social work entails; we have a glimpse of the meaning which this experience commonly has for the student and, I hope, some feeling for his needs and strivings in this learning process. We have presented briefly the general educational principles by which professional learning may engage adult strivings and facilitate maturation rather than impede it. We come now specifically to the classroom instructor as practitioner.

It is desirable that the educator at whatever level he functions be a learner as well as a teacher. This long has been stressed as imperative in professional education; in fact, until recently it has been one of its distinguishing marks as differentiated from other forms of education. The concept of being a learner has been contingent upon continued activity in practice and often also in research. It is beyond the scope of this article to reflect upon the various factors which have made this continuance in practice less habitual in social work education than in certain other professions. It is of interest to note, however, that in a field in which only yesterday all education was conducted within agencies by practitioners, today it is customary for a proportion of the faculty to have withdrawn from practice and to be occupied in full-time teaching. There is a general tendency, however, on the part of these same teachers, out of their concern to contribute to their field of practice and out of their need to draw sustenance from it, to participate from the side lines in social work activity. It is usual also for the school of social work through its faculty, individually and collectively, to occupy a position of leadership in its social work community, locally, regionally, and sometimes nationally. It would seem, therefore, that the majority of social work educators are in touch with practice even though not regularly engaged in it. Perhaps it is more important that systematic practice continue in some areas of social work teaching than in others if the educator is to contribute to the advancement of knowledge rather than merely to keep abreast of its changing content. Social work is concerned with the education and re-education of individuals and groups. Hence the experienced practitioner has some enduring insights and methods to take into the classroom if he but uses adaptively in this situation what he has learned elsewhere. Certainly, however, it is clear that not all practitioners can teach, and that when a practitioner does teach he must extricate himself from a specific job in order to see and convey the field of instruction beyond the limits set by a particular agency in a given community. Furthermore, he must be something more than, or other than, a practitioner. He must find himself as a teacher. A teacher, however, must make practice come alive in the classroom. All that he conveys of knowledge and understanding and skill must be oriented to changing practice.

The classroom instructor teaches the what, the how, and the why of his particular field of practice. The learning experience commonly is thought of as being divided into three parts: the classroom, the field of practice, and research. A trichotomy does not exist, however, in terms of the content of learning. It might be said that in the classroom, knowledge and theory are imparted predominantly, whereas in the field, instruction is concerned primarily with their application, that is, with the development of skill.[2] It might be said also that in both classroom and field it is only as the student acquires a research attitude of mind, that is, a way of thinking and feeling which is the essence of the research spirit, can he learn to think originally, creatively, independently, and in the process of learning gain a basic competence. One of the strong arguments for the practitioner in the classroom is that he is skilled. He is not there, however, primarily to teach skills. One of the weaknesses of the instructor who has remained primarily a practitioner and has not found himself as a teacher is that he may center his attention too closely on the "hows of doing." This may result in the teaching of techniques removed from the context of actual practice. This method fails of its purpose, the development of skill. It fosters working by precedent rather than by principle. The novice will make of techniques a body of well-established procedures or routines to be used in general or in this or that type of situation. As I have said elsewhere, when they are so used they inevitably are misused.[3] Skill in practice has come to mean the art of dealing properly with specific situations. Within a profession we are drawn back to the early meanings of the word, which signified understanding, discernment, differentiation, comprehension, and judiciousness. Professional skill stems from these capacities, hence

[2] For discussion of "What Can Be Taught in the Classroom," see paper by Helen Harris Perlman, *American Journal of Orthopsychiatry* (publication pending); paper read at Annual Conference of the American Orthopsychiatric Association, 1948.

[3] See Charlotte Towle, "Underlying Skills of Case Work Today," in *Proceedings of the National Conference of Social Work, 1941* (New York: Columbia University Press, 1941).

its development implies a primary emphasis on teaching the content of knowledge which constitutes the substance of the subject and conveying a body of working principles or general conceptions which constitute the philosophy, the rationale of the profession. It might be said, then, that the classroom emphasizes the teaching of the philosophy and science of social work, whereas the field emphasizes the art of doing in the light of this orientation.

In spite of this differentiation, there is considerable teaching of skill in the classroom. For example, in case discussion courses the student practices vicariously so that how to attain certain ends is continuously considered, always, however, in relation to other factors, such as, notably, what is known in this instance and its significance in the light of our general knowledge; and why this is done this way in this instance, again in the light of general knowledge and working principles. A decisive element in professional education lies in a continuous focus on the whys of feeling, thinking, and action. If one were to differentiate the learning on the job of apprentice training from the educational method of the professional school, a major difference, I believe, would be this emphasis on the whys of thinking and action. Here again, the practitioner in the classroom who is primarily a practitioner and only incidentally the teacher may focus on the what and the how of doing and overlook the whys. This is not because he does not know them, but because they have been so incorporated into his skill as to have become unconscious. In his practice he acts judiciously with comprehension and discernment and he teaches judicious and discriminating action, but because he no longer needs to figure out the whys he may have given up the articulation of them. This factor, the "why," is a decisive component in teaching, for it promotes the assimilation of knowledge and method. A student often will find the knowledge and the rationale of procedure quite irrational until he understands why we have come to feel, think, and do this way. Thus confusion and hence anxiety and resistance in learning are lessened or eliminated.

The what, the how, and the why come together in the classroom as one teaches two major areas of learning which are the very core of content throughout the casework course series. These are repeated to varying extents through direct presentation and application in other fields of instruction.[4] These areas are a way of thinking and a way of feeling and responding appropriate to social work and essential for an adapted use of the scientific method.

In social work we have come to use the process of scientific inquiry as a diagnostic tool and as a basis for action. In social casework it has been used also as a therapeutic measure, and this function has modified the process. The body of knowledge and theory of which social work is comprised, as well as skill, is involved in the differential use of scientific inquiry so that it truly enlightens and facilitates rather than impedes the furtherance of some definite human good. Social work education is continuously concerned with teaching students to help people meet their needs. The range is from helping an individual meet his own personal needs to helping groups of individuals procure, organize, and administer resources for others in areas of unmet need. In attaining this end there is always a problem presented for solution. The classroom instructor must insistently teach that we do not work by "guess," and the student must repetitively experience in classroom and field the orderly way of thinking, the steps in which are as follows: (1) observation and gathering of facts; (2) scrutinizing the facts in the light of certain knowledge; (3) formulation of a tentative hypothesis; (4) testing of the hypothesis through further inquiry and sometimes also through emergent action which has been guided by the initial tentative thinking; (5) formulation of an interpretative or diagnostic statement; (6) action recommended or taken on the basis of the diagnosis which is tested further and revised in accordance with the results of the action; (7) throughout the process a continuous self-appraisal by the worker to discount his own bias.

[4] Charlotte Towle, "Professional Skill in Administration," *News-Letter of the American Association of Psychiatric Social Workers,* X, No. 1 (May, 1940) 11–17; Charlotte Towle, "Some Basic Principles of Social Research in Social Case Work," *Social Service Review,* XV, No. 1 (March, 1941), 66–80; Charlotte Towle, "Teaching Psychiatry in Social Case Work," *Family,* XX, No. 10 (February, 1940), 324–31. See also Perlman, *op. cit.;* Helen Harris Perlman, "Content in Basic Social Case Work," *Social Service Review,* XXI, No. 1 (March, 1947), 76–84.

As the educable student gradually masters, that is, begins to incorporate this way of thinking, he becomes increasingly competent to think and to function independently and creatively. Thus as through his own "know how," order comes out of confusion, his dependency is lessened, his defenses lowered, and his resistances overcome. Furthermore, in this intellectual discipline he has a means to self-understanding. An intellectual process is set in operation through which feeling may be objectified if the student is not too involved emotionally in a given situation to be free to think. This method of thinking, once deeply incorporated so that it is ingrained, can serve an experienced practitioner well, even after he has been removed from regular practice and has become more teacher than practitioner. In any field of instruction within social work this method in the hands of a teacher with no experience can become an academic exercise and produce abstractions divorced from the reality of social problems, group life, and people. All social work thinking and action come back, in the last analysis, to the human individual in and of himself and as he participates in group life. The practitioner-teacher directs this intellectual process within the context of his own first-hand knowledge and understanding of social problems, of community resources, and of human behavior. The social work teacher, regardless of his field of instruction, needs a more thorough understanding of the dynamics of personality structure and the dynamics of group behavior. A weakness in present-day social work education lies in the fact that faculty members, by and large, are unevenly educated or even uneducated in this area.

A way of feeling and responding appropriate to social work is taught continuously and insistently in varied ways, but comprehensive discussion of this area of learning is beyond the scope of this paper. Very early, the student encounters the often disturbing reality that some of the prejudices, convictions, ways of thinking about, and ways of doing for and to, people which until now he has cherished and found useful must be modified or scrapped. Furthermore, the demand immediately must be made that he act in ways appropriate to the profession regardless of his feeling. The educable student will bring much from his past that is appropriate and useful to counteract the threat of change. Furthermore, what is not useful will not be serving such a deep purpose and be so rigidly entrenched that it is not subject to change. Even so, there will be a discomfort in this area of learning, and defense of the old way of thinking and feeling may be anticipated. The last-stand defenses before the student gives up the old for the new frequently are strong and fraught with intense feeling.

Educable students are searching for security in this decisive life venture, and consequently they have all their "feelers" out to identify with those who have what they have not got. Normally, they "feel out" toward those authorities to whom they have entrusted themselves for learning. They move into the relationship with ambivalence but with a predominant tendency toward identification with, rather than rejection of, their mentors. Hence, unless they find in the conduct, attitudes, and response of the instructor something objectionable or something which rebuffs or inhibits identification, they will begin, through their emotional acceptance of their faculty, individually and collectively to take in, and gradually through their own use to incorporate, professional ways of feeling and responding. The practitioner-teacher is reassuring to them. He knows first hand the what, the why, and the how. He has survived threatening demands. He brings the "feel" of his practice into the classroom, and the students' response is a lively one unless he is a very poor teacher, one who in the long run cannot help them learn what they need to know in order to gain competence. A classroom teacher removed from practice must have some capacity to keep alive and to continue to envisage the field of practice realistically. Students react apathetically even to the profound thinking and fine teaching of an instructor who has lost touch. There seems to be great variation in the capacity of social work instructors to retain the "feel" of practice.

This appropriate way of feeling will be conveyed didactically and through class discussion of course content in a number of fields of instruction. It will be imparted, as I have indicated, largely through the instructor's way of feeling and responding to the content and to his class members, individually and collectively. Thus, throughout the curriculum, in so far as faculty members have a positive attitude toward people, students will be prone to develop that attitude: for example, an attitude that a client is eligible until proved ineligible; that a client is competent until proved incompetent; that an agency official is coöperative until proved uncoöperative and that in such an instance the uncoöperative response is something to be understood and rectified if possible; that a student's point of view is something for serious consideration and understanding. Hence, an unwavering intent to understand is the positive attitude to be enacted in all classroom instruction. We, teacher and students, bend our hearts and our heads to understanding, not as an end in itself but in order to help, in order to rectify, in order to effect social change.

This is not to say that an instructor does not have and should not reveal negative feeling. Strong feeling, both positive and negative, is essential for social work. It takes us into this field of endeavor and it endures, hopefully waxing strong with the years to serve as a motivating force for leadership in the attainment of human good. Professional integrity compels righteous indignation over social injustice, deep sympathy with the underprivileged, definite commitment of feeling and of opinion as to the right and the wrong. Emotionally charged thinking has a place in the classroom. A teacher, therefore, condemns, passes moral judgments, criticizes; in short, he "stands up to be counted" in no uncertain terms. He acts, however, that he may understand through scientific inquiry and orderly thinking in order to find a solution, or in order to help students face realistically why certain problems at present defy solution. He leads them to find out and to consider what must happen first and to see why we must accept frustration now. Thus frustration may not spell submission to defeat. The leaders of tomorrow, the students of today, need help in the acceptance of frustration in order not to become defeatist. To inculcate a will to understand rather than to tolerate should be the social work educator's insistent aim.

It is the classroom instructor's responsibility to set an example for a way of responding that is truly professional, the very way of responding which, hopefully, he has enacted in practice. He may teach didactically the necessity for objective evaluation of cause-and-effect relationships but if he enacts condemning attitudes he impedes his own purpose in trying to help the student to become objective. Thus he may criticize freely but he may not caricature individuals whether they be clients, students, faculty members in other disciplines, board members, or the unenlightened director of a welfare program. Caricature does not show respect for the individual; moreover, it distorts and weakens the intent to understand. If an instructor is sarcastic in his critical evaluation of the part played by a worker in a situation under discussion, or if he ridicules a student's thinking or responds subjectively to the student's response of differing with him, he undermines the student's inclination to become understanding. The will to understand is inculcated and strengthened in so far as students experience understanding in the classroom. Furthermore, in participating in an objective evaluation of their own or of someone else's work, students frequently are enabled to take the first step in the development of autocriticism.

A classroom instructor is responsible for the management to productive ends of his relationship to the class as a whole. It should be a working relationship, and hence the instructor must keep it directed realistically to the student's learning purpose in relation to the school's educational goals. It should not become one in which students are absorbed in the instructor per se or the instructor in the students' response to him. In other words, the instructor should not stand between his learning content and the receptive capacity of the student. Studied efforts which place method before content put the self-conscious instructor in the foreground, and no instructor, regardless of how intriguing his method, belongs in the foreground. Likewise, the instructor whose personal need for recognition leads him in one way or another to win a response to himself rather than to his subject matter interferes with learning. When this happens, the dependency authority conflict implicit in the adult learning situation may be intensified so that resistance is aroused; or the instructor's need may entangle students so that they become identified to the extent of losing their own identity. When this occurs they may "take over" without "taking in." Followers rather than leaders are developed when the emotional pressure of the teacher engenders the dependency, the anxiety, and the confusion which in the long run result when a student's professional orientation merely reflects that of an influential person.

In this whole area of learning a way of feeling and responding appropriate to social work, one would expect the skilled practitioner to bring to the classroom discipline in the regulation of his own need in order to bring about concentration on professional purpose. Capacity for objective management of relationships derived through practice now should stand him in stead. Unless, however, he finds himself as a teacher and is secure in this role, he may need reassurance as a person and unconsciously fail to use his skills in this new situation.

Social work always has been practiced under urgent conditions. Social workers have had to be men and women of action making emergency decisions under pressure of changing circumstance, timed by forces beyond their control. It is easy for social workers to come to dread deliberation and to cultivate immediacy. As event follows swiftly on event they can self-deceptively pretend that every decision was mothered by necessity. Thus every defeat and every stupidity is felt to be well justified. It is essential, therefore, that social work education instill a philosophical frame of mind. This will be done as the curriculum throughout emphasizes working principles, imparts and helps the student to formulate philosophical concepts, stimulates comparative thinking, and conveys historical perspective. Historical perspective is gained only as students are habituated to an historical approach. Historical courses of the narrative type which are little more than the recountal of a series of events will not develop this attitude of mind. Historical courses dynamically presented have an important place. When the present is viewed in the light of its retrospective and ongoing connection with major social trends and changing purposes, then the significance of the past comes alive in the present. However, it is as students experience repeatedly the truth that out of hindsight comes foresight that they may habitually look to the past to enlighten the present and the future. Experiencing history's power "to evoke and to solve problems still unstated and unrecognized" can occur again and again throughout different fields of instruction. It may occur as they explore the onset and development of present social problems. The problem may be one in the life of an individual client, or it may be one in agency administration, or in community attitudes, or in the social and economic structure which is creating unmet need. Problems are timeless, and there are repetitive elements in changing conditions so that prior causes and solutions, or failures of solution, may be significant today for tomorrow. If social welfare leaders of the future are to become less visionary, less escapist, and more judicious under pressure than many of their predecessors have been, their professional education must foster the reflective mind.

In conclusion, I stress the importance in education for social work of a positive relationship between learner and teacher. As I have stated elsewhere, this relationship "should have as its core not only the students' respect for the competence and integrity of the instructor but also trust in his essential friendliness. . . . A learner who regards those from whom he must learn as being against him rather than for him will be more prone to submit than free to engage actively and responsibly in learning." [5] For a relationship conducive to learning it will be essential that the educator continuously be concerned to meet valid dependency adequately, to affirm the student's potentials and use his strengths, to avoid making unrealistic demands, and, finally, to hold the student accountable and help him meet the reality demands of the educational situation. These principles basic to social work practice should guide him in the educational situation in the selection of content, in methods used, and in relationship proffered.

At present, the educator's contribution to the advancement of knowledge in some areas of social work is limited by his re-

[5] Towle, *op. cit.*

moval from systematic practice and also from research. Through prodigious effort to keep in touch he may keep abreast of changing content. He is, however, in the position of imparting and interpreting the observations of others. His creative contribution largely is that of preparing students to go beyond him in the advancement of knowledge. Certain exigencies in the social work scene have dictated that the social work educator be more teacher than learner. This constitutes a problem for future solution if social work is to become less dependent on related fields of knowledge.

It is important that the social worker on becoming a teacher not abandon as irrelevant those basic insights and skills which have served him in helping people. As a social worker he has been concerned continuously with individual differences and personality growth. Learning and growth are synonymous. As a social worker he has been engaged in the education and reeducation of individuals and groups. All classroom instruction goes back, in the last analysis, to the learner as an individual in and of himself, and as he participates in the group learning process. The social work educator has an advantage in that he can direct this intellectual process within the context of disciplined knowledge and understanding of human behavior. As he consciously transfers his professional learning to professional education he might well make a creative contribution to professional education in general. This is the challenge of today for tomorrow, to create conditions under which the natural urge to learn, the inspired response which characterizes the student preparing for life work, may find full expression.

Psychiatry Experiments with Selection

HENRY W. BROSIN, M.D.

NUMEROUS STUDIES in the selection of men for the armed services during the recent war accelerated the progress made by previous studies in this field. In spite of much prior work it was generally conceded that most existing tests for personality organization and stability were inadequate. Examiners found that test scores were not helpful; that regardless of the score, the most valuable service rendered by the testing procedure was the opportunity furnished to study the quality of the individual reply, or the method used by the candidate to solve the problem. This recent experience, as well as the acute need, has stimulated many workers to continue their efforts in this challenging field after returning to civilian life. We chose medical students as an object of study because we live with them, but, obviously, the basic problems in this area transcend occupational lines and are probably universal in their significance.

In reviewing the published work on selection of medical students, it is apparent that there was a need here also for tests which gave information about personality stability and aptitudes, since the well-known Moss studies were not satisfactory. This technique tried to measure both intellectual ability and aptitude but failed to include those methods which would describe essential aspects of behavior which are of critical importance. Competence to study medicine and practice successfully involves many organizational properties which are not easily measured since they are not unitary functions and are related to the more obscure, unconscious aspects of personality. It is desirable to know how well the candidate is motivated, how economically he handles his anxieties under stress, the ways in which he relates himself to people, how much free energy he has for genuine productivity in contrast to neurotically driven competitiveness. We are interested, not only in eliminating men who will fail in medical school, but in choosing those who will bring the richest gifts to their calling.

Unfortunately, two large, relatively unexplored areas must also be considered before we attempt to define the properties of a good candidate:

1. There should be general agreement upon the qualities which identify the successful physician. There are undoubtedly many kinds of successful physician, thus leading to the inference that great caution should be exercised in forcing all candidates to conform to rigid requirements since otherwise we might lose invaluable men who do not happen to pass through our particular sieve. Dr. Alan Gregg suggests that in any selection program at least 10 percent of the class be chosen outside the testing program for a control. This danger of losing good men is reinforced by the increasingly competitive premedical education area which discourages some high-minded young men, who cannot bring themselves to live at the necessary economic levels. There is a danger that highly vital selection has already occurred by the time the student presents himself for admission to medical school.

2. The second important area which must be studied in relation to selection is the effect of the training process upon the student. There seems to be a wide difference in schools in this respect, although no valid comparisons can be cited. Any acquaintance with schools, however, reveals the widespread anxiety which is the fate of most students. That this anxiety may act as an inhibitor of the categorical or abstract attitude and thus decrease the scholarship of the student where it should be best is a matter of real concern. The Rorschach protocols present material which strongly suggests this probability. Further experimental verification by more objective methods may be possible by utilizing the methods of W. C. Halstead as outlined in *Brain*

and Intelligence.[1] These preliminary remarks are offered to give some background for the exposition of the methods used by us. Attempts to solve the larger questions will be made as relevant material is acquired, but we cannot make publicly verifiable observations at this time.

Since expense eliminated the possibility of actually examining premedical students, it was decided to do pilot control studies on the incoming freshman classes for a number of years at two medical schools, follow their academic progress through four years, and, so far as possible, do follow-up studies after their internships and residencies. Concomitant studies at two schools by a team seemed to have some advantages in mutual stimulation and the possibility of comparison. It seemed much more likely that pertinent sociological differences would be noted when two different social systems were simultaneously under scrutiny; for, to some extent, the effects of the systems upon the students should be apparent.

Two classes at each school have been examined, a total of 450 students. Actually, many more from other classes have been seen for therapy so that our information is much greater than that provided by these classes. We also have comparable data from several prewar classes. At one school, an experienced psychiatrist, Dr. L. W. Earley, himself saw 330 students in individual interviews in addition to doing individual Rorschach examinations on two thirds of them. The other one third had individual Rorschachs performed by trained clinical psychologists, but Dr. Earley did all the interpretations. In addition, the following tests were performed:

1. American College Entrance (for comparative value)
2. Strong Interest Test (for prediction value)
3. Allport-Vernon Study for Values (for minimal information on attitudes)
4. Group Thematic Apperception Test (Murray) in modified form (an excellent projective technique revealing something about motivation both peripheral and central, goals, needs, and social factors exciting goals)

[1] W. C. Halstead, *Brain and Intelligence* (Chicago: University of Chicago Press, 1947).

Two classes of 130 students were examined at the second school, utilizing the following methods:

1. Individual interviews (by a team the first year and by one psychiatrist the second year)
2. Individual Rorschachs (not completed)
3. American College Entrance (L and Q score and total score)
4. Group Rorschach (Monroe check count)
5. Group Thematic Apperception Test (Murray), modified
6. University of Chicago Reading Test
7. University of Chicago Writing Test
8. Kuhlman Intelligence Test (P.A., I.Q., speed, accuracy)
9. Primary Mental Abilities Tests (Thurstone)
10. Minnesota Morale Test
11. Minnesota Social Adjustment Test
12. Minnesota Emotional Test
13. Minnesota Conservatism Test
14. Allport Theoretical Test
15. Allport Economic Test
16. Allport Aesthetic Test
17. Allport Social Test
18. Allport Political Test
19. Allport Religious Test

Tests, numbered from 3 to 19, were divided into thirty-five variables and studied by two skilled, professional, statistical psychologists, Dewey Stuitt and Harold P. Bechtoldt, in the American Association of Medical Colleges office of Dean Carlyle Jacobsen at Iowa City. These variables have been analyzed in terms of the criterion of first year grade point average for three quarters. Dr. Bechtoldt reports:

> The results of this preliminary analysis were uniformly disappointing. Only two of the Chi-Square values were significant at the 10 to 20 percent level (such values are expected by chance alone in 10 to 20 percent of the samples). Eight additional variables resulted in Chi-Square values falling in the 20 to 30 percent area of significance. Since either inadequate criterion measures might account for these results, the second step in the analysis was to investigate the relations among the five courses constituting the first year program. The results indicated wide variation in the distribution of the grades by courses and some evidence of little or no association (correlation) between the grades in certain courses and the grades assigned in other courses. The range in the percent of students making A or B grades

was from 95 percent in Gross Anatomy to 44 percent in Physiology. From the viewpoint of discriminating between "achievements" of various students, the Physiology department is apparently finding much wider differences between students than is the Anatomy department. Since the same students took these courses in the same year, it would seem either that different (non-comparable) standards of evaluation were being used by the various departments or that the abilities required for success in the various courses were not highly correlated. Studies on intercorrelations of adequate achievement measures, however, generally show marked positive correlations between such measures for college courses.[2]

Other attempts were made to evaluate the interrelations between the five courses and to relate grades in the two most significant courses (physiology and bacteriology) with ten variables of highest significance on the tests. Dr. Bechtoldt, in summary, said:

> These results are interpreted as indicating some slight chance of a useful differential prediction of success from these thirty-five measures when the 1946–47 and 1947–48 data are combined and analyzed. Further analyses against total grade point averages are considered as less promising than analyses against averages in separate courses. Because of the lack of discrimination found in some courses, rank in class or ratings in deciles would be more useful for research purposes than letter grades.[3]

When the grading system was revised for more consistent criteria of success in the course work it was apparent that these criteria were only theoretical. The factors which showed some slight significance were the over-all prediction of success, the sum of separate ratings, and the Monroe check list count for devious points. This small success in using larger units supports the clinician in his quest for those dynamic units which have more meaning to the total organism and which may some day be more useful. If the statistician is given more relevant data he may become more helpful in this type of investigation.

This preliminary analysis clearly gives us little hope that these tests, the best available to us, will furnish the means of differentiating students. This is not a new story, but it may be worth while to indicate that we want to help the psychologists on our

[2] Personal communication. [3] *Ibid.*

team to get material which may be useful to them. We intend to utilize the best known methods as they become available, dropping out each year those which are definitely noncontributory.

I will not review the role of intelligence tests in selection studies since they have not contributed much in most schools. The excellent article by Waggoner and Ziegler[4] covers the principal subjects. Although direct comparisons of our data with theirs is not possible, it seems likely that our students fall within the same ranges as theirs. Their experiences with various achievement, reading, and personality tests parallels ours. They make a concrete observation of interest: that men whose I.Q.'s are below 130 on the Binet Test will find the competition severe, both in medical school and after graduation.

The projective techniques do offer solid hope for finding an improved selection technique. Incomplete summaries prevent a comprehensive report at this time, but a few facts are noteworthy. The group Rorschach was distinguished by the frequency of abnormal responses. The comment was made that "very few of the records would have seemed out of place in a collection of clinically disturbed people." This supports the opinion of Dr. Earley and myself in evaluating individual Rorschachs that we must study intensively a large collection of these protocols and their authors in order to evaluate properly the wide limits of inefficient behavior, including manifest psychological disturbances. Dr. Emil Oberholzer has repeatedly emphasized both the need for a wide range of normal controls in order to do more sensitive interpretations and the difficulties of obtaining a reliable series in the heterogeneous American population. As in other control series of normal individuals, including college students, nurses, and organic medical cases, we find that an enormous amount of disturbance is tolerated by many people. It is our task to identify the assets of the ego which permit a person to work effectively in spite of his burden. The patterns revealed in the group Rorschach are those apparent in the individual tests and in the interviews: anxiety of many types and severity;

[4] R. W. Waggoner and Thornton Woodward Ziegler, "Psychiatric Factors in Medical Students Who Fail," *American Journal of Psychiatry*, CIII (November, 1946), 369–76.

conflicts about human relationships; oppositionality; marked constriction and rigidity in many with a few showing extreme looseness of affect; and strongly dependent trends not infrequently coupled with hostility.

The Thematic Apperception Test of Murray duplicates some of the Rorschach findings. The psychologists, Anna S. Elonen and Mrs. Harriet Moore, report:

> It is more useful in discerning the organization of energy in work, attitudes toward authority, toward the weak and distressed and peers. Among the students who did poorly, we found frequent inhibition of work effort sometimes self-destructive in nature, sometimes related to extreme dependency and to inability to channelize energy toward a goal. Among the successful ones there were many difficulties involving dependent needs, sexual relations and oppositional trends. However, the successful ones generally showed relatively uninhibited work motivation and intellectual activity. They were differentiated by their ability to follow the directions, to maintain a basic intellectual structure in the face of the stimulation of fantasy.[5]

From the current material it seems unlikely that these group tests alone or in combination with other tests can provide significant differentiation for success or failure between incapacitating patterns of behavior and those disturbed systems which are compatible with achievement. Perhaps future work on the crippling effect of strong dependent needs coupled with hostility, the advantage of being able to maintain intellectual control when faced with emotional stress, or the manifest advantages in a school system of extreme compliance by a constricted personality, may make these group tests much more valuable. If increased expertness in design of projective methods is possible, and there is no reason to doubt that it is, we can expect progress in this field, because (1) units of this type and those relating to motivation; (2) ego strengths as shown by the capacity to withstand frustration; and (3) flexibility in mastery of emotional challenges are more meaningful also in the clinical idiom, and can be studied with the benefit of information from this field.

The individual Rorschach in conjunction with the individual

[5] Personal communication.

interview by a psychiatrist is by all odds the best method known to us for selection purposes. It is well known that the Rorschach has splendid potentialities for providing cues to many facets of the personality both in health and disease, if the interpreter is a skillful clinician with large experience and some talent in this field. Such patterns as outgoingness, introversiveness, nature of emotional control, aggression, intellectual drive, capacity for thinking abstractly, concretely, and imaginatively, "type of intelligence," and orderliness are often available on the protocol to the expert.

The range of behavior shown on these records is incredibly wide, including most of the common reaction types and dynamic defense systems. As in other studies, we find that superior abilities are no guarantee of success since personality factors, including motivation, are more important. Relatively poor intellectual equipment, as revealed by the I.Q. and other tests, is not always a deterrent to high class rank. One of the men with an I.Q. of 113 and no unusual obvious assets is in the upper 15 percent of his class; this is quite unusual, however.

The composition of the postwar, 1946–47 classes in the two schools is markedly different, for the average age is much greater in one than in the other, due to the inclusion of a large number of veterans. The 1947–48 classes in both schools have many veterans, but the age level has decreased. These variables make generalizations hazardous until we have more comparative material. A few observations are justified.

For a large number of all our students the principal personality constellation is that of "coarctation" as described by Rorschach. Often this is a matter of a long-time life adjustment which is closely related to the obsessive-compulsive, sometimes depressive (acute and chronic), adjustments. Interviews and T.A.T. protocols support the inference that over 25 percent of the students show major coarctation. An unpublished work by H. F. Faterson happily suggests that expansion of these test indicators occurs following completion of the internship. Some individuals, not uncommonly found, have essentially "hysterical" character organization; they live principally by repression, but do very well in medical school with respect to grades. Often they are ruthless, do not really care about people, manipulate them skillfully as objects, live in a stereotyped, conventional manner.

Close examination of the Rorschach of the top sixteen men in one school shows a common factor in their high ego integrity as shown by (1) accuracy of perception; (2) freedom from obsessional concern with small detail; (3) freedom from interference of extraneous material together with freedom from superficial anxiety under this pressure. The fact that they are not stimulus bound, retain the ability to shift easily to relevant material, enjoy the use of better abstracting ability, and are able to maintain better boundaries, to use the language of K. Goldstein and others, makes possible comparisons with the experiments and hypotheses of other workers in several fields. More systematic examination of these processes is now under way with the hope that more intelligible patterns will emerge. As mentioned before, if a man has some of these basic stabilities, he can achieve a splendid work record in spite of much concomitant personality disturbance. It is essential to recall constantly that evidence of personality conflicts in interviews or tests does not disqualify a person from achievement.

Discussion of direct interviews involves many variables which can only be touched on briefly. With the assistance of the dean, the freshmen are told that they are participating in an important investigation to help us understand the selection and medical education process. Most of them are very coöperative, especially after being reassured that all material is held in strict confidence and that it will in no way affect their class standings. Every effort is made by the staff to live up to this policy. If a student at any time requests therapy, the selection material is utilized. Most of the group tests are given during the five days of the orientation week before classes begin, taking care to avoid fatigue phenomena as much as possible. Individual interviews and tests are scattered throughout the first months of school.

The team method, using six psychiatrists to examine the students, has many disadvantages when there are not frequent conferences to check on the material obtained. During the last year one psychiatrist at each school has interviewed all the students in one class, making notes during the interview where feasible or dictating them immediately after the interview.

The doctors soon learned that interviewing freshman students differed from interviewing patients in several respects, even though there are often similarities when the student is willing to discuss his difficulties frankly. It seems to me that we should recognize these differences and define them where possible, for the setting is important in a single interview, even though the time is not limited. The students are not requesting jobs or help, nor are they being evaluated for service in the Air Corps or the Office of Strategic Services, or for other special duty. It is essential to gain their interest and rapport. Most of them answer direct questions, but this fact-collection is not adequate, even though it permits the meticulous investigator to obtain an impressive set of comparable records. As examiners gained skill they were able to encourage spontaneous associations which were much more valuable for later review. This was true even for the more constricted, inhibited personalities mentioned earlier. The examiners found growth in their own ability to listen to and evaluate the productions without too great concern about the possibility of an incomplete record. In the case of students whose defenses were too great to permit easy communication, it was possible to characterize these defenses with definite value to the study. Our goal is to encourage highly fluid interviews in which the student takes the initiative in describing his personal adjustment. Pedantic efforts to retrace his developmental history and work record must be sacrificed to some extent, but the final opinions have more life and individuality. Some interviewers are not secure without a developmental history, and this phase must be investigated. Where the students recognize one examiner as a real "friend" because of the good will built up through many therapeutic contacts, the barriers are considerably lowered. For this reason alone it is worth while for a school to try to keep one doctor at this job over a number of years.

The summaries include an over-all estimate of the man's abilities, assets, and liabilities, some estimate of the nature and amount of his anxieties, and the methods utilized to dissipate them. Special dynamic features are, of course, recorded. An estimate is made of his probable class rank or position in the first, second, or third group of the class. If it seems likely that he will fail, greater effort is made to describe the reasons and also to see him again in order to smooth the way for future contacts. Unfortunately, we have had several men who dropped out of school precipitously and could not be interviewed although extensive efforts were made to get them to come in. We hope that close liaison with the dean's office will enable us to see these men for more detailed interviews in order to understand the active pressures that caused them to take such a drastic step. It is too early to attempt a description of the emotional organization of a class, the way in which the students mobilize their hostilities toward various instructors, the homogeneous methods of handling some problems, and the highly differentiated reactions to others, although this would probably help us understand the failures much better than by merely describing internal dynamics. We are also interested in the nature of the libidinal investment of the student in the content, particularly in the experimental data, how this is fostered or altered by the academic work, but we have no stable conclusions. In the follow-up studies, efforts will be made to correlate personality structure with the choice of specialty.

The students give many curious reasons for entering upon the study of medicine, in addition to the usual stereotyped replies that they are interested in people or in making money, or in gaining prestige and social position. These conventional answers cannot be taken at face value in most cases. This is especially true for the women candidates who have problems of competition with men and conflicts about marriage. One of our psychiatrists believes that our current women students are much more feminine than were those in earlier classes.

We have instituted no formal "control" interviews with examiners and senior psychiatrists in order to check methods of obtaining the data. It is hoped that we will be able to do this in the future, utilizing several different methods, including (1) a review of the interview dynamics of one interview by a senior physician; (2) staff review of the interview dynamics; (3) staff review of a sound recording of the interview; and (4) staff review of interviews by two or even three psychoanalytic psychiatrists. This method has been popular at the Institute of Psychoanalysis at Chicago in interviewing candidates for analytic training because candidates may give entirely different impressions if they are interviewed by three people in quick succession on the same day. It is helpful if one of the three examiners is a woman. Apparently, the effects of one interview may alter significantly the candidate's orientation in succeeding interviews. This system mitigates against collecting detailed histories for research purposes, but it provides more valuable data for genuine understanding of the person.

The selection investigations have been of much practical value in detecting potential failures, but it would not be wise to say that such identification has high reliability. Probably the contact with a psychiatrist has made it easier for some students to return for help, a fact which in itself is a gain.

Several suggestions, which are practical even though not novel, are apparent from these studies:

1. It is desirable to select as medical students candidates who are reasonably healthy and free from anxiety; others are apt to become technicians.

2. It is desirable that environmental pressures be reduced, as suggested by Waggoner and Ziegler, Moon, and others. The well-being of the student should be conserved.

3. There should be better long-term follow-up studies of the careers of our graduates. In the immediate future we will maintain close interest in the failures and in therapeutic cases as well as in the men with high achievement potentiality.

4. Caution must be exercised by school admission committees to avoid an artificial homogeneity in the composition of a class, whether this occur because of too great a dependence on grades alone, or on tests, or on both. First-hand, personal knowledge of the man is more helpful in determining his desirability.

Pilot Study: Criteria in Selection for Social Work

SIDNEY BERENGARTEN

WE HAVE AMPLE REASON to regard with satisfaction and pride the rich substance of social work education today. We need not be defensive about social work meeting the requirements of a profession. So long as we have students who are educable, there is a body of scientific knowledge and skills which has been validated clinically and can be taught and applied. However, our knowledge and understanding of whom to select for training in social work, from among the many candidates applying, have not advanced *pari passu* with developments in educational content and method. That this situation is not peculiar to social work can be readily attested by the recent interest of the allied professions of psychiatry, clinical psychology, and public health nursing, as well as by the more traditional professions of medicine, law, the ministry, and education in conducting experimental studies to determine more clearly the personality endowment and the aptitudes required for growth through education, and for successful professional performance and attainment.

Why is it that the more established professions, having had not a half century but many centuries in which to accumulate and integrate their knowledge and practice, have so recently begun to evidence interest in the personal characteristics that make for a better doctor, lawyer, minister, and educator? It is from the contribution of dynamic psychiatry that the professions have come more to the realization that in any type of work with people, relationship is of extreme importance. Thus, the possession of a healthy personality is being accepted increasingly as a basic qualification for these fields. Mastery of professional content alone is not enough to insure effective service to others. Every profession is involved, more or less, in working through the medium of interpersonal relationships, in addition to the unique content and contribution of its own discipline, but as we cut through the circle of the professions that deal with human relations, we find psychiatry, clinical psychology, and social work at dead center with the others in an array extending outward toward the circumference. It is obvious that, without the medium of interpersonal relationships, there could be no practice in any of the three allied disciplines mentioned. Thus it behooves us to know, apart from the intellectual capacity required of a candidate for assimilation of the formal body of concepts and practices of the professional discipline, what it is more specifically that he brings to the learning experience in the form of basic interests, skills, aptitudes, and personality equipment in particular, which would help clarify his potentialities for growth as a self-disciplined, helping person.

Social work educators have a grave responsibility in this matter of selection of students for training, not only to the candidates and the professional field, but most of all to the future clients of social work agencies. To the candidates we have, I believe, a dual responsibility: (1) to make certain that the candidate with good potentials for professional development is given an opportunity for training; and 2) to accept an advisory role with the candidate whose qualities clearly contraindicate his selection of social work, either for the present or the future.

There will undoubtedly be a wide difference of opinion on the second point. We would like to say, however, that it has been the unanimous sentiment of the several hundred students and candidates interviewed in the pilot study authorized by the New York School of Social Work in March, 1947, that they could not accept denial of their application for admission without a clear understanding of the specific basis for the decision, a knowledge of whether their personal limitations for social work practice were considered modifiable, and information concerning the best means, if any, of effecting change for those who were still interested in professional training or in entering the field in the future. As a logical extension of the same theme, the more adequately we understand what the admitted candidate brings in the way of personal equipment and skills from experience, the more intelligently can we help in the planning of his educational program, especially in the selection of the crucial first field placement, in order to permit optimal use of his personal endowment, as well as sound advising in the choice of an ultimate field that will further his personal and professional growth.

In considering the selection of candidates, we are told that the shortage of properly trained social workers to meet the requests that have increased because of the rapid expansion of health and social services, will undoubtedly have an adverse effect on the future of social work. It has been estimated that there is a minimum of three times as many positions as there are workers who can meet the educational and experiential requirements—a situation which often compels agencies to employ untrained workers.[1] Without question, the pressures that the professional field is experiencing for extension of services are becoming increasingly great, and there is an urgency in them. There is also a corresponding increase of interest and demand for training on the part of experienced workers in the field and among the more recent college graduates, taxing far beyond capacity the available facilities for professional training.

It is important, however, that we should not be misled by the number of candidates applying. The two main external precipitants to the accelerated expansion of social work during the past two decades have been a devastating and prolonged economic depression and our involvement in a global war, bringing in their wake vast social, economic, and emotional dislocations. The highly trained and skilled personnel, in their assumption of leadership, performed so admirably and demonstrated so clearly the efficacy of social work in their handling of so many complex and troublesome problems facing the country that the demand for extension of social services grew accordingly. However, because skilled personnel were drained off on trouble-shooting as-

[1] Irene Farnham Conrad, "The Organization, Objectives and Program of the National Council on Social Work Education," *Compass,* XXVIII (March, 1947), 3.

signments and the professional schools did not have the facilities to meet the increased demands without seriously lowering their educational standards, the agencies were often compelled to employ staff members whose qualifications, both personal and professional, were marginal. The motivations for entering the field were diverse and not always positive. This experienced but untrained group constitutes a large proportion of the candidates, perhaps fully 50 percent. Special attention has been paid to this group in our study, and our observations are presented in later pages.

As the wartime emergency pressures have been gradually eased, and agencies are once again in a position to do some long-range planning, a number of these people are under considerable pressure from their agencies to secure professional training. Some workers are feeling the competition of younger, more skilled, and trained staff. Others are now finding opportunities for advancement blocked unless they have the status which a professional degree affords. It has not been uncommon in our experience for these candidates to express resentment because the graduate program in social work, which requires supervised field work, did not permit the acquisition of a degree by entire attendance in the evenings, as is possible in earning undergraduate and certain graduate academic degrees. Although this attitude was attributed at times to the economic factor, it was clearly indicative of marked resistance to involvement of self in the learning process. As supervisors and educators, we know that personal problems are reactivated for some individuals in social work, both experienced and inexperienced, when they are introduced to the content of the mental hygiene courses and even more so in a field work assignment. Many might never have had these deeper unresolved conflicts precipitated to the surface had they been spared this unique type of educational experience which requires so much personal involvement. We realize, too, how damaging and unsettling failure may be to the experienced person. In planning for social work education in the next fifty years, it seems to be of timely importance that we turn the spotlight rather quickly on this intriguing and complex problem of selection of candidates.

In March, 1947, the New York School of Social Work authorized a long-term study to determine the best method for selecting students for training in social work. Funds were appropriated for the purpose, and a member of the full-time faculty was released from his regular responsibilities to act as director of the study. A faculty advisory committee, consisting of a psychiatrist who taught the social psychiatry courses at the School, a casework instructor, a casework field adviser, and a social group work instructor, was appointed with the Dean of the School serving as an ex-officio member of the committee. It is important that we stress the fact that the study was not undertaken because of any particular concern about the students who had already been admitted. It was conceived and envisioned as a pilot study in the more precise formulation of personality criteria for social work and in the development of better procedures for selecting students. It was hoped that the findings and recommendations would not only be utilized by the New York School of Social Work, but would also be shared with other schools of social work and the professional field at large.

The following specific objectives were formulated by the Faculty Advisory Committee:

1. To establish more scientifically the qualities and characteristics that make for good vocational aptitude for social work in general, and the candidate's field of special interest in particular

2. To determine what content and techniques in interviewing candidates would prove most productive in clarifying point 1

3. To determine which psychometric and personality tests (both group and individual) would prove to be adjunctive, useful devices in clarifying point 1 [2]

4. To discover the correlation between predictability based on initial interviewing and test findings with actual achievement measured by degree of success or failure in field work, since it was felt that in field work there was a real testing-out in a modified job situation that predetermines the degree of effectiveness

[2] We should state at this point that the testing has not yet been administered. It was considered advisable to concentrate our efforts on the interviewing objective for this beginning period, until some common patterns would emerge, before attempting to incorporate the testing as part of the study.

of the individual. It was also planned to carry the correlation further with the candidate's performance on the job after graduation when he could hopefully be evaluated without the safeguards, protections, and support inherent in a learning experience, but rather against the expectations for qualitative performance and ability to cope with the quantitative pressures present in the reality of a job situation.

It was felt that as students advance in training and move into the field of choice, important criteria may emerge regarding factors of personality equipment and motivation which mobilize the student toward a selection of field. By an empirical approach in following the student through the educational experience and out on the job, we hoped to build up and clarify a comprehensive picture of the gradation in success or failure and, concomitantly, more knowledge about the individual characteristics which lend themselves to the different fields, as well as about the basic qualifications of personality which would be expected for success in all fields of social work. We anticipated emerging correlations from which we could develop knowledge about potentials, motivations, and special aptitudes which would give bases for sounder selection and also vocational advising offered early in the student's educational experience. It was recognized, and this has been confirmed by our experience, that it might not be possible until after two to five years of study and correlation to isolate the criteria which might be applicable in the selection process, and for those admitted early in field experience, which would prevent the traumatic effect of delayed recognition of lack of aptitude for the profession or for a particular field.

A panel of nine interviewers of both sexes, including the director of the study, was selected from a large number of persons who were recommended by the Faculty Advisory Committee and other members of the faculty. The qualifications for the interviewers were that they should be mature, experienced caseworkers, not only with good clinical aptitude, but also with extensive backgrounds in supervision, administration, personnel, teaching, and field work advising, with competence in evaluating skills from experiential background as well as from personality equipment. They were to be either graduates of the New York School of Social Work or very close to the School through field supervision, teaching, and field advising, and thus well integrated with the School's educational program and objectives and well aware of what it had to offer a candidate as well as what it would require of him intellectually and emotionally. I might add that we were very fortunate to have obtained the services of such a highly qualified group of interviewers, and the fact that we still have the same interviewers after one year, despite the considerable personal sacrifice of having to devote from two to three evenings weekly to the study, attests to their positive identification with its aims and objectives. At first it was suggested that we set up a much larger panel of interviewers in order to benefit from many divergent viewpoints, but we felt that the larger panel would have the greater disadvantage of introducing too many variables which would be difficult to equate. Moreover, excessive spreading of the interviews would mean less volume for each individual interviewer, thus reducing the possibility of growth in this experience and his usefulness to the study in the ultimate evaluation of the findings.

In giving consideration to the question of whom to select as participants in the study, it was deemed best to start with students already admitted to the School and in their first quarter rather than with candidates or with more advanced students. With the latter, it was felt that we could not get at potentials for development as readily as with the beginning student, inasmuch as it would be very difficult to know then how to evaluate the conditioning factor of the learning experience. We did not feel that we were prepared to interview candidates until we had completed sufficient research so that we could develop and test some tentatively formulated criteria. The students newly admitted to the School were the closest to the candidate experience and could more readily recapture the feelings they brought to the application process. Actually, in order to make the most productive use of the students in the incoming class in the spring quarter of 1946–47, it was felt advisable to select a small unit of six fairly representative students from among our second and third quarter casework, group work, and community organization students without previous social work experience to help the interviewers sharpen and adapt their own interviewing skills to this type of interviewing experience, and to test some criteria to apply to the students who would be interviewed subsequently.

The entire student body was advised of the purpose and objectives of the study. In a memorandum from the Dean, the students were assured that the individual findings would be kept strictly confidential and would never become a part of the student's permanent folder at the School nor shared with any faculty member. The Faculty Advisory Committee had felt that if the students were to feel free to share what they were consciously aware of and what was of vital importance to us, confidentiality would have to be assured, and this has been strictly enforced from the inception of the Study. In order to insure anonymity, code numbers were assigned to the students and candidates interviewed. The recorded material is locked in the files of the director of the study, entirely inaccessible to the School administration or to any member of the faculty.

It was planned to have each participant interviewed by three different interviewers, preferably with both sexes represented on the interviewing team. It was also agreed that the interviewers were not to share the content of the interviews with each other during the sequence of the interviews, and an attempt at correlation of the interviewers' individual impressions was to be made only at the completion of the three interviews. What was wanted were judgments arrived at independently rather than impressions influenced by an interviewer having had access to the preceding interviewer's material and directing his interviews to themes previously developed and unfolded. In this connection, except in a few experimental situations at the beginning of the study, the interviewers have not been consulting the student's School folder material prior to the interviews. Although it was felt by some, at first, that the students' folders could be used productively to high-light any significant diagnostic clews and perhaps enable the interviewer to establish and sustain purposeful direction in the interview, there was strong opinion that the interview should be conducted without preliminary analysis of the folder material, in order to determine whether sufficient skill in interviewing could be developed to arrive at a sound prognosis unaided by other material. Without laboring the point, we might add that our experience with the students and candidates interviewed has confirmed the validity of our not having used the folder material. The students and candidates have been very free in acknowledging that the autobiographical sketch, in many instances, was consciously conditioned to give the School "what it wants" rather than a frank sharing of their limitations as well as their strengths. In more extreme instances, the application report was submitted to as many as six or eight persons in the professional field for review and suggestions to help strengthen the candidate's chance for admission. Their frequent objection to the written material as a primary source for an admissions decision was based on the lack of provision, as part of regular procedure, for a personal interview, not only to permit further elaboration and clarification of the content, but also to be actively helped in the production of material pertinent to the School's understanding of their capacities and potentials for training. They felt, too, that it would afford them the privilege of thinking through with a representative of professional social work the soundness of their decision to enter the field, since they had often little more than intellectual appreciation of what was involved and required of them in this type of educational experience. Furthermore, since they would not see the person who would do the evaluating, and since they felt that a frank acknowledgment of negative experiences and relationships would not be accredited, they had deemed it prudent to be self-protective. I might add that, wherever possible, pre-admissions interviews have always been made available to candidates at the New York School of Social Work. In view of the fact, however, that so many of our students applied from distant states and foreign countries, the routine requirement of a personal interview presented a serious administrative problem.

In considering how the three interviewers might each have a purposeful discussion with the student or candidate in the Pilot

Study, it was felt that the area of focus might be the individual's personal-social adjustment and that through a discussion of concrete experiences, past and present (educational, work, recreational, social), some basic attitudes and pattern leads could be determined. Motivation for entering social work, with knowledge of the individual's psychological orientation and identifications, and his basic ability to adapt in the relationship area, were felt to be of primary interest. Rather than restrict each of the three interviewers to some specific area of discussion, it was agreed that the content of each interview would not be delimited, but, instead, an attempt would be made to have a fluid interview geared normally to natural areas (for the interviewee) from which to start. Because of our intense interest in determining which interviewing methods and techniques would prove most productive, as well as in the specific content necessary to arrive at a sound decision, it was decided that the interviews were to be recorded in detailed process, with each interviewer having the responsibility for preparing a diagnostic summary and evaluative statement. Our actual experience in the interviewing has convinced us that using attitudinal reactions in the interview situation alone is hardly a sufficient basis on which to form an opinion of the individual's potentialities for training and, without question, that specific knowledge of more significant historical content and observation of the candidate's functioning and relating during the interview are both required. We shall comment further on the interview process when we discuss some of our findings on several groups.

A form was devised which enabled the interviewers to rate the interviewee on basic qualities and characteristics tentatively deemed desirable for social work training, as well as to give him an over-all rating for social work in general and for the interviewee's special field, if any, in particular. In addition to the individual's physical appearance, demeanor, voice, and verbal facility, the component qualities to be rated were his warmth and responsiveness; sensitivity; intellectual capacity; maturity of thought; judgment, and discrimination; subjectivity-objectivity; his psychological-mindedness, particularly his insight into himself and his empathy with others, which might include the interviewer, family, clients, groups, characters in plays, books, etc. Any symptoms or parapraxes noted were to be listed as well as any historical material of special importance. Other areas of particular significance, with a space for comments on the rating sheet, were the individual's work capacity, recreational and cultural interests, and his social and political awareness and views. The component items on the rating sheet were to be supplemented by the interviewer's summary, which was to be concentrated primarily on an evaluation of the individual's personality pattern, his capacity to establish object-world relationships, his adaptive mechanisms, his motivation, and a prognosis of his potentials for growth and change through the educational experience. A ten-point scale was devised, with those graded 5 and below regarded as unsuitable or rejected for training, and those rated 6 being mediocre or doubtful. All persons rated 7 or above would be accepted, with 7 considered as average in potentials, 8 above average, 9 superior, and 10 top grade. The interviewee's final rating would then be the arithmetical average of the ratings submitted by the three interviewers. Through frequent seminars, at which the processed interviews are read and analyzed together as a group, greater uniformity in thinking and evaluating has been attained among the interviewers, reflecting itself in a trend toward fewer divergent ratings.

A parallel form for the student's field work performance was prepared to measure the same qualities and their translation into practice. This form permits evaluation of the individual's intellectual endowment, personality equipment, emotional acceptance and use of supervision, and skills and productivity, with the total of eighteen component items and the over-all rating to be checked as above average, average, or below average for each quarter's performance in field work. In addition to the statistical rating, a descriptive, evaluative comment related to the main topical headings is prepared on each student each quarter. To insure as much uniformity as possible, the field work advisers rather than the students' field supervisors are asked to prepare these charts, and in evaluating the students for the study, to use the criteria already in use by the School. These charts then serve as the basis for correlation with the original ratings and impressions of the Pilot Study interviewers to determine whether the positive and negative qualities recognized by the interviewers were manifesting or modifying themselves throughout the educational experience.

At the end of the first year of the study, 258 students and candidates had been interviewed, of whom 62 had been seen as candidates. A random sampling of all candidates from the New York metropolitan area for the fall, winter, and spring quarters participated on a voluntary basis. Although interviewed by the Pilot Study before the Admissions Committee's decisions were announced, the candidates for the fall and winter quarters were assured of confidentiality. In order to determine to what extent candidates were able and willing to share in a pre-admissions interview when the material did have a bearing on their admission, the candidates for the spring quarter were advised that although they were still participating on a voluntary basis, the Pilot Study interviewers would be submitting a recommendation to the Admissions Committee. While the recommendation would not be binding on the committee, it would be given due consideration, together with the other supporting material presented by the candidate. It is interesting that sixty-eight of the seventy-seven candidates invited, or 88 percent, responded to the invitation although only thirty could be seen in the study. We would like to add that it was the general impression among the interviewers that, as a group, these candidates seemed to share more and be more eager to participate than any other group previously interviewed, which would seem to indicate that the loss of confidentiality by the submission of a recommendation to the Admissions Committee had little threat.

At this point we would like to present our first attempt at an over-all qualitative analysis of the findings of the first three quarters in the study's experience. It is of utmost importance that we emphasize the fact that this is only an interim progress report on trends and merely suggestive. At this phase in our research study we cannot recommend criteria for selection based on our impressions with any definitive conviction. As we mentioned earlier, we believe that several years of corroboration and correlation of impressions with actual performance are necessary before we can speak with more assurance.

For this over-all analysis of collective findings, we selected the recorded material on fifty interviewees, constituting 28 percent of the students and candidates interviewed during the first nine-month period. The fifty interviewees were forty-three students and seven candidates; of the latter, five became students, so that forty-eight of the fifty were full-time students at the time of the analysis. The method of selection of the fifty was to start with every tenth person interviewed during the entire period, then every fifth, and finally every third until the quota of fifty was met. Statistically, the sampling of fifty compared favorably with the entire number of students and candidates interviewed during the period as to sex, age, and experience, as well as in the distribution of number of interviews among the nine interviewers and in the categorical ratings for all the interviewees.

For purposes of analysis, the group of fifty was divided into the following groups, using as the common denominator the over-all rating of the Pilot Study interviewers: above average, average, between doubtful and average; doubtful; and the lowest category included those between reject and doubtful, and reject.

There were sixteen men and thirty-four women in the group of fifty. The median age was twenty-seven with the quartiles being twenty-three and thirty-two. The median age for the above-average interviewees was twenty-three and a half; for those designated average, twenty-three; between doubtful and average, twenty-eight; doubtful, thirty-six; and the last category, twenty-seven and a half. The heavy concentration of the younger students and candidates was in the two highest groups. The oldest group was predominant in the doubtful area.

In order to determine whether any common patterns and leads were beginning to emerge from the Pilot Study material, the data on each of the fifty selected for this report were charted and analyzed in the following areas:

Previous education (major)
Initial interest in other fields
Previous unrelated vocations and reasons for change
Previous related vocations and reasons for change
Training plans and interest
War experience
Familial relations
  1. Parental relationships
  2. Sibling relationships
    a) Ordinal position
    b) Key sibling (*s*)
    c) Others
Economic status of parental family
Marital relationships
  1. Spouse
  2. Children
Extrafamilial relationships (earlier)
  1. Individuals
  2. Groups
Other significant developmental history
Organic conditions
Clinical (psychological or psychosomatic) symptoms
  Type and period of treatment
Personality evaluation
  Ego defenses
  Capacity for insight
  Adaptive capacity
  Personality pattern
  Capacity to establish object-world relationships
  Motivation
Reaction to current educational experience
Progression (or lack of it) in the Pilot Study interviews

Because of the space limitation, we shall be able to report on only three of the five groups. A summarization of the evaluation of these different groupings by the Pilot Study interviewers follows:

1. *Above average.*—It was believed that most of the students were relatively free and uncomplicated, and with several the comment was made that they were mature beyond their chronological age. The indications were that they were people with sensitivity who related easily and readily and had good intellectual

equipment, emotional stability, objectivity, and a marked degree of independence. The students appeared generally to have made good adaptations to reality situations. There was evidence, not only of increasing insight, but also of self-discipline. In the course of the interviews, they manifested unusual ability to analyze the importance of more significant experiences and their contribution toward their emotional maturation. There was evidence also of increasing ability in the interviews to regard those persons who were very close personally with more objectivity, yet with warmth, understanding, and acceptance.

It was generally believed that these students had a healthy identification with emotional problems and with people in difficulty. They had tolerance for a wide variety of people and concern for broad social problems. The interviewers were of the opinion that most of these students were conscious of a relatively deep sense of satisfaction in their current personal individual relationships, and many of their past relationships were of a sustained nature and had a more lasting quality. Although their own parental relationships had some negative aspects, there was an easy and ready sensitivity to other people's feelings, and they appeared free enough to permit themselves to be used constructively by others. There was a noticeable lack of hostility among most of the students, but with two, it was thought that their empathy was more selective than was that of the rest. One student seemed to overidentify with adolescents struggling against authority and with the severely disadvantaged, and the other had some difficulty in working with children who expressed over-aggressive and hostile behavior. What was noticeable even with these two students, however, was the presence of sufficient insight into the basis for their overidentification and rejection to lead the interviewers to believe that these characteristics would not necessarily prove to be insurmountable deterrents to the students' becoming superior social workers. It is interesting that the student who recognized her problem with over-aggressive children in group work slanted her training program toward the administrative and program-planning level of practice for which her experiential background fitted her admirably, arrived at through a more mature awareness and acceptance of her limitations.

With several, the motivation for selection of social work appeared to stem from very positive identification with both parents, who were outgoing and actively helping people in the community, or from having had the satisfying role of an older sister with a younger sibling. Although the other students spoke of their great personal satisfaction in being in a helping role, there were several variations. One student recognized that it was an extension and prolongation of her mother role with her younger siblings, but expressed good awareness of her need, and felt that it was easier for her to give freedom to others at this time, especially to children. Several believed that their identifications were strong primarily with their mothers, who had engaged in many volunteer activities. With others, it was felt that there was identification with deprived persons, in part because of the students' own unhappy childhood; but again the self-awareness of these students was excellent. It is interesting that the initial reason given for selection was usually a philosophical one—their conviction of the importance of doing preventive work with children particularly, to forestall breakdown as adults. These students, however, were able very quickly to move into personal content and examine their motivations with minimal defensiveness.

In practically every situation the interviewers were in agreement that the students and candidates in this group related warmly and responsively from the first interview and with almost no exception maintained the same attitude throughout the three interviews. They identified positively with the interviewers of both sexes, and with the objectives of the study. There was little blocking or hesitation in discussion of self and personality, and yet their free expression was not self-absorptive but rather directed to an objective understanding of personality and motivation, of equal interest to the interviewee and the study. These students and candidates were able to take considerable initiative in organizing their thinking around the study's objectives from interview to interview, and easily assumed responsibility for introducing new areas for discussion, of interest to them and related to the basic themes, and in moving the interviews forward. There was a noticeable undefensiveness and lack of anxiety and hostility, with adequate evidence of freedom to express factors of difference objectively and analytically. Although responsive, they were not necessarily conforming, and there was a healthy give-and-take in the discussions.

2. *Students and candidates rated as average.*—The majority of these students impressed the interviewers as being essentially undefensive. The degree of insight evidenced varied, but there was a sense of progression in analytical ability in the interviews and in the sharing and handling of material more personally oriented. With some of the students, it was felt that the self-awareness manifested was primarily intellectual, but in general the potentialities for acquisition of insight were considered good. In the remaining situations, there was some variation in the interview series, with some students beginning defensively with passivity, hostility, projection, intellectualization, and withdrawal all in evidence, but in the subsequent interviews giving evidence of a lowering of their defenses with increased autocritical ability. It was felt that they could face negative aspects of their personalities, and their potentials for insight were also good.

With one student who was so completely undefensive in the first interview and shared such productive material so freely, there was a retreat to intellectualization in subsequent interviews, but even then the interviewers believed that she displayed good self-analytical ability.

The interviewers were of the opinion that the students had adequate or good adaptive capacity, even in several situations where the students themselves had a self-demeaning attitude and felt that it had been difficult for them to adjust to new situations and experiences.

Although in several instances there was some divided opinion among the interviewers, the dominant component in the personality structures of the students in this category appeared to be dependency in different stages, evidencing itself in various forms. With several, the dependency manifested itself in overacceptance of authority, stemming from a strong need to be loved and approved, with the student's dependency needs having been unmet in the past. Identification in one instance seemed to be with a submissive, self-sacrificing mother, and the origin was unclear in another, except for excessive identification with the young and weak against a frustrating and hostile environment. With several others, there was evidence of pronounced need to excel, with much striving for status to obtain parent-persons' approval, resulting in unusual demands of themselves and a feeling of unworthiness and loss of esteem when it was difficult to attain their goals. These students had rather good intellectual understanding of their problem, but their hostility was more deeply internalized, and it was questioned whether they would be able to integrate their awareness emotionally through the educational experience alone.

Another recognizable trend in the dependency range was that of the students who were ambivalent, wavering between submission and independence, with both hostility and compliance expressed toward authority. Although these students had not yet worked out their feelings in relation to conventional and restrictive parental attitudes, they appeared to be making progress in the steady assertion of their independence. Several of these students had been extremely active with campus groups concerned with social and economic problems. One of these students stated that her inability to establish more meaningful personal relationships probably accounted for the hyperactivity in this other direction.

Several of the women seemed to have had much conflict about their feminine role, and their aggressive reactions were not too successfully sublimated.

There were more variations in pattern of relating in this group than among the students in the above-average group. Although the students were generally characterized as warm and responsive, a more narrow range in selectivity and ability to form and sustain relationships was recognizable in this group. With more than one third, again based so much on knowledge of their feelings toward the key persons in the family constellation and with others in the same relationship, it was anticipated they would have more difficulty in relating to authoritative persons, especially those in a superior position. There were several interesting facets, however. One student "froze" when criticized, and her need to conform was so great that it not only reflected itself with parent-persons in authority as her supervisors, but also with clients. Another student attempted to control her supervisors in past job experiences "by making them over" and also had particular difficulty in working with controlling mother-persons among her clients. One student seemed to relate herself easily to others and did not find it difficult to evoke strong positive countertransference reactions in clients, but because of her strong negative relationship with her mother and mother-persons and the absence of mature father-persons during her own psychosexual development, a problem was anticipated in that she might relate less adequately to adults of both sexes, especially with controlling and hostile mother-persons. Another student had difficulty with men in supervisory positions and was in marked rivalry with them, and her empathy was readily seen as being greater with women.

Quite a few students were felt to be much more comfortable in their relationships with children because of their own more positive identification with the emotionally deprived child. In one situation the student herself, because of her deprived childhood and residual feelings, thought it might be better for her not to work with children since she was not sure she could handle her feelings as well as with adults. The interviewers, however, felt that she was capable of working more effectively with children because of a more positive identification based on her own negative experiences, and her keen intellectual and analytical ability would probably prevent projection. It was also anticipated that several students would have more difficulty in accepting aggressive behavior in children because they had not yet resolved their conflicting feelings toward their siblings, but these students had demonstrated beginning insight and some modification of their attitudes and feelings.

Although several students had a real feeling for other people, they had a tendency to overidentify with the person in difficulty, with excessive fear of hurting people. The approach was more intellectualized and cautious, and ability to handle emotional content with clients more circumscribed, seemingly directly related to fear of their supervisor's rapid penetration of their defenses at this time.

The frequent response given by students and candidates to the question for motivation for selection of social work was, "I've always liked people," "I've always wanted to work with people," and, on occasion, the extreme response of having "a great urge to do something constructive for humanity" or "to try to make world conditions better." Those students who had more advantaged economic backgrounds frequently referred to an initial stimulation coming from sociology and economics courses, with an introduction intellectually to negative social and economic conditions which would have been foreign to their own personal experiences. When explored a little further with the students who presented as their motivation an interest in bettering society or doing good for humanity, they were often able to show evidence of more self-awareness and produced material indicating identification with those who were underprivileged in some way. In general, the motivation seemed less positive than with the above average group. With some of the students there was evidence of self-absorption and the desire to learn more about oneself; or the need to be important to somebody; or difficulty in competing successfully with others in fields that they believed required more intellectual ability; or avoidance of competition with siblings or parents who were very successful in their profession as well as others who were in direct competition with them. There appeared to be less positive identification with a loving parent or sibling and without as much self-awareness evidenced as in the above-average group of students.

The interviewers felt that almost all the students and candidates had responded positively to them and were identified with the aims and purposes of the study. Although several students had a tendency to begin the interview with what seemed to be aloofness and a cautious, guarded attitude, they quickly responded to the warmth and interest of the interviewers, and as they became more secure in the interview situation, shared personal content and expressed their feelings rather freely. Some seemed to require more support and reassurance from the interviewers; others showed varying degrees of warmth and responsiveness with the different interviewers, either because such meaningful content had already been shared in a previous interview, or because a preceding interviewer had been particularly stimulating in helping the student to "piece things together," thus making the interview experience a constructive part of the student's own learning process; or because the student's identification was relatively more positive with one interviewer than with another because of the sex factor. Some of the students commented that, apart from the increased understanding and self-awareness and the opportunity to clarify their views and attitudes toward their professional career and interest which were derived from the project experience, they learned much about interviewing skill and techniques. Where blocking was more conscious, either because the student felt that additional time was necessary in order to do some more thinking about the subject under discussion, or owing to heightened feeling when intrafamilial relationships particularly were discussed and not seeing clearly enough the connection with the study's aim of understanding motivation, in subsequent interviews these students showed evidence of having given more thought to the previous discussion by moving the interviews forward more productively and more freely.

As might be expected, the ratings of the three interviewers for each of the students were in close agreement.

3. *Students and candidates rated as between reject and doubtful, and reject.*—The interviewers were almost unanimous in agreeing that this group of students and candidates was rigid and highly defensive. Projection, repression, intellectualization, passivity, denial, aggression, withdrawal, were observed repeatedly with almost no variation from interview to interview. The members of this group appeared to be fearful of self-awareness, were unanalytical, and had very poor potentials for development of

insight, being uncommunicative when personal feelings or content were approached. At the most, several verbalized intellectual self-understanding, but it seemed quite apparent that the self-critical ability or capacity for independent thinking was minimal.

These students generally made poor adaptations to new situations, and essentially they were poorly integrated, with a low threshold of frustration tolerance.

It was felt that these students had not made a mature emotional adjustment. They were basically dependent, ranging from an extreme of primary narcissism to those who presented themselves as actively struggling with their dependency needs. Outwardly, they were predominantly passive and unaggressive, but had deeply repressed hostility. With a number there was a characteristic feeling of worthlessness and inadequacy, lack of self-esteem, and excessive self-preoccupation. Several were particularly described as having a compulsive type of personality, evidenced in their rigidity, orderliness, indecisiveness, and perfectionistic drive. Their feeling of deprivation was so great and their need for acceptance so deeply rooted that it was questionable whether any modification in personality was possible through the educational experience alone.

It was felt that several were quite dependent upon persons in authority, yet hostile toward them, and there was a need to exert controlling force over others. A few seemed more energetic and ambitious with evidence of a strong ego drive but were basically rigid and dogmatic, and their values seemed to rest on external symbols, such as convention, attainment, and position.

A number of these students had given evidence of superior intellectual ability, having made excellent undergraduate academic records. One person had the intellectual awareness that the striving for academic attainment was compensatory "to show them that I could amount to something, that I was not an inferior person."

The students in this category generally found it very difficult to discuss their intrafamilial relationships and experiences, and their defensiveness and inability to accept the assurance of confidentiality were much more pronounced than were those of the other groups.

It was the opinion of the interviewers that these students would have great difficulty in relating to clients on any but a superficial level. Based on knowledge of their having had few and poor object-world relationships, the prognosis for growth and empathetic ability was considered minimal. Because of their basic hostility, and with as much self-absorption and self-preoccupation and fear of involving themselves with others as appeared to have been true of this group, their being accepted for any field of social work seemed contraindicated. The great majority had had such poor relationships with parent-persons—apparent both from the interviewer's knowledge of the specific parental relationships as well as from those situations where more personal content might have been lacking but in which very negative feelings were repetitively expressed toward persons in authority—that it was felt they would have difficulty working with authority. Several, despite their own conflict with authority, had strong need to be controlling and were apprehensive of personal relationships except in an authoritative role. A number who had been in social work previously had experienced serious difficulty in relating to supervision. Many were quite threatened and insecure in any competitive experience with peers and superiors. These students had a narrow range in their preference for working with individuals and groups. Several expressed fearfulness of groups but also had little success in working with individuals. With some, it was quite apparent that excessive responsibility was repeatedly delegated to the client in order to sustain the relationship. One student appeared to be deriving narcissistic satisfaction from working with groups in an active, physically participating relationship, but was very uncomfortable when working with adults and with very young people. This person's tendency was either to overidentify or to reject with minimal insight.

Although most of the students in this group initially responded that they had "always liked people" and "were always interested in people," when the reason for selecting social work was discussed, as they became somewhat more secure in the interviews, several acknowledged that security and status were the primary factors. As one individual expressed it, there would always be a need for social workers whether economic conditions were good or bad. Attributing motivation to concern for "all mankind" was a frequent expression of those who had been extremely deprived libidinally. With several students the selection appeared to be very important as ego-supports and reassurance of their ability to relate to others. With some students, it was felt that the primary motivation was the need to know about themselves, or because it was felt that social work was a less competitive field than other professions.

Although several of these interviewees felt that they were attracted to working with underprivileged people because they had experienced certain hardships in early life, this group appeared to be singularly lacking in positive identification with others in motivation for selection of social work as a career.

The over-all impression that this group made on the interviewers was overwhelmingly negative. There was some slight variation in their relating in the interview series. Some approached the interview with passivity and diffidence and in subsequent interviews were able to express their hostility more freely toward the attempts of the first interviewers to have them discuss more personal content. Others started by attacking the study as invalid or voicing resentment in the beginning and sustaining this attitude throughout the sequence of interviews when personal material was discussed, with very strong defenses in evidence against involving themselves in the interviews. It was hard for them to accept assurance of confidentiality; in the second or third interviews several members of the group expressed alarm at having revealed so much personal history, while others expressed guilt at having suppressed data which they could accept intellectually only as pertinent to the study's objectives. Some termed the interviews a "threatening" experience, especially where the interviewers did not give as much direction as the student would have preferred. The group seemed to have poor autocritical ability, with several members taking direct objection to any effort to unfold themes related to an understanding of causation, and asking with much feeling whether there always had to be an explanation.

Again space prohibits any detailed discussion of the correlations of the field work advisers' ratings with the Pilot Study interviewers' impressions. We should state, however, that up to this point the correlation on the average group is excellent. Of a total of twenty-seven ratings received on these students, only one was below average. Too few field work reports beyond the first quarter have been received on the above average group to draw any conclusions, although they were all functioning at a level of average or above average at the time. The group which interests us particularly is the Pilot Study's reject group of students. There was close correlation with field work ratings on half the students. The other half, however, appeared to be performing adequately. As we follow these students through the remainder of their educational experience and later in job situations, we hope to learn more of their capacity for adaptation or modification of the personal qualities which influenced the Pilot Study interviewers to regard them as having poor potentials for professional development.

As a follow-up in our analysis of these fifty interviewees, we shall begin a similar evaluation of an additional fifty as a basis for further confirmation or evidence of any differences in trends and patterns observed among the first group. It is extremely important that we re-emphasize the fact that whatever conclusions and interpretations we have made in this report are highly tentative, since they are based on limited numbers and on only an initial period of correlation with field performance.

May we say that on the basis of our experience we have the utmost conviction that, regardless of what other methods and devices are used to aid in the selection of students for social work training, the *sine qua non* of any cluster of screening methods is the personal interview.

Part III: Vistas in Human Relations

The Scientific Spirit and Human Welfare

L. C. DUNN

IN THE RAPID MARCH of material progress, science and human welfare have seemed to be so intimately connected that we have come to expect a continuation of these gifts without inquiring too closely what they are, how they are produced, and what the prospects are for their continuance in the future. The external facts are too well known to call for repetition. The scientific revolution which began in the Renaissance, gathered momentum in the nineteenth century, and proceeded at so rapid a pace in our own century has transformed our material culture, and has provided the means for a better life. Whether the spirit which animated this scientific drive was primarily concerned with human welfare is a debatable question, since the primary purpose of research is the pursuit of knowledge, but the great potential benefits which have resulted have been real even though they may have been by-products.

Some of these huge promises of things to come which the poets and social thinkers and scientists of the nineteenth century foresaw, and which appeared in the prophetic stories of H. G. Wells in the decade just before and after 1900, have been more than realized. Yet we know now that we have somehow failed to reap the whole harvest of human happiness which was then offered to us. The discoveries of science, applied through medicine and public health, have made it possible for each human life to be both longer and richer; and yet we know that if war comes again the lives of vast numbers of men will be both nastier, shorter, and more brutish. This same world in which such splendid technology is possible is filled today with desperate people. We have lived in this kind of world too long to believe any longer that they are desperate by original sin. A large part of the world's population has been made desperate by sorrow and uncertainty and hunger and fear—and every one of us faces the immediate prospect of becoming just that kind of desperate person who today wanders through the rubble of the destroyed cities of Europe and the Orient.

Against the great accomplishment and promise of a benevolent science, let us for a moment pose the dilemma of the scientist of today as representative of the modern man of the West. Here he is, with unparalleled power over materials, a power which he has not yet learned to use for his own good. This is not primarily because the progress of science has outrun moral development, as is often alleged, but because men are still unwilling to base their beliefs and hence their actions on the kind of reasoning which has been shaped by the hard empiricism of science. They are still shocked when an objective statistical inquiry is made of their sexual behavior, although no zoölogist would dream of holding serious views about the factors which influence the life of any animal species in the absence of a study of that sort. We pay attention to, and allow our votes to be influenced by, the most absurd appeals to unreason. We permit unreasonable attacks upon the methods of science itself, which once were made by an old theology but which now are taken over by committees of Congress. Even among the scientists are some who have almost the same distrust of science as a guide of life which Tolstoy had, and which many humanists and moralists profess.

I shall examine some of this reaction against the scientific spirit and seek for its causes, for only if we understand what is implied by it can we hope to assess the future effects of science on human welfare. My thesis will be that we suffer not from too much science but from too little; this superb instrument of human reason has been harnessed to the production of materials and of energy with results both magnificent and terrible. It has hardly been tried against those problems by which as a human species we shall survive or perish—the problems of social and economic organization, and the underlying problems of human motivation, of the needs and wants of human beings as animals, as social persons, as men who strive for happiness. We should know why this state of things exists three centuries after Newton's apple fell and Galileo turned his telescope on Venus. It is now nearly a hundred years since the great indignant outcry against Darwin and Huxley and Spencer, who dared to call man an animal and include him among the objects of scientific study as a part of nature. I fear some part of the battle has to be fought over again, for I believe we can escape from our dilemma only by a diffusion of scientific understanding so wide that all people shall have access to it. This is one of the chief educational problems of the immediate future, and has to be faced, not merely by the secondary schools and colleges, but by the schools of the university where the leaders of professional life are trained. The goal of science in professional education is not to make scientists but to have the methods of proof from evidence and the logic which underlies science absorbed into the mental life of all the students. Whether its goal is achieved can only be judged by the extent to which all questions concerning man's material life are examined in a scientific spirit. By this criterion, science has not penetrated very far into the culture of our people.

There are some peculiarities of science itself, of scientists, and of all human beings which have tended to keep science out of the social and human sphere. There is first the pursuit of science for its own sake. Fundamental learning proceeds best when it is free to follow its own interest. This has fixed an individualistic character upon scientific research which has made it resist control and application. While this has been true for the deepest truths, there is much science which now could proceed at the group level, and did so proceed during the war when most scientists were organized into teams. Just as art for art's sake is applicable only to individuals, so science for science's sake need apply to the few lonely discoverers, not to science as a social activity. There is much evidence of change in this direction, although the inertia of individualism is still strong. We should like to think that the scientific spirit in the individual pursues knowledge, while in the group it pursues a common purpose which includes welfare. This view is possible though not proved, because the value of the individual's interest, his craving for knowledge, underlies that of the group. The interest of the group, of society, is best protected when scientific interest is free to arise in each member; that is, when a wide diffusion of opportunity provides for wide participation in scientific work. This is an ideal of a healthy society; for we know that in science, learning has meaning only when the learner reaches it as a conclusion by an effort of his own. He acquires the spirit of science by using it.

There is, secondly, the inertia of custom among all men which leads us to escape the discomfort of change by taking refuge in what we indulgently call our higher natures. We are not realists unless we train ourselves to be so. For long ages we preferred supernatural to natural explanations, and now we tend to protect our superhuman nature, which we equate with the divine, from examination except by introspection. We treasure, as we say, our illusions and pity the man who is disillusioned, even though these ancient illusions, for all the joy they may give the individual, doom the species as a whole to recurrent wars and terrors as horrible as any primitive tribe has ever faced.

In the social sphere it will be time to turn to metaphysics when we have exhausted the benefits which physics can give. The comfort of spiritual elevation is cold indeed when the body is miserable. For the solitary individual this may induce a mystical experience in which his suffering is transcended, but in a whole society it can lead only to revolution and violence.

We had better look our higher natures straight in the eye, for it is disastrous to confuse illusion and reality, and the values of both the real and the ideal may thereby be destroyed. In *Reason in Religion,* Santayana speaks of the poetic value of religion as being greater even than that of poetry itself because religion deals with higher and more practical themes. But he goes on to say:

> But this initial advantage is neutralized in part by the abuse to which religion is subject, whenever its symbolic rightness is taken for scientific truth. Like poetry it improves the world only by imagining it

improved, but not content with making this addition to the mind's furniture—an addition which might be useful and ennobling—it thinks to confer a more radical benefit by persuading mankind that, in spite of appearances, the world is really such as that rather arbitrary idealization has painted it. This spurious satisfaction is naturally the prelude to many a disappointment. . . . Religion remains an imaginative achievement . . . but it becomes at the same time a continuous incidental deception; and this deception, in proportion as it is strenuously denied to be such, can work indefinite harm in the world and in the conscience.

It is certainly not to displace faith that science strives, for science has perforce a faith of its own, a view of order without which it could not plan or perform the simplest experiment. Science is rather concerned with that other factor in the old equation of faith plus works, and with avoiding, by active steps, the self-deception to which we so easily fall prey when we substitute a fiction, however beautiful, for a fact of nature.

It is not strange that this inertia by which the citadels of belief are defended should persist so widely in the public when scientists themselves take refuge from reality. An example is found in the eloquent address delivered by my friend and colleague Professor E. W. Sinnott at the one hundredth anniversary celebration of the Sheffield Scientific School of Yale University. Professor Sinnott is now the distinguished director of that school and, in 1948, president of the American Association for the Advancement of Science, so that he speaks with the prestige and authority of a leader of American science. His address, as published in the *American Scientist* for January, 1948, is entitled "Science and the Whole Man." It is primarily concerned with the relations between natural science, on the one hand, and the humanities and religion on the other, and with its conclusion that science alone is an insufficient base for education there can be no quarrel. But he asks a timely and pertinent question about science and answers it in a way that reveals one aspect of our trouble today. "What we seek to know," he writes, "is really this: is intellect the only guide to truth and do all ultimate certainties come through science, or are there other valid avenues, different but worthy of exploration, which we should not neglect?" Later on, after recounting some of the material accomplishments of science and the usefulness of the scientific method in discovering truth, he nevertheless answers his question in these words:

> But there is a wide terrain into which this newest highway of the mind can never penetrate, a country where are found the rich facts of experience—subjective, primary, immediate,—our emotions, desires, purposes, values, feelings of beauty and ugliness, of right and wrong, of love and hate. These are hardly accessible to analysis by the methods of cold reason or understandable by science.

Of course, we have no present evidence of the successful application of scientific method to the inner life of the individual, and we shall probably always appreciate the good and the beautiful by canons not determined by reason alone—and yet the categorical predictiveness of that word "never" seems to reveal that Professor Sinnott does not want that inner sanctum invaded by rough reason. The "emotions, desires, purposes, values, feelings" of which he speaks have been the mainsprings of human behavior. Would Professor Sinnott wish us to conclude that, since rational methods have not been applied to human behavior, therefore the very domain from which our present misery arises will be forever immune from rational control? All our experience with scientific method should protect and warn us from such a premature and hopeless conclusion. It will not do to abandon the position which has been won with such difficulty. The desperate situation of society today can ill afford further delay in applying to it the best methods we have discovered, nor will the ills of the great majority of mankind be helped by the old admonition, "Tighten your belts and cultivate your souls."

Within our own lifetimes we have seen domains of human behavior invaded by rational methods which may well be the spearheads of new advances. It is not long since the knowledge and practice of contraception spread over the Western world against the weight of inertia and prejudice and made possible, in some countries of Northern Europe where it has been encouraged, that control of population increase which is one of the most essential powers of a society built on reason. But this invasion is still resisted, only now in different form, as is shown by Lionel Trilling's review of the Kinsey report, *Sexual Behavior in the Human Male,* in the April, 1948, issue of *Partisan Review.* One gathers that Professor Trilling would have preferred to remain ignorant of the sexual life of his contemporaries, if it must be disclosed by the method of establishing facts used by the Kinsey group. The report, he says, "has an extravagant fear of all ideas that do not seem to it to be, as it were, immediately dictated by simple physical fact." The bias disclosed by this abhorrence of facts as such vitiates much of the otherwise cogent criticism which Professor Trilling directs against the report; and I believe it is symptomatic of the reaction against science amongst the humanists.

In so far as it finds and exposes the weaknesses and limitations of the scientific method and of the narrowness and pettiness of much that is published in scientific journals, this reaction is good and useful to scientist and nonscientist alike; but I fear that much of it stems from the old fear that if our beliefs and actions are based entirely upon reason, what are called "values" would disappear from life. This seems to me a dangerous and unproved *non sequitur.* Why attention to a good and sound foundation should interfere with the construction of a superstructure of beauty and grace has never been clear to me.

Moreover, what the scientific spirit has to offer for the improvement of man's life and society is tangible and clear. It is not only the chemical identification of the necessary elements of his diet, the synthesis of substances which will control and eliminate the parasites and pathogenic organisms which prey upon him and all the devices by which his life may be made safer and more comfortable. It is not only the control over the vast sources of energy which has recently been gained (for we do not yet know whether this will benefit him or ruin him), nor the prospects of life without labor which this may produce. It is such benefits, of course; but more than this it is the proven ability to solve such problems, and the actual ways and means of scientific discovery. In science the important thing is not what one knows, but how one knows it, how it is to be found out. The primacy of evidence, the giving of credence only to that which can be repeatedly subjected to objective demonstration, the reference of all material questions to the court of nature by experiment and observation—these have given modern science its strength and confidence, and these are ready to be used in the service of man. J. T. Merz, in writing of the rise of science in the nineteenth century, characterized it as "the statistical view of nature," and it is certainly in the mathematical and statistical approach to problems of society that the method of science is immediately applicable to social and human problems. To examine all things methodically and to reduce them to an order which reveals the relationships among them—this is the spirit of science whether applied to atoms or to men.

The older mystical or magical view of nature and the spiritual panaceas founded upon it are nebulous and uncertain, and have not prevented the plight in which we find ourselves, in which needless hate and suspicion make an armed camp of a world of which all the inhabitants are, by the testimony of science, of one blood brotherhood. We need not fear the loss of the unlearned values inherent in the human spirit, for it will stubbornly persist as solace and as consolation and, one hopes, as the seat of that faith which may be saved from death by works.

Now, it is a most important fact that the first of these, the scientific spirit, must be consciously invoked and learned. It is artificial, a creation of the human mind, not an uncultivated gift to be produced by prayer and fasting. It requires effort and the preparation of a milieu, and that is why it had to contend for educational place amongst the older disciplines of learning. And in its train it brings deliberation and conscious planning. One of the major effects of science will certainly be to widen the area of planning until it includes the whole of what Graham Wallas called "the Great Society." Not only does this result from the diffusion of scientific ways of thinking, its cultural effect, but it is now perfectly evident that technological and mechanical effects of scientific discoveries already made will impose the necessity of planning and control. Laissez-faire was already dying, but once the first atom bomb had exploded, even a child could see that if any society was to survive, it had to control that force and arrange itself deliberately in relation to the new power.

The duty of those in social work to appreciate these implications of modern science is clear. Beyond the materials and the special techniques it can provide, the great gift of science is understanding, and this can confer an attitude of confidence and power of which those who devote their lives to human welfare stand in special need today.

One need not have had much experience of life to know that at present the surest way to promote human welfare is to prevent human misery. That the human mind and spirit have great potentialities for happiness and achievement is a testimony of all human history. There the song of the slaves has been heard above the sound of their chains. It is true that we cannot cause that song; we can only remove the chains so that those with the will to sing can use, not only their voices to relieve the suffering of their bodies, but their freed hands to build the only certain protection against recurrent misery. This bulwark is not only sound government and free political institutions, not only the institutions of practical prevention and cure—the hospitals and social service devices of all kinds; it is also the institutions which search out the causes of things so that we may know the hidden sources of trouble; above and beyond all, our only sure defense is the diffusion amongst all the people of practical scientific knowledge and the will to use it for their common purposes. In order to learn we must first have shaken off some of the physical limitations of hunger and cold and disease, and our efforts must always be directed against these, not only because they are bad in themselves, but because they interfere with learning itself. Our learning must be used to diminish ever further these barriers. We trade a little knowledge for the opportunity to learn more, and the physical comfort we gain is but the interest on a greater capital. This surely is the way the scientific spirit operates among those fortunate few for whom today it can be the effective guide of work and some portion of their lives. Their best discoveries are not vacuum cleaners or even vacuum tubes, but new problems. They discover, as Columbus did, something new to be ignorant about, that is, something to learn, and so they know that they build, not merely a new world of materials, but a new world of knowledge.

This is the real savings bank of our race; for if the soil of the New World is depleted of the nutrients which supplied its corn and wheat and cotton and tobacco, if its oil and coal and iron, even its uranium, run out, then, if we have with sufficient foresight invested in knowledge, we can go to that bank for new coins when the old ones are spent.

The peculiarity of that bank which gives us hope for the future is that the credits in it are in the common currency and cross-transferable. Physics and mathematics deposit at one time, and chemistry and biology use the credits at another. The laws and methods of science are, by definition, of a general character since they deal with elements of matter and energy; and this makes possible the collaboration amongst scientists which we see to-day even in the midst of specialization. It is particularly important that the social sciences, upon which so much of the understanding and manipulation of human institutions depends, use the same bank, and that both the natural and social sciences share in the common credit.

It ought not to be forgotten that the methods of the sciences have been developed by and for dealing with material things and their strength is greatest when directed toward the material basis of human welfare. Whether happiness follows material welfare is another question, but at least in our crowded world of today, a certain level of material welfare has come to be a condition, not only of happiness, but of continued social existence, and this comes to rest increasingly on an expanding science.

Finally, although I believe that the spirit and methods of science have been insufficiently used and appreciated as a basis on which the welfare of society may rest, it must be clear that for the individual life, science provides beginnings and not endings. He whose life is based upon the kind of reason which has been shaped in the long struggle to understand the physical world will still look both inward and outward, and find questions and answers about ends which he believes transcend the means. Perhaps the fact that some of the older fears have disappeared with clearer sight will permit him to face his newer, more material problems with a greater calm.

Science and Philosophy: Sources of Humanitarian Faith

EDUARD C. LINDEMAN

THE FORCES OF DEHUMANIZATION which now seem to pervade the modern world, dictating national policies and serving as motivation and method for political parties, will, if they continue to spread, destroy both the humanistic tradition and humanitarian faith. Individuals and entire nations will lose their liberties by means of swift strokes of external power. Authorities constructed through the slow processes of indigenous conflict and consent will be supplanted by abrupt seizures of power, often exercised by persons or groups alien and unknown. Imposed uniformity will take the place of internally achieved unity. Finally, man will cease to believe in himself and will transfer his faith to objectified symbols of power which control his physical existence, determine his needs and desires, and dictate even those aesthetic forms which, in order to be truly enjoyed, must belong to his inner, his private, life.

In such a world there will be collaboration without friendship, and association without fraternity. The fellowship of scholars will disappear completely since the scholars' tasks will become assignments emanating from sources of power. A vast network of police will be required to keep this power structure in order, but the will to resist will finally wither and die. Discipline and subserviency will become primary virtues. Life itself will have become a conditioned reflex, a response to derivative concentrations of power, all receiving their authority from a centralized bureaucracy or dictatorship. Propaganda, which knows neither right nor wrong but only what its wielders want, will have taken the place once occupied by education.

Is such an outcome possible? Is it believable that the "human enterprise" may culminate in this type of black defeat? Is it likely, to state the issue in other terms, that the collective will to die may actually supersede the individual's will to live? And, if this denouement belongs to the realm of possibility, is there no workable alternative? Are we caught in a web of inevitability, a mechanical sequence of fate from which there is no escape?

My answer to these disturbing questions is both simple and direct: I do most certainly believe that this tragic eventuality is possible but I emphatically do not believe it to be inevitable. I do not believe that a necessity exists which must turn man into his own nemesis. On the contrary, it is my firm conviction that none of these existing or impending evils is the outcome of anything predestined in natural law or in human nature. This conviction is integral to humanitarian faith, and it is this faith which I must now strive to validate.

Humanitarian faith rests upon the assumption that the essential resources for dealing with human problems are resident in nature and in human nature. This constitutes a bold article of faith, and whoever announces it must be prepared to answer a series of difficult questions. For example, what manifestations of human nature furnish assurance that man is capable of mastering his fate? What is the character of these resources which are resident in nature and in human nature? How have these resources thus far made themselves manifest?

The shortest, although perhaps not the most felicitous, answer to these questions is to be found in a restatement of the humanitarian faith in the language of scientific promise. A concise statement might take the following form: Science is the instrument which is potentially capable of making man's habitat, the earth, not merely a tolerably suitable home, but one in which poverty may be eliminated and disease reduced to a minimum, an environment in which all basic human needs may be satisfied.

This is the promise of science, the proposition which justifies, so I believe, the faith that a humanitarian world is feasible. Its logical composition is simple indeed; what this proposition affirms is the belief that man's intelligence expressed through scientific method is potentially capable of creating a beneficent relation between nature and human nature, between the natural environment and the human organism. If this proposition is false, then the hope of a humanitarian world in which human welfare rises to cumulatively higher stages must, of course, be abandoned. Upon this instrumentality, science, our survival depends. If this proposition is not true, then despair will and must become a reasonable human trait. In this case, the humanitarian faith will be supplanted by an outlook such as was ironically expressed some years ago by a British intellectual who proclaimed:

> All form of life, all organisms in which it is manifested, are engaged in an unceasing struggle to maintain themselves against the disintegrating forces of nature. All are in conflict with each other for the means of life, clan against clan, individual against individual. Each exists at the expense of others, and keeps its foothold only by success over the rest. . . . How deep it goes, this warfare, you may conjecture if you remind yourself that the very trees of the forest are battling with each other for the light of the sun, and that the plants have their defensive armour, the rose and thistle their thorns, the nettle its sting. Make your heart iron within you, when you remember that to live you must kill, either plants or animals.[1]

The above exercise in rational pessimism precipitates at least three varieties of doubt which need to be cast upon the scientific promise before it can become the basis of human faith.

Will the historic sequence of scientific development be fulfilled? Will science continue to move from physics to biology, from biology to psychology, and finally from psychology to the realm of social relations? If this sequence is not completed, then we shall still be equipped with an instrument which we cannot utilize for human ends since the physical and biological sciences will be frustrated by disparity and uncertainty respecting the proper uses of scientific facts and technological inventions. (This dilemma is presently illustrated by our confusion regarding atomic energy.)

The second doubt stems from the first. How are we to be assured that the power released by science will not be used by po-

[1] W. Macneile Dixon, Gifford Lectures delivered 1935–37 at the University of Glasgow, in *The Human Situation* (London: Arnold, 1937), p. 82.

litical agencies seeking power for ulterior ends? How can we know that scientific power will not be transmuted into political and military power, utilized, perhaps, to meet some of man's animal needs but only these, thus dehumanizing him in the process? In other words, is it not obvious that the outcome of the scientific promise depends upon a future alignment between science and politics, politics, that is, in its noblest sense?

The third doubt is philosophical in character and may be stated thus: By what means may it become possible to bring science and philosophy into a working relationship? If this cannot be achieved, then the conflict between facts and values will deepen with the consequence that ideological warfare will become the norm, culminating in military warfare and the progressive waste of natural resources and human life.

Although the task of finding answers to these misgivings and doubts is the chief business of the intellectuals of this disturbed and anguished age, I am compelled to admit that no easy and simple optimism awaits the inquirer who embarks upon this quest. My faith in the ultimate outcome is strong, but I foresee a long and arduous mental struggle in which contradictions, paradoxes, and dilemmas must be attacked, dissolved, and resolved. The available intellectual and emotional tools required for this purpose are inadequate, and some have not yet been forged. I can only suggest as an initial approach that you join with me in exploring a few affirmations which lie in the direct pathway of the great assertion upon which human welfare and happiness depend. We shall be seeking a new dedication to a faith which is not in essence new since some of its roots are certainly to be found in ancient Greek and Chinese thought. But in spite of its durable history, we shall be obliged to redefine this faith for our time only if we are prepared to grope our way along channels of ignorance, superstition, confusion, and downright ill will. I shrink from giving this faith a name lest I shall be called upon henceforth to defend the title rather than the function for which the faith stands as symbol. Those who call themselves scientific or naturalistic humanists hold this faith, but they sometimes express it too narrowly, too exclusively.

Why does any reasonable person doubt that scientific method

which has demonstrated its capacity to reveal so many secrets of nature may be applied also to the complexities of human personality and the social process? That this doubt is both widespread and deep-seated we can no longer question. When, in 1946, the Senate debate and hearings on the proposed National Science Foundation were proceeding, an attempt was made to include the social sciences as deserving subsidy along with the physical and biological sciences; the response was negative. Leading American scientists testified on behalf of exclusion. They insisted that man and his behavior are not a part of nature and cannot, therefore, be studied as basic or "pure" science; that the methods of the social sciences are so widely at variance with those of other sciences that the two could not be administered jointly; that social research is especially in danger of corruption by pressure groups and by governments; and, finally, that we already know the solution of human problems and all that is needed is education respecting the eternal verities and stronger appeals to moral fervor.

In contrast to this testimony I make a completely contrary, antithetical proposal: If the sequence from the physical to the biological and from the biological to the psychological and sociological sciences is not fulfilled, we cannot even solve the basic elementary problem of food, and hence neither poverty nor war can be avoided. And if poverty and war are to be accepted as necessary ingredients in human affairs, we cannot attain genuine freedom, and democracy must be abandoned as a way of life. Our present lack of social policy with respect to our food resources alone makes a normal, healthy diet for the world's population utterly impossible. Without a social policy concerned with population control we are caught in an endless frustration, since each increase in food supply will be followed by a corresponding increase in population. "The tide of the earth's population is rising, the reservoir of the earth's living resources is falling. . . . There is only one solution: Man must recognize the necessity of coöperating with nature." [2]

[2] A statement made by Professor Paul B. Sears in a review of *Our Plundered Planet* by Fairfield Osborn, New York *Herald Tribune* "Weekly Book Review," March 28, 1948.

How does man relate himself to nature? In our age and time he does so through the intervention of science. This is, however, a superficial explanation. The plain fact of the matter is that man relates himself to nature through his culture, that web of habits, customs, folkways, beliefs, and traditions which determine his values, purposes, and goals. It is culture which allows man to waste his natural resources, to reproduce in excess of available food supply, to perpetuate societies in which poverty persists even while plenty beckons.

I have chosen a simple but, I believe, graphic example to illustrate my thesis, man and food. The earth is now populated by approximately 2,250,000,000 human beings, and the rate of increase is 50,000,000 per decade. My proposition is this: If the biological and physical sciences are left to themselves without supplementation from the psychological and social sciences, the only methods for dealing with the world's population will continue to be starvation, disease, and war. I say this in spite of the exaggerated claims on behalf of the potentialities of atomic energy.[3] It must be remembered that what atomic fission can supply is a new volume of energy, more power. But power has been cheapened and multiplied constantly ever since the invention of the steam engine. Power is only one element in the productive enterprise and not the one upon which human existence on this planet primarily depends. Human life rests upon a scanty supply of organic matter which is very unevenly and sparsely distributed throughout restricted areas of the earth's surface. This resource, fertility of the soil, augmented by sun and water, could be utilized much more efficiently through improved uses of power, but unless we find some way of controlling population increases this measure of efficiency will once more reach a point of diminishing returns.

Merely to raise this question is to realize that science alone is not sufficient to sustain our faith in a humane outcome. We now know what some of the latent possibilities of science when transmuted into technology may mean to the life of contemporary and

[3] There will be attendant benefits such as have already become evident in the use of isotopes, but the basic meaning of atomic fission is power, or energy.

future men. Each successive stage of technological development, from tools to machines, from hand machines to power-driven machines utilizing the energy of coal, from coal to the release of energy in oil, gas, and electricity, and finally from electricity to atomic energy, has revealed a new and an augmented source of power. Within the short span of the last thirty years we have witnessed an acceleration of power which has radically altered space-time relations. But we also know that as space has become shortened, transportation speeded, and communication made almost instantaneous, human relations have deteriorated. Long, long ago Francis Bacon sensed this coming dilemma when he asked this pertinent question: "Is truth ever barren? . . . Will it not raise man's mind above the confusion of things? Shall he be able thereby to produce worthy effects and to endow his life with infinite commodities?" [4]

Alas, our answer to Bacon's query must still be couched in the form of dubious wishes. The reality is this: we live within an adult, matured pattern of technology striving to adjust ourselves to its resulting dynamics with an adolescent pattern of human relations. The consequences are frustration, friction, war, and a type of collective "insanity."

What remedies have been proposed? There are some who would prescribe a moratorium on science, assuming that if no

[4] A recent sonnet, inspired by these haunting questions of Francis Bacon, has been written and published by Thomson King. It reads as follows:

> Three hundred years and more have come and gone
> Since Bacon's busy pen and curious mind
> These questions to the centuries consigned;
> How reads our answer, if there should be one?
> Truth is not barren, benefits have flowed,
> At first a trickle, then a torrent broad
> From springs and wells of science; all applaud
> Her gifts and gains, so lavishly bestowed.
>
> But is man's mind above confusion raised?
> How stands the audit of his aims and life?
> Worthy effects are by but few appraised.
> The many listen to the siren's song
> Of greed and ease, or wake to sterile strife
> While Bacon's vision waits, how long! how long!

This poem, "Three Questions," is to be found in *Scientific Monthly,* LXV, No. 6 (December, 1947), 497.

further inventions were to be permitted for a space of, say, a half century we might then use the intervening time for "catching up," for bringing our social, economic, political, and cultural adaptations into harmony with technology. Others have sought refuge from science by attempting a resurrection of principles and beliefs which existed in the prescientific era. And still others appear to find a solution in depriving scientists of their freedom, of restricting the range of their researches to problems and situations set for them by nonscientific authorities, that is, by moralists or politicians.

These are not in any true sense solutions. They are impulses of fear and ought not to be taken seriously save for the fact that such statements are often espoused by otherwise sane men who have come to look upon science as a villain and technology as a criminal.

Solutions lie in other directions, not in denials of knowledge and intelligence, not in retreats from fact, not in suppressions of science. On the contrary, the logical equation at this point seems to me clear and obvious. If science has shown the way of solving some human problems, why is it not to be expected that an extension of science will serve to illuminate other problems not yet subjected to scientific scrutiny? Where is the flaw in the argument which states that the remedy for the difficulties which a partially scientific age has precipitated lies not in less but rather in more science?

There is, so it seems to me, no real flaw in this argument. The proposition that science can and should be extended to human and social affairs involves, nevertheless, a serious difficulty. The argument stated thus baldly is not sufficiently inclusive. It states the problem of life but not the problem of a good life. It defines the human situation in the language of means without ends. There are solid grounds for believing that science, when extended to the psychological and sociological realms, might produce a world without starvation and the fear of starvation, without war and the fear of war, but this might easily be a world populated by well-fed, well-housed, and well-clothed individuals, relieved from the basic insecurities which have bedeviled our age, and yet people lazy in spirit, aesthetically benumbed, and morally sterile.

The truth of the matter seems to be that science cannot fulfill itself. It can furnish the means but not the ends, the instruments but not the goals, the facts but not the values. The discipline of science is capable of carrying man to a high eminence, and also of leaving him there cold, lonely, and frightened. It may give him a healthier and a longer life, and an emptier one. The faith which we may and should place in science is a valid faith but an incomplete one since it cannot imbue life with meaning and purpose. Man does not live by facts alone. That which makes him human, endows his life with more than animal significance, and makes him a morally responsible being is fact infused with value.

This task of infusing facts with values, of discovering values and new sources of value, of bringing values into coherent relations with each other and with experience, is, initially at least, the obligation of philosophers. But, even if philosophers performed this function effectively, we should still be confronted with a cultural predicament: how are we to bring about a reconciliation, a working partnership between the humanistic discipline of philosophy on the one hand and science and technology on the other? We live at the moment in the midst of a bleak contradiction. The scientific pattern cannot merge with the philosophical pattern because the cultural pattern stands as barrier. The notion that science and philosophy are opposites, irreconcilable antitheses, is so deeply ingrained in our cultural habits that the very practitioners of these two disciplines are themselves the chief perpetuators of this myth. I doubt whether the ordinary man who is neither scientist nor philosopher would cling to this "nonorganic" conception if he did not hear the reiterated echo of the voices of dissident specialists. He, the ordinary man, would in that case look to his experience where he would surely discover that fact and value are the inseparable components of daily life. When he acts, he acts in pursuit of an end. To pursue an end is to posit a value. Or, in the language of the late Justice Oliver Wendell Holmes, "To act is to affirm the worth of an end, and to persist in affirming the worth of an end is to make an ideal."

Confronted with this awkward contradiction of modern life, some have reasoned that we must begin and end with the simple discrimination alluded to above, namely, that science represents the means of life, is its instrumental resource, while philosophy symbolizes the ends of life, the goals for which the means are to be utilized. Satisfied that they have now erected a plain and simple distinction, they proceed to regard this separation as a true antithesis. Some specialists will, then, in the light of this separation, deal with the means, and these will be called "scientists"; others will be concerned with ends, and their name shall be "philosophers," and never the twain shall meet. A convenient trick of language thus becomes first a tenet of belief and then an ingrained habit of thought and action. But means and ends cannot be so easily divorced. If we should turn for a moment from the beguiling symbolism of language and concentrate our attention on observations of actual behavior, we would soon realize that no such distinction between means and ends is permissible. In actual experience, we find ourselves involved in an unending sequence of responses in which means and ends are so intimately intermingled that it becomes impossible at any given moment to designate a unit of behavior as being wholly an "end" or a "means" operation.

> Show us not the aim without the way,
> For ends and means on earth are so entangled
> That changing one, you change the other too;
> Each different path brings other ends in view.[5]

No, I fear that there exists no such easy escape. Scientists cannot avoid responsibility by confining their attention solely to the "means" aspects of life, nor can philosophers be helpful if they continue to recommend ends which cannot be employed because there are no means, no mediating resources with which to move forward.

"The ends," said Ralph Waldo Emerson, "pre-exist in the means." And so they do. Psychologists will affirm this. They will demonstrate that organisms become what they do. The notion

[5] Ferdinand LaSalle, "Franz von Sickingen."

that good ends may be attained through the use of inappropriate or faulty or incompatible means is not merely false in terms of logic, but is an unscientific, rather, an antiscientific conception. At this point I find myself utilizing scientific and philosophical tools conjointly, and this is precisely what I intended to demonstrate. I have referred to science in order to validate a principle of philosophy, thus preparing the way for a fresh affirmation: Human problems are not scientific and philosophical; they are at one and the same time scientifically philosophical, or philosophically scientific. Every unit of behavior is a complex of ends and means, values and facts, purposes and methods.

Is it feasible to join these two disciplines, to put them to work on common problems, to harness science and philosophy in the interest of human welfare? Yes, I believe it is possible to place scientists and philosophers in a team relationship, to utilize both as joint problem-solvers, as collaborators. This goal cannot be reached, however, until both practicing scientists and philosophers are re-educated and future generations of scientists and philosophers are trained within the context of a new pattern of social responsibility. (A third personnel factor must be included in this equation, namely, administrators.) This, the educational outgrowth of my thesis, belongs to another occasion, and I shall content myself for the present by furnishing two illustrations from experience which demonstrate the worth as well as the difficulty of effecting such collaboration as I have proposed.

Some years past, I was asked to lead a conference of scientists who had been working for many months on a problem of serious importance to the people of the United States and of the world. They had been assigned the task of developing an annual type of sorghum (which is a perennial plant) to be used as a future source of sugar for human consumption. A part of the scientific and technological problem involved was to invent a processing method which would be capable of extracting the sugar content of the new sorghum economically. Both researches had reached the point of near completion, and my responsibility in this conference was to ask the scientists to discuss the following basic questions:

1. When, and in terms of what related factors, should the new sorghum seed be put on the market?

2. Should the processing inventions also be introduced to private enterprise and thus made part of competitive economy, or should these inventions remain the property of government?

3. What probable consequences would flow from the introduction of this new source of sugar, for (*a*) the beet-sugar industry; (*b*) the economies of foreign nations dependent upon cane sugar; and (*c*) the economies of those regions of the United States which are now predominantly tobacco- and cotton-growing areas, namely, the Southern and Southwestern states, the specific regions suitable for the cultivation of the new sorghum?

These questions were, patently, moral in character, or shot through and through with moral implications. They were, in short, philosophical questions, and as such the assembled scientists and technologists refused to accept their assignment. They insisted, and with fervor, that questions of this order ought never to be placed before scientists. They were all government employees, plant-breeders, chemists, physicists, engineers, that is, men trained as specialists who believed that their whole responsibility to themselves and to their government had come to an end. The consequences of their inventive work, they insisted, were to be regarded as a completely different problem which lay entirely outside the realm of their competence and their responsibility.

Finally, an appeal to sportsmanship led them to accept the assignment, but only if it were understood that they were acting outside their proper province and that the exercise should be considered as an extracurricular activity. The conclusions they ultimately reached were of a very high order. Whether or not these conclusions became the basis of public policy I am not able to state.

My second illustration is derived from a conference held at Columbia University in 1947. On this occasion the participants consisted of persons engaged in practical planning, employees of the Tennessee Valley Authority, municipal and regional planning bodies, technicians of social and economic planning, and teachers offering academic courses in planning. This group was balanced by a coterie of social scientists, psychologists, and a sprinkling of philosophers. The main discussions revolved about situations presented by the practical planners. I shall cite but one of these situations in order to indicate the interrelationship between philosophy and science.

In the Tennessee Valley live two farmers who are neighbors. In fact, their farms are on two sides of the same road. Farmer A. had adapted himself to planning, and his farm enterprise is operated under the discipline of some seven or eight contracts initiated by the TVA. As a result of these contracts, which constitute in essence a plan for his farm as well as for the region, Farmer A. made a net profit in one year of $6,000. His neighbor, Farmer B., resists the planning discipline. He refuses to have anything to do with the TVA. He will not sign a single contract. During the same year in which his neighbor cleared $6,000 from his enterprise, Farmer B. made a net profit of less than $400. The question which these practical planners thereupon placed in the laps of the social scientists and philosophers was: What is to be done with Farmer B.?

In this instance we are again confronted with the inevitable sequence. There comes a point at which all scientific and technological achievements are transmuted into moral or philosophical issues. We cannot escape this conclusion, but our educational indoctrination, that is, our culture, will not, as yet, permit us to act upon this knowledge.

The implications of what I have said are, I trust, clear, and they apply to all professions. But the profession of social work bears a peculiar relation to my thesis. It is a profession which, by definition, emanates from and exemplifies humanitarian faith. If social workers are not thus motivated, they must ultimately become cynics. Casework, group work, and community organization—the three major operational fields of social work—are all founded upon the assumption that science can help human beings to lead a better life by applying scientific principles to personal, individual, family, neighborhood, and community processes and situations. Practitioners trained to function in these various spheres of human adaptation and adjustment accumulate their subject matter and their techniques from many scientific and technical sources, inclusive of psychology, psychiatry, physiology, biology, medicine, sociology, anthropology, economics, social psychology, history, pedagogy, government, and, indeed, all disciplines which have attempted to reveal facts about human nature and social relationships.

The social worker's task is indeed one of broad inclusiveness but also of delicate refinements. A professional person who assumes the prerogative and the responsibility for conditioning the behavior of other human beings should possess skills of a high order. But such a person must achieve something more than technical proficiency. Those subtle personal and societal interrelationships with which he deals and which he strives to guide are the very stuff out of which human happiness or human tragedy emerge. Human relationships, are, in fact, the matrix of values.

As William James once pointed out, an isolated human being on a desert island would have few if any moral problems, but once he is joined by another human being, his whole life becomes fraught with moral issues. Social ethics is the consequence of human interactions, of human relations. Thus it happens that when a social worker interviews a prospective client he has taken a plunge into the realm of ethics. Even though his client is merely a citizen who has qualified for public assistance, what takes place between the social worker and the citizen constitutes a moral equation. At this point the intrusion of science, in the person of the trained social worker, disturbs the client's entire web of relationships, involving his status, his self-respect, his citizenship, his conception of responsibilities, in short, his philosophy of life. It therefore becomes unthinkable that a professional person trained in the techniques of human relations should be lacking in an understanding of philosophical insights and methods. In this profession, the practitioner must be both scientist and philosopher.

The New York School of Social Work has been a pioneering institution throughout its fifty years of existence. My personal pride in its achievements is heightened by the knowledge that during the last quarter century it has included in its curriculum courses in philosophy, thus demonstrating in practice what this essay has been proposing in theory.

I sincerely hope that the School and the profession which it serves will not, in their zeal to attain professional status, permit themselves to be separated from either the rigorous discipline of pure science or the humane influence of philosophy and the various arts. From these sources arises the faith which sustains our hope for a better world. In a university setting, the social studies may be thought of as the connecting link between the sciences and the humanities. The student thus equipped will become something more than a skilled craftsman, something more than a well-meaning idealist: he will become what universities have always sought to produce, namely, the cultured man or woman who is also useful to his time and place.

The World Moves toward Professional Standards in Social Work

SIR RAPHAEL CILENTO, M.D.

I HAVE BEEN ASKED TO OUTLINE the factors that seem to indicate that the world is moving toward professional standards. Perhaps it might be well at the outset to consider how the world itself, and particularly the New World, has moved in the fifty years since the foundation of the New York School of Social Work in 1898. That was, if you remember, the year in which Great Britain was contemplating her last major adventure in imperialism—an adventure that resulted in the Boer War, the annexation of the Cape Colony, Natal, and the Transvaal, and, within a few years, the establishment of the free, independent, and sovereign Union of South Africa within the British Commonwealth of Nations.

By contrast with the last great imperialistic adventure of Great Britain, you may recall, that same year 1898 saw the first widespread expansion of the United States of America overseas; the annexation of Puerto Rico, the Philippine Islands, and Guam by the Treaty of Paris; and the hoisting of the American flag over Wake and Midway Islands—setting a chain across the Pacific from east to west; and the preliminary discussions for the tripartite treaty with Britain and Germany, by which American Samoa—a point of dominance in the South Pacific—was also to fall under United States control in 1899. The people of Hawaii, pressed by a variety of circumstances, ceded the sovereignty of their islands (and a base for the control of the Northeast Pacific) to the United States in 1898, so that in many ways 1898 was a point of departure for major political and social activities.

During the next fifteen years, the United States saw the greatest flood of immigration in history, which reached its peak in 1907 and provided the country with huge numbers of masterless men, crowded out by the pressure of population against subsistence in the Old World and turning hopefully to the New World and its immense opportunities. The situation was a new one for the New World; it was an old one for the Old World; and it is still producing reactions here which (with due allowance for time and circumstance) are like those that occurred in the fifteenth and sixteenth centuries in England during the reigns of the cold and calculating Henry VII, and the much married Henry VIII and his three children, Edward VI, Queen Mary, and Queen Elizabeth.

In that period, too, there had been a financial, economic, and ideological revolution in all Europe. It had been produced by many factors, among others, the closure of trade to the East by the capture of Constantinople by the Mohammedans, and the blocking of the sea and land routes; the discovery of America; the Renaissance, the Reformation, and the religious wars; while in England itself the repercussions of these great events had included, among other results, the confiscation of the monasteries, chantries, and almshouses by the King, and distribution of them and their dependent peasants by favor or by purchase; a fantastic rise in prices; a great flow of population to the cities; and a great increase in unemployment. Throughout most of Europe, however, there had been a change quite as fundamental as the economic revolution: the defeat of the Church and the replacing of the Church and its social philosophy by the State and its social philosophy.

The great influx of unemployed and masterless men to the cities produced problems of the greatest urgency. They had passed from the subsistence-level sufficiency of meager peasant life, and the social institutions of the family and the village church, to the double insecurity of the cities, to a situation where, with insufficient individual or collective purchasing power, they were a greater and greater burden upon the body politic.

Statesmen, influenced partly by the humanitarianism of the

Renaissance, partly by the religious reformers, partly by the ambition to gather into their own hands all the threads of social administration, and partly by the danger from the growing resentment of the increasing mass of the unemployed, set themselves to organize a secular system of poor relief to replace the Church system that had been destroyed. In other words, they set themselves, as we are setting ourselves, to reorganize civilization in order to steer it through a dangerous period of transition between conflicting economic and social ideologies.

Before we develop this point in terms of the twentieth century, however, let us recall the social theories of the sixteenth century by paraphrasing, with apologies and my own modifications, some of the ideas so ably set out by R. H. Tawney in his book *Religion and the Rise of Capitalism.*

Society, as late as the fifteenth and sixteenth centuries, was still regarded as a pyramid of all mankind, embracing all human interests and activities, with religion as its apex. The most common simile for corporate society was the human body. Like the human body, human society was grouped into members with different functions, each entitled to receive the means suited to his station in the whole plan, and forbidden to claim more. Within each group there must obviously be equality between individuals, but between the different groups or members it was just as essential that there should be inequality, since otherwise a group could not perform its unique functions or enjoy its different and unique rights. "Hand helps head, and eye helps foot, and foot helps body, and thus should it be in all parts of the Church," says a medieval preacher, "and if one part leave his work that God hath given him and take the work of another part, sinful wonder is in the Church." As a basis of social policy, this doctrine was at once productive and repressive.

So far as social relationships and social institutions were concerned, the Church, embracing all mankind, had obviously complete and final authority, and no matter how Catholics, Anglicans, Lutherans, and Calvinists differed on points of doctrine, Luther and Calvin, Latimer and Laud, John Knox and the Pilgrim Fathers were all emphatically agreed on one point: social policies and social morality were exclusively the province of the Church!

Right from the fourth to the fourteenth centuries, indeed, the Christian basis of social work or voluntary service to others had been partly a means to perfect one's own personality, and partly a means by which the almsgiver "made Heaven his debtor." "If there were no poor," said St. Chrysostom, "the greater part of your sins would never be excused; it is the poor who are the healers of your wounds." This last produced an outlook that had behind it neither the knowledge nor the moral energy required for the institution of programs of regulated and organized relief directed toward the improvement of the individuals of the social groups that needed relief.

The defeat of the Church and its social philosophy reversed the whole machinery of medieval charity, with its mendicant orders, its fraternities, its festivals and pilgrimages, and its idea that merit could be acquired by almsgiving. It not only rejected the view that almsgiving was meritorious in itself, and that the mendicant was an opportunity "to make Heaven one's debtor," but it insisted that indiscriminate almsgiving depraved the depressed classes still further.

Basing itself on St. Paul's admonition that he who would not work should not eat, the secular State sought to stamp out mendicancy and, at the same time, to correct unemployment by rigorous measures of repression. In three generations it succeeded in demonstrating only that vagrancy was not produced merely by innate idleness, but was an inevitable consequence of faulty economic adjustment, and that the whip had no corrective influence on men who must either beg or starve.

Meanwhile, the social worker, seeking as always to approximate principle and practice, had sought, as early as the reign of Edward VI, to determine the basic essentials required for a reorganization of society in the light of the newly accepted principles. If, in fact, the State was to find its justification, not in religion, but in the so-called "laws of nature"—in plain words, in the necessity for mutual protection and the need for mutual assistance—and if the acquisitive instinct was not to be rejected as the sinful basis of usury but was to be considered a vital and essential social dynamic, the object of society became a rational regulation of economic endeavor, extending to all levels of the community. The idleness of the mendicant must be considered a social evil as well as a sin against God, and the enterprise of the tradesman was at once a Christian virtue and a social benefit. Conduct was to be governed essentially by the very letter of the law, and the law was to be modified to meet changing circumstances.

In theory, schools, hospitals, and asylums for the aged were to be established in every town, and provision was to be made, not for the maintenance of a fixed hierarchy with religion as its apex, and salvation as its sole objective, but for a scientific series of separate and parallel activities—political, commercial, devotional—between which a due balance must obviously be maintained, but without vital connection one with another. Social work was to reject that promiscuous charity that corrupted both the giver and the recipient, and was to concern itself with aspects of education, health, and employment—a significant subdivision—and was to be based upon the theory that true charity involves the development in every individual of an industry and a self-denial that makes relief unnecessary.

By the year 1600 there had been instituted a chain of measures and enactments to control prices, to control food supplies, to stabilize employment, to check unnecessary dismissals of workmen, to prevent evictions, to establish funds for providing employment or for aiding struggling tradesmen. An enormous amount of private effort was also directed to the re-establishment of almshouses and hospitals. New colleges were founded, and universities were further endowed. Moreover, the first strong effort was made to organize the medical profession, which, indeed, had won from King Henry its first recognition as a profession. As the last link in the chain, the social reformers brought under the State the control of the indigent poor in the celebrated series of acts of Queen Elizabeth which, amongst other provisions, first imposed a compulsory poor rate and required judges and local authorities to "set to work all sturdy beggars and vagrants."

In fifty years the social theories of the Church had already become antiquated, and the social theorists of the time had pinned their faith to the possibility of establishing a controlled economy. It is true that they had adopted the attitude toward this objective of one who hopes to hold a wolf by the ears! Their fears were realized. It is the essence of trade to push the acquisitive appetite into a position of solitary dominance, and the sixteenth century was no exception. Every opportunist already had his teeth in the body politic. The economic urge broke the grip of the theorists, and the wolf was out among the rabbits.

Theories that replace those upon which Church and State have both been established for many centuries cannot be replaced in practice by other theories merely on the basis of logic, and during the uncertainties of any period of ideological conflict, perhaps more than at any other time, men take the road of self-interest. The demonstration that unemployment was largely due to economic causes was accepted with indifference, and with little sense that the victims of economic causes had a legal right to be safeguarded by society. The procedures for social reform collapsed in practice, and were subordinated to political and economic exigencies, in virtue of the acceptance, as the guiding principle of national life, of the doctrine of economic expediency.

Three hundred years ago, in 1648, the Treaty of Westphalia ended the last of the religious wars in Europe, and set the stage for the first of the wars of economic nationalism. The same year saw the end of the English Civil War, the trial of Charles I, and the rise of the Commonwealth of Cromwell. It saw also the collapse of the public and private schemes for social welfare, poor relief, and the maintenance of employment. It was followed by a marked decline for a century in education, health, and procedures for the protection of labor, and the loss of almost all professional safeguards in the social field. The policy of England, along with that of all her European competitors, was based on a ruthless materialism which was determined at all costs to wrest from other nations the markets of the world, and to secure, by colonial expansion, the spheres of interest and the great sources of raw materials that had been brought to notice by the rise and fall of Spain and Portugal.

The identity of human nature throughout the centuries produces a broad identity of pattern; and where economic or ideological circumstances produce a new transitional period, public apprehension provokes a political solicitude that results in broad, placatory, and stereotyped measures—measures which avoid the essentials of the situation because the essentials defy control. The crisis of the seventeenth century and the crisis of the twentieth century have many features in common, but they have this great difference: the Old World watered down the urgency of social reform with the aid of colonial expansion in a half-empty world; the world of today is gripped within the confines of a continually shrinking, interdependent economic structure. Essentially, however, the situation is the same, and the stereotyped measures required for its correction comprise all the measures we include under the general heading of social amelioration, with perhaps the added factor that there appears this time to be no escape from the necessity of finding an immediate solution, and not one spread over three centuries.

It is quite inevitable that the solution required should embrace all those activities that lie between the recognized fields of health, education, and labor that we call "social welfare."

It was not at random that I mentioned the great expansion in the political field that had marked the progress of the United States of America since 1898. The position that this country is called upon to occupy during the present period of economic and ideological transition is a natural consequence of her economic and geographical situation vis-à-vis the countries of the Old World, and particularly those which were the cradle of modern civilization as we know it.

Similarly, it is not for nothing that social welfare has taken greater strides toward professional status, and indeed a more inclusive as well as a more exclusive view of its scope in the United States than has been the case in older countries where, as the result of the logic of events, the term is still most commonly used as a generalization for the less-defined or marginal aspects of education, health, and labor. Social work and social institutions in the United States are an expression, naturally enough, of what is known as the "American way of life," motivated by the ideology on which that way of life is founded. There is not the slightest doubt that in the United States the assumption that social work is a profession and, indeed, a great and growing profession, is accepted as self-evident. It is also obvious that the solution of the present ills of the world must be found by the newest of its nations, and pre-eminently by the United States of America and the Union of Soviet Socialist Republics. It is, therefore, of particular importance and significance that there appears to be a wide divergence between the viewpoints of these two great powers in respect of social work and its significance.

Let us, however, consider the points that determine professional status and, while accepting them for the United States (where since 1945 at least one state has legislated for the registration of social workers on a professional basis), consider how they are regarded in other parts of the world. We require answers, perhaps, to the following six questions:

1. Has social work a well-defined scope and function, with a content and method peculiarly its own?

2. Is the practice of social work limited, or is it tending to be limited, by local or professional regulation, to persons with approved professional training?

3. Is there, in fact, a systematic and standardized training that insures competence in certain well-defined subjects and skills which are recognized as obviously the province of the profession of social work?

4. Is the required training recognized as appropriate for inclusion in the curricula of universities on an equality with other recognized professional studies?

5. Does the compensation received by the social worker indicate his acceptance by the community as a member of a recognized profession?

6. Is there a philosophy permeating the profession that transcends sectarian, political, and geographical boundaries?

For the United States of America there is no question that social work is acquiring, or has acquired, professional status, and there is a tendency in the same direction in every country influenced by the United States and its literature. Elsewhere, however, the situation is not so well defined.

Recently, one of my colleagues in the Division of Social Activities of the United Nations Secretariat undertook to examine for me the views of member nations on the professional and economic status and the training of social workers in their countries. The replies have been extraordinarily interesting and revealing. Nations in which community life is based upon the family, or in which community life is based upon religion, have an essentially different social outlook from those in which social work is based, as a normal feature of life, upon acceptance of certain civic responsibilities.

In response to an inquiry as to the significance of the terms "social work" and "social worker," one Arab State replied, like an echo from our own earliest centuries: "Our social administration and our social services are governed by the Koran which, as you may not know, is the sacred book upon which all Moslems base their lives and institutions."

One Latin American country defined "social workers" as "society women who devote their money and their leisure time to helping the poor." Another country with Spanish traditions provided three concepts of extreme interest. The first, which was widespread, is as follows: "The social worker is a person active in the raising of funds for charity, and the prominence of the social worker is measured by the amount of money he or she is able to raise." The second, equally widespread, was: "Social work is an activity directed primarily toward acts of charity for unfortunate members of society: it is palliative rather than constructive"; while the conception held by those few professional social workers who are influenced by the literature of the United States had the following familiar phrasing: "Social work is a professional service for the purpose of assisting people as individuals or groups to attain a satisfying standard of life and personal adjustment . . ."

Let me interpolate from personal observation made during a

recent visit to a few Latin American republics some recollections of conflict in views as to social policy. Some of those governments were desirous of instituting organized social welfare services based on New World conceptions of social work, with a standardized course of training, standardized examinations, and ready fields for service in the rapidly growing industrialized areas of the country.

The attitude adopted by several of the dominant families, however, was one of flat refusal of any suggestion that social work should be other than voluntary, or other than a spiritual exercise to perfect the character and conscience of the social worker herself. The suggestion that they should coöperate in this regard with the government was equally unacceptable. One woman, head of a large school of social science, quoted to me the Biblical aphorism: "Render unto Caesar that which is Caesar's, and unto God that which is God's." Pressed by me, she admitted that her school, which could take fifty pupils, had no more than twenty, owing to the severity of selection; that selection was based upon conformity in certain religious particulars indicating vocation; that of all the young women who had completed the course in the last fifteen years, only six were still working in established schools with groups of student learners; and that wherever one of these leaders died, left, or was married, the local organization concerned simply collapsed.

The suggestion that the State might give authority and permanence to the work she had so much at heart, was answered by this head of a school with the statement that States were transient and this work was eternal, irrespective of the contradiction between her statement and the actual facts of performance. When I pursued the subject further and suggested that the universities, at any rate, had a permanent mission and might offer an excellent alliance for this work, she rejected the suggestion even more violently on the ground that such an association would make social work a career, and possibly might even lead to professional registration and all the evils associated with such a change of approach! Here, in 1948, was the viewpoint of 1498.

Nevertheless, this almost perfect survival from the Middle

Ages is not so remote from reality as it might appear. In some ways, social thought has rounded the circle. Economic expediency has discredited itself by the results achieved when it operates unchallenged, and there is beginning to be in some lands a vigorous reversal toward the practice of social work upon a mystical or spiritual basis, just as in some other countries there is a vigorous drive toward organization on a professional basis in the interests of economy and efficiency. Political propaganda by means of the social approach has also begun to appear as an unwelcome attendant, or even a dominant factor, in social action in several countries.

The long history of social service in the United Kingdom, and the process over generations by which the content of what in the United States is called "social work," was considered to be sufficiently distributed among the subjects of health, labor, and education, leads many intelligent people, other than social workers, throughout England and in other members of the British Commonwealth of Nations to regard social work, at the worst, as an aberrant expression of what should normally be included in the better-recognized professions; and, at the best, as well-intentioned work characterized unhappily by a considerable degree of amateurishness and lack of efficiency.

This widespread misunderstanding of the professional nature of social work services produces a situation where, as one English report said: "It is not an uncommon experience for a voluntary agency to have a person recommended as a potential social worker, either on the score that he or she is not technically qualified for any other profession, or even, that he has problems of his own to meet!" It is also to the point that the United Kingdom, in its magnificent expansion of the social services controlled by the government, appears to have made no deliberate provision within its civil service for any great increase of recruitment or employment of trained social workers in those services. Yet in terms of population, these services are easily among the greatest in the world. However, there is at least one other viewpoint, and it has been voiced by various Eastern European powers. They have taken the stand that the very definition of social work condemns it as an activity per se. If it is necessary to make a highly paid and widespread profession of an activity that is intended to assist people as individuals or groups to attain a satisfying standard of life and personal adjustment, this is a gross reflection on the political or economic system. It is quite unjustifiable, they say, to allocate to an individual profession and the private practitioners of it, working in many instances for profit, the responsibilities that are so obviously the basic and fundamental purpose of any properly motivated government.

In brief, therefore, on this one question alone, the preliminary indications are that social work may be regarded as: (*a*) an individual family responsibility; (*b*) an individual and community obligation, based upon a religious duty; (*c*) the basic purpose of government, requiring no specific isolation; (*d*) an expression of the marginal activities between the health, labor, and educational aspects of social work, and sufficiently covered by extensions of those activities; and (*e*) a specific area of the social field outside the health, labor, and educational aspects, with an identity, a content, and a method of work peculiarly its own.

This last conception, which is undoubtedly appropriate to the special problems of the present transitional period, is appealing increasingly to intelligent workers in many lands. One point of identity that stands out amongst these different conceptions should, however, be mentioned. The term "social work" is recognized as applying to services, whether administered by statutory or voluntary bodies or both, that are designed to promote the well-being of those members of the community who, for any reason, require special protection and assistance, and where the services in question, whether they exist as such, are either exclusively, or primarily, or frequently directed toward solving problems associated with, or created by, poverty.

If, after this lengthy dissertation, we take the second question —"Is the practice of social work limited, by legal or professional regulation, to persons with approved professional training?"— we find again that while this is indeed the tendency, it has by no means been achieved; and, moreover, that in many places the urge of the best members of the profession toward that desirable aim is defeated by governmental and other agencies in the very process of seeking to implement new laws that require the provision of trained social aid of various kinds.

In a few Latin American countries I found that laws directly derived from United States inspiration had been placed on the statute books. Manufacturers had been called upon to do certain things, but, with the best will in the world, they could not perform their statutory obligations because of the absence of trained personnel. By tacit agreement, they have either ignored the law, or appointed completely untrained persons to figurehead positions. This difficulty is a serious one in all countries, particularly since the war.

No great gulf yawns between the trained and the untrained social worker, like the gulf that separates the registered lawyer or the registered physician from unqualified persons in those professions. In fact, it may be true, as is sometimes claimed, that there are occasionally untrained social workers who are more effective in the practice of their craft than many badly chosen but adequately trained social workers. It is true that those who are good without training will be even better with training, and that it is fantastically wasteful to allow people to discover by trial and error, at the expense of the public, what they could learn through training. Moreover, while one must take into account the need to protect the community from the fumbling and often harmful administrations of untrained social workers, one must also realize the discredit that these bring upon the profession itself.

There is still another point:

I recently read an article on the legalizing of professional social workers which contained the following statement: "The lawyer, the physician, the clergyman (or anyone else) may, with legal impunity, invade the field of social work, and commit acts which, in the opinion of qualified social workers, are lamentable errors." The boot is not always on that foot. There are many social workers, trained and untrained, who suffer from an overadventurous spirit and provoke antagonism by rushing in where the lawyer, the doctor, the clergyman, the teacher, the labor inspector, or some other operative, who actually has the acquired right, has on the soundest of grounds decided to take no action. Such well-meant instrusions not only handicap the acceptance of the social worker as a professional and ethical colleague, but provoke others to proclaim the right to territories that the social worker might legitimately aspire to possess.

The situation with regard to training presents two points for consideration. On the one hand there appears to be considerable acceptance, among people directly concerned with the administration of social welfare programs, of the conviction that special training is essential for the persons who perform the relevant social welfare functions. The second and opposite view, reaching back into the traditions of the past, that a "sense of vocation" was sufficient to insure the competence of the social worker, perhaps explains some of the reluctance of businessmen, politicians, and others, to admit the need for professionally trained workers in social work activities.

The answers we are receiving to our questions show that there is wide divergence in formal practice also. Some countries insist that a certain type of social work should be performed only by fully trained persons; others, that the same work shall be performed by partially trained persons; and still others, that the same work shall be performed by persons with no training whatever; while the anomalous situation existing in certain countries permits the same social work to be performed by fully trained, or partially trained, or quite untrained persons, depending on whether they are employed by this agency or that.

While it is true that the shortage of trained personnel and the great limitation of resources for training may be responsible for much of this confusion between theory and practice, there is a real danger in its continuance. Wherever untrained persons are accepted for social work activities, the door is open to political patronage and nepotism, or plain indifference, and the profession itself suffers an obvious and an occult depreciation greatly to be deplored. There is an old proverb which says "bad currency drives out good," and it is nowhere more apparent than in the early days of the establishment of any profession seeking to base itself on ethical standards. It is therefore regrettable that ideas as to what constitutes adequacy of training are far from uniform, either from the quantitative or from the qualitative point of view. It is true that there appears to be a strong and growing conviction that formal training in a full-time course of theory and related practice in an approved educational institution is a prerequisite for professional social work, and the attitude of universities is significant. Some universities accept social science as a "certificate" course only. Others go further and provide a degree. Some universities provide both, but mere acceptance is significant. One of the essentials, it would appear, on the march toward professional recognition is to establish absolute standards as to the basic preparation required for social work, and to insist that these shall not be modified except after the most careful consideration and acceptance of the proposed change.

The situation with regard to the economic status of the social worker is similarly variable. Members of professions are not, it is true, motivated primarily by the expectation of large economic rewards. There is usually a very real sense of service. Nevertheless, professional people who spend considerable time and money on their training have certain legitimate expectations regarding their future standard of living; but sentiment and tradition on the part of the public still promote a tendency to assume that the social worker is a person who has dedicated himself or herself to the work without regard to appropriate economic return. In most countries the situation is not satisfactory, and the predominance of women in the field is partly the result of the low salary offered, partly a cause of it, and partly an argument for those who consider social work the field of the sentimental amateur. Something of a vicious circle is created by this situation.

As to the question of the permeation of the whole profession by a philosophy that transcends sectarian, political, and geographical boundaries, I feel that I need to say nothing.

In this very sketchy survey I have deliberately emphasized the gaps and the deficiencies, because I think they should be emphasized, and because I feel that it is a healthy, if somewhat disturbing, exercise to shift the spotlight from the home scene to less familiar but equally important fields. I have deliberately avoided specific reference to the achievements and the progress made in this country.

I think we should pause for a moment to recollect how, in 1898, the first six weeks' summer institute for social workers from all parts of the United States was sponsored in New York City by the Committee on Philanthropic Education; how practicing social workers, with indefatigable industry, gained recognition from the universities and an incentive for unifying the profession under one educational discipline with the establishment in 1919 of what is now the American Association of the Schools of Social Work. We should recall also how, several years later, in 1932, equally intense and devoted efforts resulted in the establishment of the first basic minimum curriculum, ultimately binding on all member schools; and the establishment in 1939 of the requirement that they should operate on a graduate level for professional education. There is still much to be done, as the Curriculum Committee of the Association indicated in its operations from 1941 to 1944 when attempting to establish its eight fields of basic knowledge, and as is shown in the continuing, earnest reexamination to authenticate and to define even more precisely the content of the subject.

No one can fail to appreciate the difficulty of striking a happy balance between an exclusive formalism and an overinclusive exuberance. The fact that the idea of social work developed from the gradual coördination and correlation of services to particular groups—infant and maternal welfare; indigents and dependents; delinquents and other persons maladjusted socially; the aged; the handicapped; and other underprivileged groups—does not obscure the ultimate concept of social activity, which can perhaps be said to be the constant and enlightened endeavor to insure that the influence of the individual upon the community, and of the community upon the individual, shall be toward a constantly improving standard of living.

Similarly, however, one must constantly bear in mind the fact that this is also the essential aim that inspires the best practitioners in the health, the educational, the legal, the labor, and the religious fields, and that social work, as a specific entity, will fail unless, with all these, it makes a complete, coördinated, and mutually coöperative pattern of effort.

The item that has given me most assurance in the present investigations into this subject being carried out by my officers and colleagues among the member nations of the United Nations has been the fact that almost all the countries that have replied to our questionnaire have evidenced an earnest preoccupation with this very question and, as a corollary, with the question of the content of the subject; the question of the basic essentials of training; and the question of the clarification of the functions of the social worker in order that they may be susceptible to legal definition for their certification or registration on a professional basis.

Intensive studies on the matter of training are actually being made in several other countries, in Norway, in South Africa, and in the United Kingdom, as well as in the United States; training facilities are spreading apace—there are already 275 educational institutions listed by us, that are offering facilities for social work training in twenty-nine of the fifty-seven member countries of the United Nations, and other schools are projected; national associations of social workers are being organized with enthusiasm in countries that have only recently entered the social welfare field, and congresses on social services have been held in these and in other countries.

Perhaps one of the most significant features is the fact that the greatest interest is being shown in countries that have the greatest economic or demographic problems, for it is obvious that these nations are looking with new hope of solution to the inclusion among their existing executives of professionally trained workers in the social field.

The increasing intensity of the internal and the external problems of human relationships, blown to a white heat by the incidents of the last thirty-five years, justified the assumption that the most urgent question before all men of good will today is the matter of social amelioration. Active endeavor for social amelioration has, several times in history, begun on the basis of fervid enthusiasms for the development in every man of the best of which he is capable; the constant threat is that its enthusiasm may be tempered by perfunctory performance until its aim is to teach adaptation, and indeed resignation, to a routine level of existence one degree above stagnation. The essential factor for the maintenance of efficiency and progress in social work is its organization along professional lines on bases of knowledge and vital sincerity; its danger lies in its organization along professional lines on bases of piecemeal expediency plus a sort of pharisaical formalism.

It is not too much to say that the eyes of the world are upon social work, and that the heavy responsibility that rests upon its advocates and practitioners is to show first that it is truly "social" and, secondly, that it "works"; and, moreover, that it has within itself the flexibility and the potentialities to cope successfully with all the problems of human life and endeavor, as one by one they emerge, more and more definitely, from the social confusion of our present period of transition.

International Horizons for Health and Welfare

GEORGE F. DAVIDSON

IN THINKING OVER what can usefully be said on such a subject as this, one cannot ignore the almost universal preoccupation with the much larger international issues which face the world today. These are insecure and troublous times in which we live. Not only social workers, but men and women everywhere are deeply concerned with the problem of security in all its many aspects. Social workers think of the problem as one of social security. But let us not forget that twice within our lifetime, twice within a generation, mankind has fought a bloody war. And for what? To establish peace and security in our way of life, in all its many aspects.

Our lives as individuals, as communities, and as nations are, in fact, bound up increasingly with this struggle for security: security of our national existence; security from the threats of those hostile forces outside our boundaries who would do harm to us and to our ways of life. What is it that we have been seeking to achieve, through two world wars, if not security for the nation, security for the people of the nation, security from outside aggression? And at the same time, what is it that we seek through our departments of health and welfare, through our Federal security agencies, through our entire network of Federal, state, and local organizations, if it is not, once again, security for the nation, security for the people of the nation, against certain hazards, certain risks and threats—coming this time, perhaps, from within the nation—over which the individual has no control?

These social and economic dangers from within are perhaps

not so startlingly obvious as the threat of danger that comes from outside a nation's boundaries. Yet, who is there to say that for the average individual, or for his family, bullets are more of a menace than microbes; or that the hazards of social and economic security may not prove to be even more destructive, in their insidious way, to the fabric of our family and our national life than the threat to our national security through aggression from outside our borders?

These questions, of course, can have no final answer. What emerges clearly is that the problem of achieving security for a nation is in reality a many-sided one. It is social, economic, political, and military, all at the same time. We fight this battle for security on many fronts; and we, as health and welfare workers, do well to remember that each one of us has an important part to play in securing, for the common people of our nations, that kind of society in which we all want to live—a peaceful and truly democratic society that offers security to all without restricting freedom or weakening initiative or opportunity.

This quest for security—social, economic, political, and military—is today not merely a matter of national concern in our respective countries. In addition to being a major, if not *the* major objective of many governments today, in terms of their domestic and internal policies, this quest for security, it becomes increasingly clear, is our major preoccupation in the international field as well. We have traditionally recognized the importance of the purely political and military factors in the international field. These have for centuries been the governing factors in the shaping of international relationships and alignments. Not until very recently have we begun to realize that in addition to political and military considerations, social and economic factors likewise play a large part in predisposing the peoples of the world to peaceful and coöperative ways of life—or, failing that, to friction, violence, and unrest which oftentimes break out beyond controlling, and lead to open war.

This recognition of the importance of social and economic factors in the international field is, I repeat, a development of fairly recent times. It has certainly come about within the last hundred years. It was the Industrial Revolution which, in fact, first set fully in motion those forces which led to countries bursting forth from their bonds of economic self-containment into a new world, a new order of society characterized by the economic interdependence of states rather than, as formerly, by their economic independence. From national economic self-sufficiency, we have moved through an intermediate stage of economic imperialism into what may be regarded as an era of economic internationalism.

Coinciding with these developments in the economic field were other changes stemming likewise from the Industrial Revolution, namely, the development of organized community health and welfare measures. It is not, of course, a mere accident that the development of these organized health and welfare activities, first of all by private agencies and later by governments, has coincided with the progress of the Industrial Revolution. Organized health and welfare activities began in the cities and towns. These cities and towns were themselves created by the very need of the new industrial techniques and processes for large concentrations of manpower at strategic points throughout the country. It was this haphazard, ill-planned concentration of masses of the population in cities and towns for the first time to meet the manpower needs of the new industrial era that led, in large part, to the emergence of health and welfare needs; then to the recognition of these needs; and finally to the provision of services to meet these needs wherever they might arise throughout the whole community.

The history of the development of health and welfare measures during this past century is also a story of the transfer of responsibility from private to public agencies and, in the public agency field, from the lower to the higher levels of government. One of the most consistent trends in the evolution of our concepts of responsibility for the development of health and welfare services is this trend which consists of lifting financial and administrative responsibilities for health and welfare measures increasingly from the shoulders of private agencies and the smaller units of government, and placing these responsibilities increasingly on the higher units of government. So forceful indeed is this trend, and so consistently clear-cut in its direction, that I like to think of it as the "upward thrust" of responsibility from the grass roots to the higher units of government in our respective states.

This is a common characteristic of all states which today are in the process of developing a modern program of health and welfare services. It does not seem to matter whether it be a federal state like the United States or Canada, or whether it be a unitary state like the United Kingdom or New Zealand—the trend is still the same. Likewise, it does not seem to matter whether the form of government be democratic or totalitarian, capitalist, socialist, or even communist—the same trend is still there, the only difference being the speed with which it may be able or may be encouraged to develop.

This upward thrust of responsibility in the health and welfare field has led us through a variety of phases. First of all, we concentrated this responsibility in the hands of private, religious, or philanthropic groups, through which developed our network of organized voluntary community welfare services. Then, increasingly, we shifted the burden to the local authorities of our cities, towns, and municipalities. From there, the upward thrust continued to our provincial or our state levels of government as health and welfare needs became greater and the resources of our local authorities less and less adequate to meet them. Finally, the last two decades have seen the remorseless, seemingly inevitable continuation of this upward thrust from the state to the Federal level.

Who can look back a quarter of a century or so in the history of the development of his country's health and welfare services (whether it be Canada or the United States) and fail to be impressed by the extent to which first the states and latterly, within the memory of all of us, the federal governments have taken over increasingly the financial and the administrative responsibilities for insuring adequate health and welfare measures to the people of our respective nations? In the light of these developments, is it surprising that we should now be witnessing, as it were, a further projection of this upward thrust into the international field?

For my own part, I regard our current interest in international social welfare and health programs as but a logical and inevitable development of the policies which have evolved in our respective countries during these last few decades. We can now at last, I think, begin to perceive the first dim outline of an international health and welfare policy which, if properly and wisely developed, will serve as the culminating point of this upward thrust of responsibility; and which will supplement and strengthen our respective national programs in the same way that our national programs themselves add to and strengthen the effectiveness of undertakings carried through on provincial, state, or local levels.

I would not, of course, suggest for a moment that the signs pointing in the direction of an awakened interest in the field of international health and welfare policy are all of recent origin. That would be far from the truth. Both on the voluntary and on the governmental levels, we have had for some time examples of planning and organization of programs beyond merely national boundaries. The international ramifications of programs such as those of the Young Men's Christian Association or the Salvation Army are too well known to require elaboration. The work of the International Red Cross is again a case in point. A few scattered examples such as these may be found extending back before the first World War. I think, however, that it would be fair to say that the first real landmarks of organized governmental concern for health and welfare policies on the international level are to be found in the developments leading immediately out of the first World War. The establishment of the International Labor Organization and the creation of the League of Nations, with its Health Section and its Advisory Committee on Social Questions, were all steps of profound significance. They heralded for almost the first time the partnership of governments in the development of means by which international collaboration could be made effective in the health and welfare field.

At long last, with the machinery for collaboration now firmly established on both the voluntary and the intergovernmental levels, it began to be apparent that the importance of economic and social factors in the promotion of peace and security throughout the world, and in the prevention of war, was gaining ever increasing recognition. This was and is the temper of the times; and the developments which have taken place since the end of the first World War have only served to demonstrate with increasing clarity the growing importance of social and economic questions both in our national and our international communities.

The achievements of the International Labor Organization and of the Health Section of the League of Nations during the interwar years provide some of the brighter spots in what is otherwise a sorry and discouraging tale of frustration in our efforts to achieve genuine international collaboration. Through mechanisms such as these, facilities were established which have made possible the fruitful exchange of information and the establishment of standards between nations with respect to health and welfare matters. The League of Nations, despite its many failures, has left a legacy for which we may yet be grateful in the machinery it established through its Health Section and through its Advisory Committee on Social Questions for exchanging information on health and welfare matters. The International Labor Organization established in a host of fields, through its Conventions and its recommendations, standards which are now regarded as minimum civilized standards throughout the world. Fortunately, too, the International Labor Organization survived the downfall of the League of Nations and continues its work today, tested and tried over a quarter of a century, recognized as a seasoned, experienced, and authoritative body in the field of international social policy. There can be no doubt that the practical results of the work of these bodies during the years between the wars has resulted in an immense advance for all humanity.

One other indication of the development of our international awareness in the health and welfare field was the establishment, in 1928, of the International Conference of Social Work. The Conference met first in Paris in 1928, then in Frankfurt-on-Main in 1932, and again in London in 1936. In April of 1948, in Atlantic City and New York, it concluded its Fourth Session, a session made significant by the fact that it was the first to be held since the interruption of the second World War, and likewise the first to be held outside Europe. These international conferences provide another channel of communication between the health and welfare workers of the various countries of the world, a channel which is useful in familiarizing representatives of many nations with the measures and procedures in force or under consideration in other countries than their own.

In the field of health, the work of these international organizations was more than matched by the freest possible interchange of information and of personnel. The interest shown by each nation in what was going on in other nations was greater in health and welfare than in any other field except that of war.

I come now to the final stage of our development to date—the very significant progress that has been made since the end of the second World War. This progress centers, of course, in the United Nations, which, in the various clauses of its charter, as well as in its organization, planning, and structure, has underscored as never before the vital importance of international collaboration in the area of health and welfare. It must be heartening indeed for health and welfare leaders everywhere to realize that recognition is at last being given to their spheres of effort. The Charter of the United Nations, written and subscribed to by the governments of most of the countries of the civilized world, proclaimed in the creation of the Economic and Social Council, side by side with the Security Council, the conviction in the hearts of many thousands, even millions, of people that international collaboration in economic and social fields can achieve as much as or even more than political or military activity in removing those points of friction which ultimately lead to war.

Let us see now what has been accomplished in the three years that have elapsed since the drafting of the United Nations Charter in San Francisco in May of 1945:

1. The Economic and Social Council of the United Nations has come into being and has already held six sessions during the two and a half years of its existence. It stands recognized as potentially the most important agency yet established to deal with matters in the field of international social and economic policy. While the hopes of those who created it are far from being ful-

filled as yet, it stands today as an agency with a vast potential for constructive, creative effort in its particular field.

2. The World Health Organization has been brought into being; and, after a waiting period of almost two years, it is now ready to pass from the Interim Commission stage to its full stature as the recognized intergovernmental organization in the health field. The establishment of the WHO to carry on where the Health Section of the League of Nations had left off emerged from the San Francisco Conference as one of the matters which the nations there regarded as being of the highest and most urgent priority. No less than sixty-three nations of the world (more than the membership of the United Nations itself) attended the World Health Conference in June, 1946, where the constitution of the WHO was drafted.

3. The Social Commission of the United Nations has likewise been established by the Economic and Social Council to act in a technical advisory capacity on all matters relating to international social policy. The Social Commission is, of course, a subordinate organ of the United Nations itself, not an autonomous, intergovernmental agency like the WHO. Likewise, it is not in any sense an operating agency, but its position in the field of international social welfare policy corresponds, roughly at least, to the position which will be occupied by the WHO in the field of international health policy.

4. Other United Nations commissions have likewise been established to deal with matters falling within the broad areas of health and social policy: the Population Commission, the Narcotics Commission, the Commission on Human Rights, the Commission on the Status of Women, and the Economic and Employment Commission. The relationship of these specific problems to the broad area of social policy in the international field is too obvious to require further elaboration on my part.

5. A number of important intergovernmental organizations have been established for the purpose of carrying out actual operations in the health and social welfare fields on the international level. Again I need only list these to indicate what I have in mind: the Food and Agriculture Organization, the Interna-

tional Refugee Organization, the International Children's Emergency Fund.

6. Certain other programs of a special character carried on directly under United Nations auspices and centering in the social welfare field add to the growing weight of evidence as to the future importance of health and welfare programs in the councils of the nations. I am thinking in particular of such special efforts as the United Nations Appeal for Children and the program of United Nations Advisory Welfare Services, under which some $670,000 has been appropriated for each of the past two years by the General Assembly to provide advisory welfare services and fellowships to foreign students and seminars in special regions of the world—all these undertakings relating exclusively to the social welfare field.

I could continue this catalogue, but to do so would merely serve to underline a point that I hope I have already made. The point is this: During the last three years we have assembled a more impressive array of machinery than we have ever known before for the development of collaboration on an international level in the areas of health and welfare. Out of the years that preceded the second World War we have salvaged a good deal of experience, a number of strong voluntary international organizations, and the International Labor Organization with its twenty-five years of solid achievement. In addition to these legacies from our previous efforts in international collaboration for health and welfare, we have added impressively, since San Francisco, a whole battery, a whole array of organizations, specialized agencies, commissions, and so forth—all of them dedicated to the promotion of mankind's weal throughout the world by raising the standards of our health and social achievements. Surely we now have the machinery to do what should be done for health and welfare on the international level. What we need now, more than anything else, is to show that we have the will and the wit to make this machinery work.

Either we let this machinery rust away in idleness, impotence, and frustration, immobilizing it with disputes, dissension, and bickering; or, if we can but find agreement on methods and procedures as we have on the declared objectives set forth in the articles governing these various international organs, we may have some hope of setting our machinery successfully to work in the broad areas of international health and welfare policy.

It is too early for anyone to say just what the results will be. Only the broad horizons of the future, whose reaches we cannot yet penetrate with our limited vision, can indicate to us the extent to which the vast potential of this international machinery created for the promotion of human health and happiness will actually be realized. We have the opportunity now, we have the equipment too, if we can but make use of it. It may very well be that the real success of the United Nations, the real opportunities for fruitful international collaboration, the real records of international achievement, now lie in those areas of international policy—the fields of health and welfare—which lay so long unexploited and unexplored, but which hold such rich promise for the future of all mankind.

The Management and Control of Aggression

MALCOLM SHARP

SOME TEN DAYS after American, British, and Russian victories had made us secure in the occupation of Japan, Mr. Byrnes and his associates in the Council of Ministers opened the London Conference. On the way over, we are told, Mr. Byrnes and his advisers decided that they must treat Russia as a threat and a danger. So far as one can tell from Mr. Byrnes's book, he and his advisers were particularly influenced by two considerations. First, Russia was acquiring territory which would make her country almost as large as tsarist Russia, and she was asking for control of the Dardanelles and a mandate in North Africa, "preferably Tripolitania." At some time, perhaps later than the trip to London, Mr. Byrnes came to regard German records of Stalin's pressure on Hitler, beginning with the Battle of France, as further evidence of a revival of tsarist imperial ambitions. Secondly, Russia had indicated a disposition to control the Balkans. Mr. Byrnes was particularly impressed by Russia's domineering treatment of Rumania in February, 1945, late in the war with Germany.

Each line of evidence will, of course, bear various interpretations.[1] Mr. Byrnes, however, began the Conference on September

[1] It is not clear from Mr. Byrnes's book when the evidence from the German archives became available to him. If it was not available before he went to London, his opinion then was formed without the aid of evidence which he later found particularly valuable, but which seems open to quite a different interpretation from that which he puts upon it. The other points mentioned in his summary of the evidence against Russia available on September 11, 1945, seem singularly inconclusive:

"I had secured the Yalta agreement on the Kuriles, Sakhalin, Dairen and Port

11, 1945, convinced that he must be on guard against the Russians, and check their culpable desire for territory and power. The Potsdam Agreement provided that in the case of each of the treaties before the Conference, the parties to the corresponding armistice should prepare the treaty, except that France should join in preparing the treaty with Italy. The other Ministers were, therefore, agreeably surprised, according to a report in the New York *Times,* when Foreign Minister Molotov on the first day agreed to a motion, recorded in a signed minute, admitting France and China to the discussion of all the treaties, although without enlargement of their voting rights.

This was the first and last hour of concord, after the war, between the United States and Russia. From then on suspicion, and its constant companion untrustworthiness, grew. Concerned about Russian forces in Eastern Europe, Mr. Byrnes seems to have been genuinely surprised that in a conference on Italian and satellite treaties, Mr. Molotov showed concern about American forces in Japan. In the background, doubtless, there was also Russian concern about American and British forces in western Germany, and particularly about British occupation forces in the Ruhr.

In the first days, France and China supported the United States and Great Britain in the discussion of the issues with Russia which immediately appeared in the consideration of the proposed treaties. The French claim to participation in settling the affairs of Europe had been belittled by Stalin from an early day

---

Arthur from the Map Room in the White House. At Potsdam we had encountered the Soviet demands that Poland be given a large portion of eastern Germany to compensate for the Polish territory east of the Curzon Line taken over by the Soviets; her demands for Königsberg; for a share in the administration of the Ruhr; and for control of the Dardanelles. Her determination to dominate the Balkan states had become apparent, and at Potsdam she had made a bid for control of one of Italy's North African colonies, preferably Tripolitania.

"This last request was especially disturbing because events had convinced me that the Soviets' interest in this territory was primarily military." *Speaking Frankly* (New York: Harper, 1947), p. 92.

Quite unintentionally, no doubt, Mr. Byrnes is not by any means frank and informing about the events of the more or less critical days between September 11 and September 22, 1945. Here as elsewhere the historian will have many problems to solve in giving us the psychological data which will form the basis of his judgments, as well as the judgments of citizens and men of affairs, generally.

in previous conferences. The Chinese claim was in some ways less strong than the French, so far as European affairs were concerned.

Molotov seems to have been increasingly troubled by the combined verbal opposition to his position. At times, judging from the New York *Times* reports, French and Chinese participation in discussion was about as effective as votes would have been. Though the point has not, so far as I know, been publicly argued, Molotov's original concession to France and China seems to have been simply a present permission, and not a promissory undertaking. At any rate, on September 22, 1945, Molotov took the position that his concession was not authorized by his government, which had been a party to the Potsdam Agreement, and was therefore ineffective.

With protracted controversy concerning the parties involved, the drafting of the treaties, and the actual terms, in our peace conferences, we have since gone on to the Balkan and Iranian crises, accompanied constantly by the struggle in China. Today, the economic, political, and military forces of the two great powers are, for practical purposes, in conflict across the face of the world.

Mr. Byrnes may have been correct in his estimate of the situation. On the other hand, he may have created the conflict which he worked and struggled to prevent.

Looking back over history, one may come to the conclusion that rational considerations, including economic considerations, have had relatively little effect in producing fighting and wars. Fear has played a great part, and such irrational factors as hostility, a source or cause of fear, have played the greatest part. Again and again, from before the Peloponnesian War, at least to the war of1914, the consciously unintended sequence of events has repeated itself. Mr. Byrnes and his advisers, like Mr. Molotov and his advisers, have simply joined the ancient dance of fear, suspicion, rivalry, blame, and hate.

The child is father of the foreign secretary, and we may therefore profitably look now for a little at the family. The family is the source of peace and of war. Children, like nations, are more or less friendly and peaceful, more or less hostile and warlike.

If we knew better why this is so, it would probably help us as teachers, parents, citizens, and practitioners of government, including law. The fact is that we understand almost nothing about the origins of love and hate, in the child or in the community.

The capacity for developing a propensity to nurse at his mother's breast seems to be present early in the child's life. It is presumably the source of the simple, undifferentiated propensity to eat and drink which is, in turn, presumably the source of the elaborately conditioned propensities which express themselves in later nutritional habits. With sexual organs, the newborn child has also a capacity for developing reproductive propensities. To a limited extent, then, nutritional propensities and reproductive propensities are "innate," or, better, they are unconditioned propensities as distinguished from conditioned propensities, or "habits."

The students of normal child psychology warn us against going further. There are differences indeed between the propensities to kill exhibited by the relatively peaceful South American monkeys and the propensities to kill exhibited by the relatively pugnacious Old World monkeys, particularly the baboons and the higher apes, our closer relations. But the most careful students of child psychology find no evidence for or against the existence of any animal instincts or impulses of hostility in any observations which they have been able to make of children before conditioning factors have appeared in their experience.

Difference of opinion on the matter appears in two classics of psychoanalytic literature. The difference of opinion itself reminds us of our ignorance. Ian Dishart Suttie thought sociable, nonerotic love, appearing with nursing, an innate propensity of first importance for the purposes of later life. He attacked Freud's opinion that the significant innate propensities are those toward erotic love and those toward aggressive hostility.

The opinions are doubtless based on clinical experience. It may be that they are to be explained further, in part at least, by philosophical, artistic, personal, and cultural influences. Suttie prefers Christian teaching, while Freud expresses himself in the symbols of the ancient pre-Socratic religion of

Empedocles. Freud's own obsessional traits and their possible influence on his doctrine have been considered by Dr. Ranyard West. Suttie's opinion is perhaps appropriate for an Englishman, and Freud's—on various accounts—for a resident on the Continent. At any rate, a psychology of psychology is developing now, and it will doubtless help us to appraise the personal influences affecting doctrines of innate propensities. Among other results, this psychology will warn readers against accepting patterns of doctrine because they like them or because they dislike them, or —still more—simply because they are the first patterns which attract a curious attention and give it security in the midst of puzzles.

A sociology of anthropology is also needed, to help us approach the anthropologist's views about innate propensities with appropriate caution. In opposition to some psychiatrists, many anthropologists have gone to extremes in minimizing the possibility that there are innate propensities to hostile aggression. In 1941 Bronislaw Malinowski did not, indeed, go so far as to deny the existence of any such propensities. Twice, however, in an article on anthropology and war, he suggested a clew to his own bias by the use of the same curious form of argument. All propensities that are unlike hunger or reproductive propensities are conditioned; hostile propensities are different from hunger and reproductive propensities; therefore, hostile propensities are conditioned. The use of definition in the major premise determines the conclusion. Moreover, "unlike" and "different from" create two different middle terms. Hostile propensities differ from hunger and reproductive propensities indeed; but they may also, so far as available evidence indicates, be like them in significant respects.

Another of Malinowski's arguments may be expressed in much the same form. All hostile activities that are unlike national wars are not wars; primitive hostile activities are different from national wars; therefore, primitive hostile activities are not wars. Malinowski was too great an observer and scientist to deny flatly the possibility that unconditioned hostile propensities exist, to dismiss primitive hostile activities as wholly irrelevant to the problems of modern war, or to put his arguments into quite such an unproductive form as the "derivations" that have just been sketched. Even in their crude form, it will be apparent that the arguments have at least a provocative force. Nevertheless, like the theories of Suttie and Freud, Malinowski's position is a reminder that hope and fear, taste, the influences of place and time, and the disposition to more or less random pattern-making, may affect the treatment of matters of vital concern, like hostile aggression.

The students of normal child psychology have singular advantages for the study of hostility. They are free from two influences which may affect the best psychiatrists: the bias which may come from preoccupation with pathological cases, and the urgent sense of necessity for working out something which may help suffering patients. Child psychologists have, ordinarily, one advantage over the anthropologist. Their subject matter is likely to be also their day-to-day responsibility. They not only study children, but they help children of various types to live pleasant, happy, and effective lives. They have, of course, limitations corresponding to the advantages enjoyed by psychiatrists and anthropologists. Nevertheless, it is not surprising that students of child life have recognized most clearly that we are still unable to determine whether the propensity to hostile aggression is unconditioned or conditioned.

It probably makes somewhat less difference than is usually assumed. Unconditioned propensities, it is supposed, are harder to manage or control than are conditioned tendencies. But reproductive propensities may be managed and controlled, to a considerable degree, in a monastery. And, on the other hand, a conditioned propensity may be extraordinarily difficult to change or manage or control. It may be due, for example, to factors in the environment which it is hard to modify, like the appearance of some administrative hierarchy in any complicated society. Or it may be due to factors which it is altogether impossible to eliminate, like the occurrence of some frustration in any conceivable society.

At the least, we know that children come into the world with an inclination, like that of all fresh protoplasm, to live and deal with the environment, and to develop the capacity and propensity to reproduce. In growing up, they develop marked similarities, as, for example, in the common appearance in nearly all circumstances of some tendency to hostile, angry, destructive aggression. They also develop marked differences in the intensity and frequency with which this propensity appears in action.

Those who observe children systematically tell us that differences in the intensity and frequency of hostile aggression are due, in part at least, to factors that may be isolated, to some extent, in study and modified, to some extent, in training and control. To refresh our minds with a figure of speech, we may observe five villains in the drama of childhood. The vulnerability these villains reveal in some circumstances indicates what may be done to eliminate them, while their invulnerability in other circumstances, and their curious way of occasionally becoming heroes, indicates the limits of management and perhaps indeed of control.

Children may learn increasingly, in future generations, to manage their rational, problem-solving capacities and their nonrational characteristics—their loves, fears, aggressions, and hatreds—alike. We cannot look forward, however, to any revolutionary improvements in these arts within the next fifteen years. Reflection on the factors in children's hostilities will serve to indicate both the possibilities of management and its limits.

We shall conclude, no doubt, that it is unsafe to trust to education for the control of the large-scale homicide that is modern war. In the next fifteen years we must expect that rather crudely trained children will be foreign ministers. We, their constituents, are doubtless no better trained ourselves. We shall make, between us, some crucial decisions. There will be the ancient tendency to make foreign policy the permitted opportunity for lunacy. Our obsessional and paranoid traits will there receive their permitted expression. In this period we shall need something besides education and management. We shall need, for all of us and not just for others, policemen and control.

Let us return to the five villains of childhood before we again discuss ourselves and our foreign secretaries. These five villains are frustration, domination, jealousy, guilt, and fear.

Frustration in one or more of its many forms appears no one knows how early in childhood. Hunger, which is certainly somewhat frustrating, is to be expected. The desire to drink will be thwarted almost inevitably, at times, for short periods at least. Training in physical cleanliness used to involve some interruption of satisfactions, some thwarting of desires. We are learning now, however, that the less the frustration, the less is likely to be the hostility, and the better in the long run it will be for the child and the community, other things being equal.

Serious frustrations and serious hostile tendencies can be traced to the mother's failure to give her love and a sense of safety and protection to the child. At some period, the parents must give not only love, but resistance too. The child misses some sense of consistent firmness in matters of which he can sense the significance. "Spoiling" is due to a kind of frustration.

A serious source of frustration, though not by any means the only one, is parental domination, the second villain. Eating, sleeping, and all the daily routine of an infant's life apparently occur in natural rhythms which a mother will do well to follow and not change. Relationships and habits will thus be established which will prepare the way for that free and coöperative development of unique personal qualities which will characterize a happy childhood and adolescence, and successful maturity in a democratic society. In a democracy there is, of course, authority; and the exercise of intelligent, understandable, and firm authority is not domination.

The third villain is jealousy. Sometimes it is jealousy of one parent for another. Commonly, it is jealousy of a younger brother or sister for the mother. Many factors, all related to some kind of frustration, appear in jealousies: insecurity, loss of control of a situation, emulation, hostility toward the other parties in the triangle, fear of their hostility, fear of one's own hostility toward them, hostility toward the self, various forms of fear derived from these other factors. It is a turbulent phenomenon, with the id, the ego, and the superego talking back to each other. It is an important source of the complex experience of guilt, and so of the blame which citizen and foreign minister alike will one day be placing on someone else. In jealousy the loved figure may become also the hated figure, who throughout the later years may constantly take new forms, such as the wife, the boss, the Jew, the foreigner—whoever is conveniently at hand to be blamed.

The fourth villain is guilt. It may appear in various connections and in different guises. Jealousy, of course, is a frequent source of early and exaggerated guilt feelings and guilt behavior. Some sense of guilt may possibly be unconditioned. Its moderate use in family administration may actually be wanted by children, and it may be advisable or necessary for other practical reasons.

This again is a villain which acts through man's later life. As blame it appears in countless forms, too readily welcomed, in courts of law. It asks for senseless reparations payments and foolish boundaries at international conferences, in 1919 and in 1947. It shifts unpredictably from guilt to blame, from the uneasiness of a nation which has fought and dropped atomic bombs, or any bombs, to the blaming of any other nation which may cause any kind of difficulty, including the frustration which results from misunderstanding.

Fear, the fifth villain, has already appeared. It is one reaction to a sense of insecurity or danger. It expresses itself in feeling and action as a disposition toward retreat, evasion, withdrawal. It is accompanied or followed, in successful organisms, by a propensity to resist by evasion not dominated by fright, or by attack. It may be both a result and a cause of frustration and hostility. Fear is commonly a factor in jealousy and guilt and in those persistent patterns of disguised jealousy and guilt which contribute to homicides and wars.

One fear is worth special notice: the child's fear of loss of love and rejection by parents. It accompanies deep frustration, and occasions hostility and resentment. It is a means of parental domination. This fear is one important element in jealousy. It is used, consciously or unconsciously, as a means of discipline and a device for creating or accentuating a sense of guilt. It appears also in response to treatment which seems, superficially at least, to be of an opposite nature: lack of resistance and firmness at times—particularly when a sense of the need for punishment has arisen—seems to indicate neglect and indifference, or some fear of himself in the parent.

Fear and insecurity themselves contribute, not only to patterns of disguised jealousy and guilt in later life, but to that pattern of activity in which a need for, or disposition to, suffering and punishment plays its part. The pattern may be closely associated with one of apparently spontaneous cruelty to others. A common element in the pattern is a manifestation of insecure dependence on others, preferably on one other, who will—it is hoped—protect and assume responsibility. It is plain how such patterns may contribute to the growth of dictatorships and, quite apart from dictatorships, to wars.

Frustration—with its accumulating or, better, conditioning or habit-forming resentments and hostilities—domination, jealousy, guilt, fear, unconditioned or conditioned thus occur in countless permutations and combinations, in infancy and later. The resulting forms of adult behavior are well known. They are more or less specifically related to particular childhood experiences, and again they appear in a great variety of combinations. There is the obsessional preoccupation with easing and saving rituals and words, picking up pins, reciting charms. Here is at least one source of that sometimes rather exaggerated concern with religions and ideologies which may appear in the events leading to wars. There is paranoid hatred. The feared, menacing, and hated figure of childhood is identified with a possible enemy, to whom menacing conduct is attributed and who accordingly becomes the object of exaggerated fear and hatred. This figure will commonly be a convenient object to which to shift our sense of guilt; he will accordingly, and sometimes irrespective of his own intentions and conduct, be blamed and condemned. The need for closeness and warmth within a group, the need for suffering, the need for an object of hostility without the group—these, among other phenomena of childhood, recur in wars. There is no problem about the appearance of these phenomena of individual life in group action. In many rather apparent ways the individual reaction is strengthened and reinforced by the group.

Nor is it clear that these phenomena are as peculiar to our own times as some suppose. There are few significant cases of consistently peaceful communities, primitive or civilized, on record. Hostile group activities or wars are characteristic phenomena of human social life. Unconditioned or conditioned, or partly one and partly the other, the propensity to hostile aggression has expressed itself intermittently in collective homicide in practically all the communities known to man.

With his subtle and ambiguous use of myth and his partly ironical temporal patterns, Arnold Toynbee shows a profound and simple but marvelously elaborated insight into the psychology of growth. At some stages of growth, cultures may be stimulated by wars, offensive or defensive, or defensively offensive. At other stages, breakdown or distintegration may have as characteristic symptoms different types of war—centrifugal wars within a culture, or wars to establish universal states or empires. The peculiarity of our time is not its hostilities or its wars. It is an institutional situation. Democracy, or, more specifically, the French Revolution, introduced, on an unprecedented scale, the mass citizen army. Technology has armed it with unprecedented weapons, of which the rocket and the atomic bomb are the most recent to have been used.

A judgment on the uses and limits of family influences in the management and control of aggression has appeared throughout this discussion. Unconditioned or conditioned, hostile aggression may, to an unknown extent, be more or less successfully managed. Some individuals and communities at some times and places are relatively fortunate in avoiding serious aggressive conflicts. Under present social and technological conditions, there is, of course, urgent biological need for minimizing violent conflicts. The family may do much to use available knowledge in training children in the management of propensities to hostile aggression. The family will thus gradually contribute to building a constituency for a world free from lethal aggression.

But no family can train an infant born this year in time for him as an adult to help get the world out of the institutionalized emotionalism of foreign affairs. Students of family life have two opportunities. One is to help in the long process of developing individuals' capacities to use and manage the nonrational human characteristics in such a way as to make life increasingly secure, venturesome, effective, happy, pleasant, and cheerful. The other is to use their knowledge and experience to help in the work of those who are responsible for government and foreign affairs. Here they may properly emphasize the difficulties of management and the urgent need for critical and powerful control.

After childhood, everyone continues to meet frustrations and to express, manage, and control hostile aggression. Learning and growth involve a constant effort to go beyond present capacities, and the resulting frustrations may be minimized, but not altogether prevented.[2] There are some frustrations, along with the opportunities for happiness, in every marriage. Frustrations are among the results of depressions and wars. They occur as a result of failure to reach the goals of business or professional ambition. Changes in religions, world views, and social ideologies may occasion insecurity and frustrations.[3]

The intellectual may easily estimate incorrectly the seriousness of these various frustrations. He may exaggerate the seriousness of religious and philosophical change for the average man. He is apt to underestimate the satisfaction which many take in moderate, competitive success in business or government. The academic intellectual not infrequently puts a high value on a rather well-

[2] See Mary Elizabeth Keister and Ruth Updegraff, "A Study of Children's Reactions to Failure and an Experimental Attempt to Modify Them," *Child Development,* VIII (September, 1937), 241, reprinted in Newcomb, Hartley, and others, *Readings in Social Psychology* (1947), p. 291; with a fuller account of the same study in Updegraff, Keister, Heiliger, and others, "Studies in Preschool Education, I," *University of Iowa Studies in Child Welfare,* Vol. XIV, No. 4 (1937).

[3] On the frustrations of mature life in our society, see particularly Dr. James L. Halliday, "Psychosomatic Medicine and the Declining Birth Rate," *Lancet,* CCXLVIII (May 12, 1945), 601–3, and "Epidemiology and the Psychosomatic Affections," *ibid.,* CCLI (August 10, 1946), 185–91, also his *Psychosocial Medicine* (New York: Norton, 1948); Talcott Parsons, "Certain Primary Sources and Patterns of Aggression in the Social Structure of the Western World," in *Conflicts of Power in Modern Culture* (1947), papers from the Seventh Symposium of the Conference on Science, Philosophy and Religion, reprinted in *Psychiatry,* X (May, 1947), 167.

safeguarded kind of security; and as a result he may overestimate the effects of the corresponding insecurity. In his concern for discovery and generalization, he may treat possible causal relationships as well established. He may idealize the past and overlook the advantages of the present.

It is possible, indeed, to look at many sources of frustration in another way. They are, in Toynbee's scheme of things, challenges. There is a challenge in a courtship, in the effort to produce and accumulate wealth, in a political campaign. The challenge, if it is not overwhelming, is the occasion for growth, for pleasurable and vigorous activity, for success and victory. Here is the aggressive struggle with the natural and human environment which permits us to speak of constructive aggression. It is the organism's activity in overcoming serious obstacles to effective life. Effective life, in turn, is apt to consist, at least partly, in just this kind of activity.

The similarity between constructive aggressive energy and destructive aggression thus appears along with the difference. Clinical experience indicates that constructive propensities may be impaired if destructive propensities are too well controlled. In particular, the man whose fear of his own destructive propensities leads him to an extremely kind and protective type of overt action, not infrequently finds himself more or less incapacitated for constructive activity.

It will have been observed also that destructive hostility has its uses in everyday life. Real enemies do appear. One who has healthy confidence or satisfaction in his own life may find it necessary to fight an enemy in one way or another, and destroy him.

If theories of frustration or other kinds of conditioning appear inadequate to explain the type and amount of destructive aggression in the human species that may be some slight evidence for a theory of unconditioned propensities to destruction. Until we are able to choose between them, or to decide on some alternative, each theory may have its own uses.

From childhood on, at any rate, there is increasing reason for accepting a certain amount of hostile aggression as a natural element in each individual's behavior. We shall not impair constructive energies by excessive fear of destructive energy. We shall accept, without too great alarm or disturbance, a certain amount of destructively aggressive behavior on the part of ourselves, our friends, and our relations. If we are wise, we shall not easily let this normal expression of life turn friends, relations, or acquaintances into enemies. It seems likely that there is less danger to the common objectives of life in the failure to recognize an enemy, than there is in the disposition resulting from our own and others' hostilities to turn friends or neutrals into enemies. When the child becomes the parent, he may thus, in turn, add to the risks of generating new hostility, created by the villains of childhood.

The familiar, everyday, hostile propensities must, like the need for independence and the need for self-support, be recognized and accepted by all of us. Various devices for making this recognition explicit have been reported. A place or time or manner may be specified, for example, in which expressions of anger are permitted. It is doubtful whether giving such significance to special conditions is altogether useful. Constructive energy and aggressiveness may lead through frustration to hostile aggression, or it may arise unpredictably in other ways, in countless varieties of circumstances, in daily life. Recognition and acceptance of the character and existence of hostile aggression will enable us to supplement the training of childhood in its use and management. We shall be able to see also that extreme forms of hostile aggression in ourselves and in others will require in the visible future the services of policemen.[4]

[4] A number of qualifications and corrections of emphasis might be appropriate at this point. The occasion for the suggestion that this paper be prepared was another paper by the author, "Aggression: a Study of Values and Law," which appeared in *Ethics,* LVII, No. 4, Part II (July, 1947). That was preceded by a number of unpublished papers, dealing with different but related matters, used in reading or speaking to a variety of groups. One paper in this series was originally read under the title "On the Neglect of Jesus in the Revival of Christian Philosophy"; it was published in November of 1947 in somewhat edited form in *Conflicts of Power in Modern Culture.*

Most of the qualifications that might be made here have been expressed in one or another of this series of unpublished and published statements; or they are apparent from what is said in this paper. Where there is so much to learn, it seems inappropriate to repeat, or to pretend to exhaust a subject. On the whole, the *Ethics* essay is a comprehensive general statement of the position taken here and elsewhere. The present paper is an elaboration of matters referred to particularly on pages 2, 5–6, 25–26, 35, and 39 of that essay.

Practices which are useful in everyday life have their place also in the negotiations of foreign secretaries and the relationships between communities. Foreign secretaries will not neglect the possibility that every powerful community is inevitably the enemy of at least one other community. If this is the case, diplomacy and war are closely related and persistent elements, whatever form they may take, in international relationships. Foreign secretaries may perhaps at this time in history take some slight chances on another view of human relationships. They may recognize and accept the normal occurrence of aggression and hostility between individuals and peoples. Then they may smile and go to work, without allowing a series of cumulative reactions to prepare for the destruction of mankind. Foreign secretaries in such a mood will recognize that any nation, including their own, may need at times to be controlled by an international force; and they will take steps to provide for the creation and operation of such a force.

These foreign secretaries will recognize that throughout history their predecessors have not done very well for us. They have acted like poorly trained children. As adults, they have failed to see in perspective the aggressive tendencies of mankind. They have not yet devised the simple means needed to prevent these tendencies from causing destruction and to release them for constructive uses.

The United States has now assumed the task of containing Russia in Eastern Europe. We are thus concerned with an area in which instructive and important manifestations of group hostile aggression have occurred since before the time of Thucydides. Take, for example, the events leading to the war of 1914. These are the events which started the three great conflicts of our time. As we recall them, we may recall further the negotiations of Mr. Byrnes, to which we shall finally return.

On a quiet Sunday in June, 1914, Serbian nationalists murdered an Austrian archduke. The assassins—or patriots—were associated with Serbian army officers, though perhaps not with the government. The aggregation of nations which constituted the Austro-Hungarian Empire was not secure. It was commonly thought that the empire had become the sick man of Europe and that it might be expected to follow the Turkish Empire into impotence and disintegration. Russia was expected to contend strongly for the position of Austria in Eastern Europe. Russia, moreover, was generally recognized as Serbia's backer. Serbian nationalists, seeking to help Austrian Serbs into a new Serbia, depended in the end on Russian support. Learning from her defeat by Japan, Russia was reorganizing and strengthening her army. The reorganization was expected to be complete in two or three years.

Germany was an ally of Austria, and the contender with Russia for power and leadership in Eastern Europe. Austria, Germany, and, halfheartedly, Italy, were allied in a combination to rival the combination of France and Russia, which had some reason to count on British support in a crisis.

The Serbian crisis, for three or four weeks, seemed to be less serious than other crises which had been surmounted in Europe. The Germans and Austrians thought that Austrian security required severe punishment for Serbia, and their responsible officials expected Europe to understand that. The Kaiser, indeed, at one critical conference apparently took the position that if he had to fight Russia, he would rather fight in 1914 than in 1917. Though less indiscreet and more moderate, he thus anticipated Governor George Earle's advocacy of the preventive attack.

With somewhat hesitant and vacillating and ambiguous German backing, Austria was more severe with Serbia than Europe had anticipated. The fears, ambitions, and hostilities of England, France, and Russia came quickly to a climax. Austria was committed to attacking Serbia, and Germany to backing Austria. For four or five days frantic statesmen on both sides tried to prevent a war without yielding their positions. Austria attacked Serbia. Russia mobilized. On the fifth weekend following the murder, the outnumbered Germans, with two fronts to protect, began the war with the attack which they considered preventive.

After the conclusion of the war, the struggle was renewed. The victorious European powers followed the habitual course of fear, suspicion, domination, condemnation, and hatred. Their conduct of affairs was bound, as we can now see, to lead to Hitler in 1933, and the battles of Britain, Stalingrad, and Midway, which, like Trafalgar and Moscow in their day, turned the war of 1939 into victory for the Allies.

There are consequences of the second World War which in their details parallel the Serbian situation. An American adviser at a 1919 peace conference objected to taking what is now northeastern Greece from Bulgaria and giving it to Greece as the spoils of her limited participation in the war. Ethnic, economic, and political considerations weighed then, as they may do now, in favor of giving this territory, with direct access to the Mediterranean, to Bulgaria. The matter was probably of more consequence then than now. Yet here is one corner of the ancient cock-fighting pit of Europe into which we have again moved. We know little about it and think little of it. Nevertheless, the intricate hatreds of Balkan politics may combine with the struggle between us and Russia, somewhat as they did in Serbia in 1914, to produce the next explosion of fear, hatred, and ambition.

It is said that, unlike the Germany of 1914, we are not imperialists, and that if we get into trouble or launch a preventive attack against Russia, it will not be our fault. In the nineteenth century, however, we conquered the better part of a rather large continent. We then rounded it out with control of the strategic Caribbean Sea. The War of 1812 and the wars with Mexico and Spain are now recognized as simple wars of conquest. It is not only for rational reasons that most of us would be unwilling to give California back to Mexico or the Isthmus to the Republic of Panama. Our fears and prides and propensities to hostile aggression have not been altogether different from those of other peoples. As we step into cockpits in the Balkans, in Iran, and in China we may get guidance from others' experience.

In fact, for a time, following 1900, we joined Great Britain in the position toward Russia which was later taken by Austria and Germany, the position to which we have now returned. That position was outlined in 1900 in *The Problem of Asia,* written by our famous systematic imperialist, Admiral Mahan. It was maintained by his friend Theodore Roosevelt in backing Japan at the time of her war with Russia, and helping Japan to get her first substantial and secure positions in Manchuria and Korea.

The position was simple. The United States must join Great Britain, Germany, Italy—on the way through the Mediterranean to the Orient—and Japan in containing Russia (then allied with France). Russian pressure must be expected and resisted, particularly in the approaches to the eastern Mediterranean and the Persian Gulf and in China. For economic reasons, but still more because of rivalries for security and power, control of China was the objective of the world-wide strategy.

After the Japanese victory in 1905 the United States and Great Britain were succeeded by Austria, Germany, and later again Japan, as leaders in opposition to Russia. Promptly on the defeat of Germany and Japan in 1945, Mr. Byrnes brought us back into our old position.

He may have acted wisely. What else could he have done? Well, Stalin does not seem to be an altogether standard type. However much theological nonsense Karl Marx may have written along with his stimulating economics, it is reasonable to suppose that the successors to the tsars are relatively practical men. There is no reason to think that they are more obsessional and paranoid, more disposed to fear and hate than we.

In the long run, we all need a policeman, and arguments have been advanced elsewhere for giving our first attention to the organization of a world military force for the protection of peoples. In the meantime, Mr. Byrnes might have considered other possibilities.

Suppose that instead of beginning at once to bargain, leaving their purposes to be inferred from their moves, Mr. Byrnes and Mr. Bevin and Mr. Molotov had spent those first ten days drinking a little and quietly talking, with a psychologist—preferably a student of children—near at hand in case of need. They might have reviewed the state of psychological knowledge, and the indications which it gave of the dangers ahead for peoples and statesmen alike, and the suggestions of means for avoiding those dangers. They might have read a chapter or two on the baboon; not, as we have seen, that we know our native endowments, but it is possible that the study of baboons explains us, and entertaining the possibility might be at once stimulating and chastening. They might have taken a look at primitive peoples, relaxing for a bit over the Todas, the Zuni, and the Hopi, deriving from them some slight encouragement. They needed most to look briefly at the long history of Asia and Europe. From the beginning, peoples have done continuously what Mr. Byrnes and Mr. Molotov were about to do, with no one able, in most cases, to apportion any blame afterward, and with uniform results thus far.

It is hard to see how the outcome could have been any worse than the actual results of the Conference. Ten days of quiet talk might have been productive. There would have been time enough in any event for resort to the ancient game of fear and hostility, with countermove anticipating move, and move leading again to countermove. Even today a conference devoted partly to fundamentals and not exclusively to old-fashioned bargaining might help restore us to our senses.

The family is indeed the laboratory and hope of the world. Its successes remind us that somewhere in us and our children are the sources of those propensities, erotic, social, coöperative, which express themselves in all the achievements which we consciously value. It is possible to go far in the management of our protoplasm and its disposition to survive and give us pleasure.

The family's limitations are at the same time the most effective reminder of the nature of our principal problem of government and law. The homicides which occurred in the House of Atreus are symbols of the appearance in family life of factors in the drama of mankind. Those of us who are concerned with families will combine our experience and make our best efforts to help one or more families succeed. We may also use our experience to warn our statesmen of the extraordinary persistence and wide distribution of propensities to hostile aggression. These propensities are to some extent subject to management by families, individuals, communities, and foreign secretaries. To some extent, however, they still require community control. The serious problems of international affairs are psychological. If they can be solved, it will not be hard to develop effective administrative agencies for the control of international hostility.

Human Relations in Tomorrow's World

JAMES B. CONANT

ACCORDING TO MY VIEW, tomorrow and many tomorrows yet to come will see, not one world, but two. Unless I am much mistaken, the hard fact of a divided world is the reality with which we have to face the future in these days.

In making this rather pessimistic forecast as the frame of reference for my remarks, I want to make it perfectly plain that I am not one of those who believe that a war with the Soviet Union is inevitable nor, indeed, even probable in the immediate future. On the contrary, I think that we are going to be living for a long time to come in a period of tension which might well be described as an armed truce.

To be sure, in this as in so many other matters, one's forecast about the future turns on one's diagnosis of the thoughts of the men who now rule Soviet Russia so ruthlessly. There are roughly three points of view current in the United States which in their extreme forms may be summarized as follows: There are those who think that the dwellers in the Kremlin are Slavic followers of Thomas Jefferson and the enlightenment of the eighteenth century, or at worst the early socialists of the nineteenth century; that all their aggressive actions are based on fear of the capitalistic and imperialistic United States. The second viewpoint, the antithesis of the first, is expressed by those who feel that the rulers of Soviet Russia are equivalent to the men who once surrounded Hitler and Mussolini; that they are military gangsters bent on conquering the world by force. A variant of this theme is that they are the military descendants of Peter the Great, bent on

Russian expansion of a nationalistic sort by force of arms. The third position, to which I am inclined, lays far greater emphasis on the ideology of Soviet Russia and on the parties which follow the Soviet line. According to this view, the leaders of Soviet Russia and the governors of their satellite countries are devoted, indeed fanatic, followers of a fairly consistent philosophy which can be traced through Marx, Engels, and Lenin: though military force would be used by the totalitarians whenever it was found advantageous, the chief reliance would be on the efficacy of their own doctrine. The very basis of the Soviet philosophy, let us remember, gives the comforting assurance that history is on their side. In due course of time, so they believe, every other nation will undergo a revolution and a dictatorship of the proletariat will be established; then, eventually, when a capitalistic encirclement has given place to a totalitarian socialistic encirclement throughout the world, the State will wither away. Thus, the ruthless rulers of the totalitarian states envisage their utopia, and they seem quite prepared to assist the course of history by keeping a steady pressure where they can.

Now I do not propose to discuss matters of foreign policy of the United States. But I submit that we cannot discuss human relations in tomorrow's world without coming to a conclusion as to the kind of world which tomorrow will usher in. If I am right, there will continue to be two worlds, and our problem is to see, if possible, that these two worlds compete on an ideological basis under conditions at least approaching peace. Our half of the divided world is committed to an open society, diversity, and individual freedom, and the only chance of peace and of our survival is to make these propositions a living reality by our deeds. To this end we need imagination, courage, and the boldness to use new knowledge.

Two important events occurred a century ago in 1848. One of them was the incorporation in New York of the Association for Improving the Condition of the Poor, one of the two parent associations of the Community Service Society. The other was the publication of the Communist Manifesto by Karl Marx and Friedrich Engels. I trust I shall not be cited for appearance on

Capitol Hill for mentioning these two events in the same breath. Nor if I further add that I am inclined to think that an impartial historian of a century or two from now would say that the motivating force behind both events was fundamentally the same. A group of relatively prosperous, forward-looking men of New York City, shocked with the conditions of the poor in an urban area rapidly undergoing industrialization, were moved to found a philanthropic organization. A few intellectuals, seeing similar situations in European countries which had always known a caste system, put forward a manifesto for their solution of a problem equally distressing to their eyes.

Now we come to an interesting point. Let us compare the developments arising from these two events. Let us turn first to the record of the Association for Improving the Condition of the Poor as set forth in the excellent monograph prepared for the celebration of its founding. Note at once how the original concept has been changed. Here we find no insistence on the orthodox pattern of the founders! On the contrary, we find written on page 10 these words, speaking of the two organizations, one founded in 1848, and the Charity Organization Society founded in 1882: "Both of these organizations continued to operate under their original titles until 1939, but as time went on they continued to be successful in their endeavors essentially because they had outgrown these names. The change in thinking which had taken place within the ranks of the two societies is made clear by the name—Community Service Society—which was selected for their combined operation." [1] A change of thinking, keeping pace with changing times—that is our American way of handling human problems arising out of the Industrial Revolution. That is the way of all true democracies, of all free nations, of all countries except those under totalitarian rule.

Let us now in our imaginations turn to another city—let us say Moscow, Belgrade, or even Prague—and imagine a celebration of the centenary of the publication of the Communist Manifesto. How different would be the emphasis! The emphasis would be

[1] "Frontiers in Human Welfare" (New York: Community Service Society of New York, 1948), p. 10.

not on change, but on orthodoxy, on party dogma; it would be argued that Marx and Engels once and for all laid down the program for the future. In the Communist Manifesto it was written, and I quote: "The first step in the revolution by the working class is to raise the proletariat to the position of ruling class to establish democracy." This was Marx's and Engels's definition of that word "democracy" a century ago. It is still the definition of their followers, both by word and action. Reporting on March 27, 1948, on a trip to Prague, R. H. Crossman, by no means a conservative, let alone a reactionary reporter, writes in the *New Statesman and Nation* as follows about his hour-and-a-half conversation with Rudolf Slansky, the secretary of the Communist party in that city. Speaking of recent events, Crossman asked, " 'How can you call this democratic?' 'Of course it's democratic. We have succeeded in purging all the parties of their reactionaries' was the reply. 'And the newspapers?' continued Mr. Crossman. 'But there, too, we were constitutional,' replied Mr. Slansky. 'The Cabinet had unanimously passed a law that only *recognized* political parties should publish newspapers. We are keeping strictly to that rule, but now all the parties are reliable.' "

What has all this to do with human relations, you may ask. Everything, according to my mind. Today's world and tomorrow's world are divided on exactly the essential point of the approach to human relations. On one side of the Iron Curtain you have ruthless, fanatic believers in a consistent philosophy that is a century old. The rulers of Soviet Russia have one answer—a revolutionary dictatorship of the proletariat—an answer to a problem which was brought forcefully to the minds of people of a hundred years and more ago by the sordid and inhuman aspects of the Industrial Revolution. On this side of the Iron Curtain we have sought a progressive and ever changing answer through an attempt to find by rational inquiry and good will a solution to this same problem. Our method has continually been founded on advancing knowledge. The Soviet philosophy, on the other hand, like a religious dogma has seemed to require no change and has been unaffected by new knowledge. Today the totalitarian rulers need no inquiries into the science of man. They need only political intrigue and the threat of force to have their views prevail, or so they think. The free people of the world, on the other hand, are committed to a totally different approach; we must press forward with great urgency to a better understanding of the problems involved in human relations.

I can illustrate what I have in mind by a personal anecdote. I was in Moscow for ten days at Christmas of 1945 as an adviser on atomic energy to the Hon. James Byrnes, at the time of one of the conferences of the three foreign ministers. I hasten to add that this does not make me an expert on Russian matters. The only official of the Soviet Government with whom I talked at any length was the Minister of Education. He was in charge of all the elementary and secondary schools of Soviet Russia. We discussed through an interpreter the possible interchange of literature on pedagogic methods. Being very much interested in guidance and all the new psychological testing procedures which have been developed in the last generation, I raised this subject early in my conversation and said something along the following lines: "Both your educational system and ours are based on the belief in equality of opportunity and careers open to the talented. We have developed methods for discovering talent and testing varieties of aptitudes and skills. What have you done? Shouldn't we exchange methods along these lines?" It was as though I had suddenly introduced some obscene subject or at least had mentioned private ownership and the profit motive. The conversation stopped and was then suddenly turned aside. Thinking that my interpreter might have been at fault, a few minutes later I tried again, and drew the same response. Still a third time yielded no indication of willingness to admit even the existence of the problems of guidance and testing among our youth and theirs as well. The next day at an afternoon party I talked with the head of the university system and the President of the Academy of Science and raised the same problem, which was turned aside not so abruptly, but with a general expression of thought sometimes heard in extremely conservative circles in the United States, namely, that it is quite impossible to tell by any tests or measures who has aptitude for any subject. All this puzzled and perplexed me until I returned to the United States and discovered what I should have known, that all testing and psychological measurements were banned in Russia some ten years earlier. By an ordinance of the Central Committee of the All Russian Communist party of July 4, 1936, modern practices in education were condemned. Dewey, Thorndike, Binet, were proclaimed unscientific and mechanistic. Existing testing programs as operated in bourgeois countries, it was declared, had been arranged to prove that the underprivileged would always fare badly and only the ruling class would receive the benefits of education! The Soviet rulers believe they can get on without benefit of the new developments concerning human nature or human relations. This fact alone, to my mind, indicates one of the weak points in their armor.

Whether I am right or not in my diagnosis, the contrast is surely striking. Compare it with the work of the Community Service Society of New York: The Society has been among the pioneers in applying the methods of the social sciences, particularly the work of social psychologists in connection with welfare work. In so doing, it has not stood alone, for throughout this country there has been an increasing recognition that social work, psychiatry, vocational guidance and education, public health practice, and applied anthropology share many of the same functions. These are all dependent on a generalized basic social science for techniques, methods, and theories. Therefore, for the carrying out of the practical objectives of the Society as a pilot plant in social welfare, it is necessary that great emphasis be placed on the future of the development of the basic social sciences.

Closely related to organized, philanthropic organizations such as this and the welfare work of organized activities of a community through its local, or state, or even Federal government are the industrial personnel problems. I may quote from a recent address by the Chairman of the General Foods Corporation:

> To attain positive industrial peace, we need something more than by-laws and compulsory rules. We need productive teamwork. We need men working willingly together toward known goals. We need, in short: workers who are informed; workers who enjoy a sense of security; workers who are given a feeling of individual dignity; work-

ers who are properly and fairly paid; workers who are given non-financial incentives.

Later, speaking of the self-analysis of top management, he asks the question:

> Do we believe that political and economic freedom are inseparable, and that they are equally the rights of employers and employees? There is no literal warrant for this interpretation in the Constitution [he goes on to say], but I happen to be one of those who believe that you cannot put freedoms in separate compartments or maintain one kind of basic freedom without the other.

This executive, like so many other leaders in industry, realizes that in the application of sound knowledge about human relations lies the possibility of solving some of the hardest problems we have to face in making our industrialized democracy work as a dynamic society of free men.

There are few today who would deny that economics, politics, and social ideals are thoroughly interwoven. The history of this century has taught all thinking men this side of the Iron Curtain that modern industry and trade do not proceed in a vacuum, that human beings do not behave in reality like economic symbols. Granted private ownership and the profit motive (which have been sneered at in certain circles, but for which I believe there is no substitute for this nation), the question of how best to keep our society truly competitive and at the same time moving toward a greater degree of equality of opportunity is no easy one to answer. I suppose few would really subscribe today to the old doctrine of "hands off." As in the case of traffic, the nature of modern society has made the public a party to what once seemed a strictly private matter. The role of government has been permanently enlarged. The political machinery of government is today meshed into our industrial life. The problem surely is to see how we can operate our private enterprises and our political institutions so that our society will be in fact competitive and thereby increasingly productive of the goods and services required.

Now it is obvious that the best minds of the country should be devoted to a study of the many problems arising as a consequence of our endeavors to keep our society prosperous, strong, and democratic. I have already expressed my conviction that the methods of certain of the social sciences have been developed to a point where studies of society by competent scholars can provide basic information to assist government officials, leaders of industry, of labor, and of education. Both fundamental investigations as to the nature of man and society and immediate studies of specific problems are required.

It is at this point that I believe our universities have a special contribution to make, not only to the welfare of the United States, but, I trust, to that of all free nations. Certain types of work in sociology, anthropology, and social psychology seem full of promise. The point of view of the younger men in these fields (and I emphasize the adjective "younger"), if coupled with practical experience in industry on the one hand or social welfare work on the other, or public education on still a third front, may be peculiarly effective in shaping the nature of tomorrow's world. For example, the applied anthropologist's position as regards a culture of a small community is just like that of a caseworker in relation to a family. Just as the psychiatrist or vocational adviser tries to bring the individual to realism with reference to his emotional problems and abilities, the applied anthropologist tries to bring realism and maturity to the thinking of people regarding their traditions and group life. A manufacturer would never dream of building a new plant in a locality concerning which he did not have accurate information on water supply, electric power, transportation, and the nearness of critical supplies. Likewise, public health officials have long since found it important to survey the population under their responsibility to discover who are the carriers of infection and to recognize the sanitary habits and methods of sanitation. But it is only beginning to be realized that the social environment likewise needs to be surveyed if one is considering the welfare of the entire community or of a particular portion of the community, such as a local industry.

To repeat, human relations in our half of tomorrow's world are the key to the survival of democracy as we understand the word. A totalitarian, socialistic nation may be able to get along with old-fashioned methods. The empiricism of the past may be a sufficient guide for the masters of a police state. But an open society with our ideals requires other instruments and a wider understanding of modern man. We need to put to use what has already been learned by the scientists concerned with the study of man. But even more important, we need to support the efforts of those who are trying to push forward the boundaries of knowledge in this vast area.

Fundamental or basic research in the nature of human relations means basic and fundamental research in sociology, anthropology, and social psychology. I am sure that those who are supporting the applied work in the field of human relations will understand from the analogy with the physical sciences how vastly important it is to strengthen the hands of those in our universities who are working far away from what may be called "practical" results. We must expect no miracles and have no shrill cries for speed. Although we are in dire need of the assistance of the scientists who study man, we must be certain not to be impetuous and thereby kill the goose which lays the golden egg. Fundamental research is at the top of our list of priorities here as elsewhere.

In conclusion, I once again offer my congratulations to the Community Service Society. Its progressive record of 100 years of accomplishment for human welfare strengthens our belief in the soundness of democratic methods. We have high hopes for increased effectiveness in the use of new knowledge; we predict a continuing improvement in relations between human beings; we expect a growing unity and dynamic stability in this free society of ours and in true democracies in every portion of the globe. With confidence, therefore, we look forward even in these grim days to the bright dawn of tomorrow's world.

Human Relations and the World Scene

BROCK CHISHOLM, M.D.

IF IT CAN BE that all the kinds of people who live in New York City can live together in peace and relative harmony, then it should be possible to extend that process throughout this entire little world in which we are all cooped up together. The world is changing, and changing fast. It is impossible to get a picture of the world of the future by gazing into a crystal ball. The crystal ball as a diagnostic procedure has been out of fashion for a long time. However, we can look a little into our past and at our present and we may be able to look a little at what we are equipped to do in the future.

Our past is not a very pleasant picture. It has been very unsuccessful. The whole history of the human race is one of competitive survival, of fighting for security, possession, prestige, power, control of others. It has been a long history of multitudes of people guided and controlled in the interests of the neurotic necessities of the few. Always a power-hungry leader has cropped up who has demanded satisfaction of his own excessive and pathological necessities for power and importance. The human race, all over the world, up to now, has been of such kind and has thought in such ways that it has been possible for such neurotic leaders to gather about them multitudes who in giving their support also gave themselves some of the satisfactions which they too needed.

This is true of all past history. It is the mechanism which has made so much trouble in the world. Blind multitudes following a neurotic leader in the interests of his personal power and prestige have been typical in all history, in all parts of the world. It is not to be expected that in the future we will be able to rid the world of neurotics. There will always be people who will require excessive degrees of importance. But it should be possible to do something about the cannon fodder. It is not beyond the range of possibility that developments may occur in that area. Competitive survival has been the mechanism by which the human race has got along in the past. It is not a truly adult mechanism. It is not the sort of thing that truly well-developed people practice in order to get along together. Civilized people, in their own personal relationships, gave up such methods long ago. They tend to get along by agreement, compromise, mutual understanding, and a certain degree of tolerance about divergent attitudes, but the human race en masse has not learned to behave in that way.

It might seem that the vulnerable spot, where an approach can be made to this problem, may be found in relation to the mass of people who even now can be led in strange directions toward socially damaging goals by people who are not themselves capable of functioning in any logical or civilized way. It may be seen if we look at ourselves, because we are the kind of people I am talking about. We are the people who fight wars every fifteen or twenty years—we have been doing that for centuries. Our thinking habits and our behavior patterns do not prevent us from fighting wars. Wars were not too important until recent years; people who fought wars did only relatively local damage. It was possible for whole races to fight other whole races with casualties amounting to merely a few thousands or a few millions, but that situation no longer exists.

The world has changed because the power of the human being to kill has changed. There is an old military saying that offense is always overtaken by defense. It is not true. Offense has reached the stage now where it can absolutely annihilate whole populations, and no more efficient offense than total destruction can be expected. So, it becomes necessary to re-examine the whole mechanism of competitive survival which has been the method of survival of the human race up to now. This whole pattern, relatively innocuous in the past, cannot be used any longer because now warfare has become synonymous with suicide. We must look at our own development, at the kinds of people we are and have been and that our ancestors have been.

We need to look at the process of developing from a child to maturity and the status of a truly mature citizen of the world. If we think in terms of small children we may see the beginning of this process. The small child functions in terms of his own feelings only. These feelings are isolated in time and space. They are feelings without any outside terms of reference. Shortly, the child learns that he is a person having feelings, and this relates him to his surroundings. He begins to become oriented in space and in time. He discovers his immediate environment. He learns methods of influencing that environment so that he gets what he wants—in the interests, still, of his own feelings. Soon he discovers the members of his family. Later, he discovers other people, outside his family; later still, the children with whom he plays, then the other children at school, and then the community. Some people never advance beyond that stage of perception. They do not develop beyond their local community. They become useful citizens of that community, but they are not capable of developing a broader than local loyalty. A certain number of other people develop a degree of national loyalty, so that they regard all the citizens of their country as entitled to all the benefits of their civilization without reservations. There are many whose loyalty is still bound to a class, group, sect, color, race, or religion, or who fail to accept people within their own national community who belong to some other social classification. Obviously, this is a failure in development, resulting in a distorted person who has not matured even to the national level.

Until recently, however, this was comparatively satisfactory. In the future, it cannot continue to be satisfactory. The world has shrunken to a very small place. It is necessary now to have enough people in enough places who are true world citizens, who have developed loyalty to the whole human race, of which we are all a part, if we are to survive. But it is not possible to do that except through complete national loyalty, and only a country that can count on enough of its citizens being truly nationally loyal—and then, as a further stage in maturation, internationally loyal—can carry on foreign relations adequately enough to prevent the kind of conflict that may in the future wipe out the human race.

In terms of time also there is a developmental process. The small child thinks only in terms of now and here, but soon he discovers tomorrow and yesterday, and after a little while he is able to save up today for something he will want tomorrow. Within a short time the normally developing child should be able to control his desires of today in order to gain something more important for himself in the future. By his early teens, he should be functioning several years ahead; by the late teens, ten years ahead of himself, projecting himself into his own future, so that he can see where he is going and what his effect on his environment will be in ten years' time. Full maturity appropriate to this stage of world development can be expected in the late twenties or early thirties, but it develops in very few people indeed. Maturity in the time field results in people functioning in terms of several generations. The truly mature personality will plan his course far into the future and will not be too much seized with the importance of the immediacy of problems. These are of great concern to the younger group, and it is fit and sound that they should be; but mature people should be thinking in longer terms, and their ability to do so is a measure of the degree of success with which they have approached this moving goal of maturity.

It is quite clear that a hundred years ago maturity in individuals did not require this high standard. It did not matter very much then if local groups or even large groups fought each other. But from now on, it does; the requirements of the civilized human being have been raised very greatly. These requirements show themselves in a great variety of directions, primarily in personal and voluntary responsibility to a social structure and social goals. The small child learns his relationship with his environment, not by what he hears, not by what he is taught at school, but by the day-to-day picture that is shown him by his father and his mother. These are the pictures into which he grows. He does not decide to be this or the other when he is a small child. He grows into the picture presented to him by his parents. That picture will always be deeply set into his personality, which is very firmly constructed by the end of the sixth or eighth year. This is not to say that nothing can be done about people after they are eight years old, but the basic structure of the personality is firmly established by that age. The conscience has been almost entirely completed by that time.

It is of the greatest importance to the world that the conscience of the next generation should be vastly different from that of this generation, because unless the conscience of the next generation includes higher degrees of responsibility to the human race than have been found in ours, there will be no generation following that. I think that we must accept these facts because they are facts, and we must consider now, before we make more and perhaps irreparable mistakes, what we must do about them.

It is painful for us to recognize that our first responsibility in relation to the world of the future is to see that our children do not grow up to be as we have been, to see that they are great improvements on the models we have shown them. We are the kinds of people who have fought each other every fifteen or twenty years for centuries, and always for reasons of power, prestige, and possessions. This is a pattern which our children cannot follow if there is to be any further development in this great developmental process of which the human race is a part. We must accept our responsibility to the next generation, and it is a long-term job we have before us. The kind of people that the next generation will be is our responsibility.

This job is not made easier by the immediate problem of the present state of the world, which is chaotic. However, conditions are being exaggerated; there is not by any means chaos throughout the world. Although it is the disagreements that get all the publicity, the United Nations itself has reached conclusions and agreements on at least fifty questions to every one that has not been agreed upon. One example is the Interim Commission of the World Health Organization. On that Commission are eighteen nations representing all the sixty-three nations who signed the constitution. These eighteen representatives have met together repeatedly, have held long sessions, have tackled extraordinarily difficult problems, highly controversial in nature, and have reached agreed conclusions time after time. They have never taken a vote on a technical subject. Indeed, in several sessions of two weeks' duration, agreement has been reached on every subject without recourse to a single vote. The Interim Commission includes the United States, the U.S.S.R., and the United Kingdom, and India and China and France, and Canada and the Netherlands, and Australia and Brazil and Egypt, and Liberia and Mexico and Norway, and Peru and the Ukraine, and Venezuela and Yugoslavia. Here is a demonstration of successful human relations before our very eyes that no one is looking at. Here is the proof that it can be done. I say in all seriousness that there has been no time in the deliberations of the Interim Commission when one could tell from what they said what country the delegates from the U.S.S.R. represented. They are responsible representatives of all sixty-three nations, they are interested in the health of the world. Their attitude is truly a world attitude. This is fact. It is true that in other areas there is much controversy and great difficulty. It is perfectly true that there are fundamental disagreements about life patterns between people in the different parts of the world.

It is just as true that the people of India, to cite one of many examples, have vastly different patterns of life from those of other countries, but they are not aggressive, and no one outside their own country is afraid of them.

A new factor has come along that really has changed the world, has changed it more than did the atomic bomb, and that is biological warfare. I assure you that biological warfare renders the atomic bomb child's play. Its potentialities for destruction are vastly greater than those of the atomic bomb. It requires no heavy industries, no manpower, no industrial development, and very little technical knowledge. This is a fact. It is a fact which permits to any belligerent small country equality with any other country of the world. All that is necessary is a few technicians and a few fanatic distributors. I submit that our whole concept of competitive survival is obsolete. We have no alternative to collective suicide but getting along with each other. It is important that we recognize this fact now, before it is too late. We must live, if we are to live at all, with all the people in the world. This necessity will be a great test of our social abilities, the abilities we must develop quickly to survive under these changed circumstances. Let me remind you that many other forms of life on earth have not survived, because they were incapable of adjusting to new circumstances. It is possible that man too will go the way of the dinosaur if he cannot make an appropriate adjustment to the new world in which he finds himself. This is a dismal prospect if we retain all our present concepts and behavior patterns, but if we are willing to start afresh, to recognize that our human relations, and those of the whole race, have not been successful so far, that we are not the people who will inherit the earth, we may have some hope for the future.

This requires drastic re-evaluation. We must consider our responsibility as citizens in relation to other nations. I must remind you that no government can outdistance its people, that any government in any international council can only represent its people; that any government which can hope to maintain such foreign relations as will entitle the race to survive, must be able to count on a citizenry which has developed a degree of maturity which makes it fit to live with a great variety of people throughout the world. We have not yet attained that standard. We have duties in this regard to ourselves, to our children, to our nations, and to the world. We have not always taken these responsibilities very seriously. There are still people to be found in international conferences, negotiating vastly important matters with representatives of other countries without having studied the history, philosophy, or even the religion of the people with whom they are negotiating. This is, of course, a fantastically ridiculous situation. It is impossible effectively to discuss anything with widely divergent people if we do not know their basic philosophy, history, etc., but these basic facts have not yet been widely accepted as standards among the people who represent us in the councils of the nations. Our lives are in the hands of these people. Their failure in human relations is what makes wars. If they continue to fail as they have in the past, the human race as a whole will suffer, or perish.

This is a responsibility that is very heavy, and it needs to be considered very seriously in relation to every election in every community in every country in the world. It is no longer safe to elect anyone to a position of social responsibility on the score of local issues. The only really paramount issue in any election of the future is the survival of the human race. Nothing else is of importance besides that great necessity. In every country it behooves the citizenry to consider the people they would elect to any office in terms of their fitness to help the human race to survive, because this is the over-all framework in which from now on the human race will live or die. We must give up much of our concern for our own little comforts and importance. We must assume a higher citizenship and accept wider values. Only thus can we hope to survive. This is the world situation with which our educational process should equip our children to deal. There is no reason to suppose that it cannot be done and done soon enough.

The very same diverse patterns which are to be found among the multitudes of people who are living peacefully together in New York City are to be found among the other countries of the world. If these people can live together, there is no reason why larger groups of the same people cannot live together in peace in the world. It requires rearrangement of our values, and the whole question before us all is whether we are or are not willing to face this fact and assume this responsibility.

I am not pessimistic, but optimistic, about the future of the human race, for I believe and earnestly believe that the necessary job can be done and will be done. There are stirrings in many parts of the world in this direction. There is an ever widening appreciation of the necessity for peoples to live together. I think there is no war in the foreseeable future. There can be a war only if there are enough people, neurotic themselves, who are willing to follow madmen, clearly demonstrated as mad by their willingness to start another war, the last war.

Index of Articles and Contributing Authors